Property of

Gabrielle Marchbanks

# DERANGED MEMORY

*A Psychonomic Study of the Amnesic Syndrome*

# QUOTATIONS

Chorus

We do not like to look out of the same window, and see quite
a different landscape.
We do not like to climb a stair, and find that it takes us down.
We do not like to walk out of a door, and find ourselves back in
the same room.
We do not like the maze in the garden, because it too closely
resembles the maze in the brain.

T. S. Eliot: *The Family Reunion*

Science never pursues the illusory aim of making its answers final, or even probable. Its advance is, rather, towards the infinite yet unattainable aim of ever discovering new, deeper, and more general problems, and of subjecting its ever tentative answers to ever renewed and ever more rigorous tests.

Karl R. Popper:
*The Logic of Scientific Discovery*

# DERANGED MEMORY

*A Psychonomic Study of the Amnesic Syndrome*

By

GEORGE A. TALLAND

MASSACHUSETTS GENERAL HOSPITAL
HARVARD UNIVERSITY MEDICAL SCHOOL
BOSTON, MASSACHUSETTS

1965

ACADEMIC PRESS New York and London

ACADEMIC PRESS INC.
111 Fifth Avenue, New York, New York 10003

*United Kingdom Edition published by*
ACADEMIC PRESS INC. (LONDON) LTD.
Berkeley Square House, London W. 1

LIBRARY OF CONGRESS CATALOG CARD NUMBER: 65-15774

PRINTED IN THE UNITED STATES OF AMERICA.

# PREFACE

This book contains the lessons I have learned about the amnesic syndrome—from observing and talking with patients, from experiments, from reading the reports and theoretical formulations of other students, and from pursuing my own speculations. Patients in the chronic phase of Korsakoff's disease were my principal subject of research for some five years. I have continued to study them and others with disturbed memory function, along with some general problems of learning and forgetting to which my research had led me. The title of this book reflects more faithfully the state of innocence in which I embarked on this research, rather than my conclusions. Deranged memory is indeed the phenomenon we observe, often with incredulity, in the amnesic syndrome. It did not take me long, however, to realize that this descriptive phrase is inadequate for understanding the mechanisms and functions damaged in amnesic patients; nor is it fully descriptive of their disturbance.

From the very beginning, my interest in the problem presented by Korsakoff's psychosis extended beyond description. In fact, I do not believe that one can embark on or pursue a descriptive study without some guidelines that are one's theoretical preconceptions. My own, if a label is to be applied, are those of cognitive psychology. Psychonomic, the qualifying term of the subtitle, though not widely used at present, may prove its worth in time. It should help to resolve the dilemma of the psychologist who pursues his subject matter with the discipline of the biological sciences but is prepared to admit that psychology may also refer to other, quite different endeavors to discover and influence the workings of the mind. The subtitle will also give fair warning to some clinicians whose expectations of a psychological study of a mental disorder I am unlikely to fulfil. My principal method of research is the laboratory experiment; my primary object of observation is achievement in performance: from these I infer mechanisms and processes. At the same time, working in a hospital and with patients, I have enough respect for clinical tools to employ them where they can point to problems as well as answer questions.

A sizeable section of this book is entirely devoted to clinical observations, and none of it is divorced from them. My major contribution, however, is the extensive and systematic experimental study of a fair-sized group of patients and a control group. It has been my rare good fortune to have available for study in the experimental laboratory, on many repeated occasions and over a period of several years, a sample of patients with a comparatively clearly defined neurological and psychiatric diagnosis. Records of their performance in various controlled tasks constitute an exceptionally comprehensive document. My goal, however, extended beyond documentation; it was to examine these records of abnormal function for the information they can provide on the mechanisms and processes of normal function. The final, theoretical, section of this book is directed towards that objective. Bridging the clinical and experimental parts is a survey of the literature in which other investigators have published their observations and conclusions on the amnesic syndrome. Since much of this material is now only of historical significance, it seemed to me inappropriate to adopt a critical point of view throughout this review. It is hoped that the exhaustive digest of reports presented here—including many in publications, and on occasion in languages, inaccessible to students of the amnesic syndrome—will prove to be a valuable addition to the history of neuropsychiatric literature. Introducing these four sections of the book is a short chapter presenting most of the data about the general purpose and design of the research that could not fit into this Preface.

One of the pleasures an author derives from publishing a book is the opportunity this affords him to thank those who have helped him with it. First, I wish to convey my gratitude to the patients and control subjects whose cooperation made it possible for me to undertake and complete this research. I am deeply indebted to my chief, Dr. Erich Lindemann, for his encouragement and for the far-sighted policy he instituted as Professor of Psychiatry at the Massachusetts General Hospital, which enabled me to develop an experimental psychology laboratory in his Department. Initially my research on the amnesic syndrome was sponsored by the Neurology Service of the Massachusetts General Hospital, and at all stages I benefited greatly from the guidance and advice of its chief, Dr. Raymond D. Adams. Professors Raymond Adams and Maurice Victor had progressed far in the clinical and neuropathological research of the Korsakoff syndrome at the time they invited me to supplement their studies with a systematic psychological investigation. The help they advanced on many occasions, in response to specific requests, I appreciated no less than the complete freedom they gave me to chart my own research.

Two of my closest colleagues, Drs. Frank Ervin and Gardner Quarton, were always ready to provide information or correct errors when I strayed outside the boundaries of my own professional competence. Their interest and enthusiasm for the topic of my research all but exceeded mine, so that I could draw freely and profitably on their fund of clinical experience and extensive knowledge of the basic sciences. I had many valuable discussions about specific patients or about general problems raised by Korsakoff's syndrome with Drs. Thomas Ballantine, Howard Blane, Stanley Cobb, David Drachmann, Miller Fisher, Thomas Hackett, Vernon Mark, Jack Mendelson, Vincent Perlo, Peter Sifneos, and William Sweet. Drs. Walter Barton and Milton Greenblatt, successively superintendents of the Boston State Hospital, Drs. Alfred O. Ludwig and Morris Chafetz, successively chiefs of the Alcohol Clinic at the Massachusetts General Hospital, and Dr. William Timberlake, chief of the neurology service at the Lemuel Shattuck Hospital, and their staffs, gave invaluable help by providing me with their patients.

My wife, Non, followed the progress of this research with interest, and helped me with the presentation of its findings in the journals as well as by reading the manuscript and galley proofs of this final report. To her and to my friend Dr. John Nemiah I am especially grateful for suggestions that improved its style and corrected errors. I am also indebted for their advice to Drs. Robert Holt, George Miller, Nancy Mello, Freda Newcombe, Ralph Reitan, Nancy Waugh, and Charles Woody, who read the manuscript or parts of it. Mrs. Alicemarie Miller, Mrs. Marilyn Ekdahl Rawicz, Mrs. Jean Cairnie Castles, and Dr. Bertram Scharf contributed to the research their skill in designing test material as well as their meticulous care in administering experiments, and assisted me in the analysis of the results.

Originally, my investigation was sponsored by a research grant to Dr. Raymond Adams from the National Institute of Mental Health; subsequently other projects, and more recently a career development grant from the National Institutes of Health, helped to support my laboratory and provided me with the opportunity to pursue my interest in the normal, as well as deranged, function of memory. Several of the experiments were first reported, in more detail than here, in separate articles published in the *Journal of Nervous and Mental Disease, Journal of Abnormal and Social Psychology, Journal of Personality,* and *Bibliotheca Psychiatrica et Neurologica.*

I am grateful to the publishers for permission to reprint much of the content, and several tables and figures from my papers, and for their permission to reproduce designs and quote from other authors to:

Teachers College, Columbia University, for Fig. 2;
Springer-Verlag, Berlin, for Fig. 5;
Pantheon Books, a Division of Random House, Inc., for part of Fig. 9;
The Psychological Corporation, for Fig. 11;
Basic Books Inc., Publishers, for the quotation on page ii from Karl R. Popper: *The Logic of Scientific Discovery*;
Harcourt, Brace & World, Inc., for the quotation on page ii from T. S. Eliot: *The Family Reunion.*

A manuscript of the preliminary version of this book was awarded the annual monograph prize of the American Academy of Arts and Sciences in the biological and physical sciences for 1961.

GEORGE A. TALLAND

*Boston, Massachusetts*
*April, 1965*

# CONTENTS

## *Part Four*
## EXPERIMENTAL

*PART ONE*

# INTRODUCTORY

*Chapter 1*

# THE GOALS AND METHODS OF THE RESEARCH

Like the other elementary biological functions of the organism, memory too we take for granted. We are rarely conscious of memory as a process unless witnessing some extraordinary feat of retrieval or an unexpected breakdown of the function. The reader admires the magic with which Proust recaptures the past, the ingenuity of Freud's explanation why he failed to recall the name of an acquaintance or a place on the map. But who will marvel at a friend when, after the interruption of a telephone call, he resumes a conversation where he left it off 10 minutes ago? Yet that too is an accomplishment of memory.

In fact, when memory assumes the form of more or less exact reproduction, such as a drive from home to office along a familiar route, it goes unnoticed. Memory becomes an object of awareness only when it fails in its availability or accuracy. This is as true of Proust as of Freud, for the reconstruction of "lost time" entails distortion. Almost all that is known about memory function has been learned from failures to achieve perfect reproduction, and that includes the realization that the process is not simply one of static storage. The amnesic syndrome, in which the breakdown of memory function is gross and extensive, may throw some light on remembering and forgetting that cannot be gained from less severe failures. It certainly offers the psychologist some problems of intrinsic interest.

In the research here reported, the amnesic syndrome was studied principally as it appears in the chronic phase of Korsakoff's psychosis with an alcoholic etiology. Adams (1959), on the evidence of extensive clinical and neuropathological studies, regards this as the third and final stage of a disease process which begins with the "acute global confusion of Wernicke's disease" and continues with an "acute amnestic-confabulatory phase." His diagnosis of Korsakoff's psychosis that provided the basis for the selection of our patients, "depends on the demonstration of an impairment of memory for recent events (those occurring before the illness began) and an inability to form memories of present experiences, i.e., to learn or memorize even though the mind is alert and attentive and capable of perceiving with reasonable accuracy and of thinking clearly about simple everyday problems. In fact, the very essence is the discrepancy between an alert, wide-awake state of mind and the memory and learning defect." A record of the neurological signs characteristic of Wernicke's (1881) disease and, in many instances, their continued presence in a residual form, provided an additional diagnostic criterion.

*Purpose.* My psychological investigation of the amnesic syndrome was undertaken with a twofold goal in view. Its first aim was to contribute to the natural history of a disease, to determine under the controlled conditions of the experimental laboratory the skills and functions that are affected in the Korsakoff syndrome. The same procedures also served the purpose of exploring the patients' remaining capacities. Much of the experimental work was so designed as to check certain clinical impressions reported by others or gained by myself. Observations made outside the laboratory thus influenced the experimental-theoretical program of the research by supplying hypotheses for testing, as well as furnishing information for the clinical-descriptive section of this report. No systematic attempts were made, however, to compare the psychopathology under investigation with nosologically distinct mental diseases or with the behavioral concomitants of certain specific brain lesions.

A second aim of this research was to contribute to a general theory of psychology. Since that which can be learned about normal function by studying only normal function is limited in scope, we endeavor to extend our knowledge by the study of abnormal function. A disorder, characterized by such a relatively clearly circumscribed psychopathology and neuropathology as the amnesic syndrome, offers a particularly valuable lesson in this endeavor.

This second objective of the research in no way hampered progress toward its first goal; on the contrary, it helped to keep the descriptive component within an ordered design. Admittedly, the order thus imposed also excluded some information that other students might have chosen to include in their scheme. The rule of selection and omission, however, was applied only to the research design, and not to its report. As a consequence, the experimental section incorporates a number of procedures and results that in the outcome have not contributed directly to my theoretical model of the amnesic syndrome. They are presented for the sake of completeness, and more particularly to students of related pathological conditions and to fellow psychologists with a special interest in one or another of the experimental methods employed.

The primary concern of this research was cognitive function, the term being used with a comprehensive connotation. A systematic analysis of certain emotional and motivational mechanisms, and more especially of those commonly traced to an unconscious level of mental function, was omitted, though not by default. The relevance of personality dynamics to the amnesic syndrome appeared, on careful consideration, tenuous and indirect if at all admissible. Theories of general psychology offered more helpful leads, and I also paid attention to neuropathological studies of the syndrome in planning my research and interpreting its results. My ultimate goal was to formulate the psychological findings in a model that could be translated, perhaps in the future rather than at present, into neurophysiological terms. Quite obviously, if a certain abnormality can be investigated by the methods of both the neurologist and the psychologist, both scientists are likely to gain if they are prepared to learn from each other. Cross-reference between the two disciplines is particularly valuable when, as in the example of the amnesic syndrome, the functional disturbance does not fit easily within the conceptual framework of either.

## Patient and Control Groups

In the study of many diseases the pathological material is the more informative the graver the disturbance. This is not true of the amnesic syndrome. The severe derangement of neurological as well as of psychological function in the early phase of the disease is undoubtedly of considerable interest to the clinician, and has in fact been fairly fully documented. Most of the reports in the literature dwell mainly on the anomalies of the acute stage of the disease, and few stress sufficiently the changes that occur when the patient settles into a chronic condition of deranged mental function. My work has been done principally with patients after those changes had taken place, and consequently some observations presented here may differ from the standard discriptions of the Korsakoff syndrome. Patients in the early phases of the disease that most commonly develops into Korsakoff's psychosis—Wernicke's encephalopathy and the transitional "amnestic-confabulatory" stage—were not included in the principal research. Observations were in fact made on 25 of them, some by means of experimental methods but in most instances only in bedside interviews. The study of those patients proved to be of interest chiefly for the light it cast on the problem of confabulation, and will be discussed in that context.

*Wernicke Patients.* Other observations made on patients in the early phase of the disease are not presented systematically, since the research was concerned with the amnesic symptom-complex, without regard to its prior development. The undifferentiated dementia of the Wernicke patient may indeed include the kernel of the amnesic syndrome but, because of its diffuseness, does not allow for its disentanglement. This is evident from Victor and Adams' (1953) detailed description of the Wernicke patient, who "is unable to focus his attention on any one topic, and may suspend a conversation to turn over and sleep. What questions he deigns to answer betray disorientation in time and place, misidentification of those around him, and an inability to grasp the meaning of his illness or immediate situation. In addition, many of his remarks are irrational, nor do these show any consistency from moment to moment. If one persists in questioning the patient, it is obvious that impairment of retentive memory especially for recent events is probably the outstanding feature of the general mental disorganization."

With a balanced diet, Adams (1959) noted a predictable change in the patient's condition, that included both neurological and mental signs. Alertness and attention improve, disorientation decreases, and retrograde amnesia, inability to learn new material, and confabulation become the characteristic defects. These observations are based on patients first treated for Wernicke's encephalopathy, and subsequently hospitalized with Korsakoff's syndrome. The etiological connection between the two syndromes rests on both clinical and neuropathological evidence. Of 13 Wernicke patients studied by Joliffe, Wortis, and Fein (1941), 12 subsequently developed Korsakoff's psychosis. Victor and Adams (1953) reported that 62 of their 80 Wernicke patients with mental symptoms were left with Korsakoff's psychosis and, in reverse, of their first 45 patients with the Korsakoff syndrome, all but 3 had evidence of Wernicke's disease on admission to hospital. The association is close but less than perfect.

*Experimental Group.* A few of Victor and Adams' 45 contributed to the present study, and the entire experimental group was drawn from the same population, a total of 11 men and 18 women, all with a history of alcoholism to which their amnesic disturbance was attributed directly or indirectly. All but a few of them also had records of the peripheral neurological signs associated with Wernicke's disease. Except for two patients, they were under custodial care in a mental hospital, receiving neither drugs nor other treatment for their psychosis. Of the nonalcoholic patients with the amnesic syndrome included in the present research, only one will be discussed (in Chapter 11).

Thus, we had an experimental group homogeneous in respect to the etiology and past history of its disease, and also unusually uniform in its social-cultural background. All but a few of the men and women belonged to the working class, were born and brought up in Boston, northern New England, or the adjacent provinces of Canada, and most of them were but one generation removed from their ancestral home in Ireland. This group was selected from a list of more than 40 patients so that it display the amnesic syndrome in its purest available form. It did not constitute a representative sample of its parent population, Korsakoff patients committed to a mental hospital. Those with evidence of other specific psychiatric or neurological diseases and completely demented patients were excluded, as they could not furnish any useful information about the characteristic derangement of the amnesic syndrome. At the other end of the spectrum, the experimental group did not include patients who had sufficiently recovered from the disease to resume their lives, more or less, where they had left off at the time of their hospitalization.

Three patients with a reliable report of Wernicke's encephalopathy and subsequently of Korsakoff's psychosis were studied in our laboratory some time after their discharge from hospital. Since no systematic psychological investigation had been undertaken with these patients while they were hospitalized, these later examinations could be of only limited interest. By their evidence one patient performed well within the normal range on every test, and might therefore be presumed to have made a full recovery. The other two functioned at levels indistinguishable from the chronic amnesic patients, and by no means as efficiently as some of those investigated in this study. Their remission appeared to be determined more by the availability of care in the home than by an intrinsic improvement in their condition.

*Control Group.* Since it was not expected that the chronic patients would recover their normal mental function, and since they had not been psychologically examined prior to their illness, in order to evaluate the areas and extent of their deranged function, they had to be compared with the performance of a suitably selected control group or several such groups. I decided to match control subjects on age and intelligence, and to control for two effects that could influence the performance of the amnesic patients: (a) the biological and social concomitants of habitual alcoholism, and (b) prolonged hospitalization.

Two control groups were chosen, each selected for one of these effects. The major control group, i.e., larger in number and available for most of the experimental procedures, was recruited from alcoholic patients who were receiving psychotherapy. None of them was known to suffer from any neurological or medical disease, and they all functioned with reasonable efficiency in their jobs. Like the chronic amnesic patients, they had no alcohol in their systems at the time of testing. They formed a pool of 16 men and 8 women, from whom control groups were drawn for each experiment to the number of available volunteers. They matched the experimental group in age, but not in intelligence as measured by three subtests of the Wechsler-Bellevue Intelligence Scale: comprehension, vocabulary, and similarities. Even though our Korsakoff patients clustered in the average range of the population, attempts to screen the alcoholic control sample so as to match their IQ proved impracticable, because that group was already preselected, representing a higher than average section of the population. It is questionable, moreover, whether screening with this end in view would have been justified, since the discrepancy observed probably reflected the intellectual deterioration caused by the characteristic disease of the experimental group, rather than basically different endowments.

The second control group was drawn from a neurological ward, and consisted of 4 men and 4 women receiving physiotherapy, who had been in hospitals for periods of 6 months or longer. They had no record of alcoholism or of cerebral pathology, and matched the Korsakoff patients in age and intelligence. In later stages of the research these two original control groups were no longer available, or not in sufficient numbers. In order to obtain some population norms, members of a social club were tested on the experimental procedures. They, as well as the psychiatric and orthopedic patients who provided the control groups for two experiments, were matched for age with the Korsakoff patients, and had a similar cultural and educational background.[1]

---

[1] Although attempts to match experimental and control groups in respect to educational achievement could not be pursued rigorously, gross discrepancies were avoided, e.g., none of the control subjects had been at college. As far as possible, all control groups excluded brain-damaged patients. Some justification may be necessary that no control group with diagnosed brain lesions was chosen, or indeed why no direct attempt was made at differential diagnosis. The obvious reason for selecting a control group drawn from the population with cerebral disease would be to determine the defects specific to the amnesic syndrome, and those shared by patients with Korsakoff's and with other brain disease. Damage in areas topographically adjacent or functionally related to the region implicated in the Korsakoff syndrome might have been of particular interest, but patients suffering from such disorders were not available for the research. Comparisons drawn between Korsakoff patients and any other class or a mixed sample of brain-damaged patients would have served no useful purpose. Of course, Korsakoff patients have in common a number of defects in mental function with many other patients diagnosed as brain damaged. They also share certain impairments with men and women who have reached old age in good health and are not clinically classified as brain damaged (cf. Talland, 1959a, 1961, 1962a). On the other hand, the pattern of psychological deficit in the Korsakoff syndrome is very different from that we have found (Talland, 1962b) with much the same experimental tests in Parkinson's disease, an undisputed example of cerebral lesion. It is hardly necessary to press home the point that the inclusion of a "brain-damaged" control group would only have given rise to confusion.

Tracing parallels and differences between Korsakoff's syndrome and other nosologically distinct diseases would have run into much the same difficulties. The prospect of such an enterprise seemed endless, unless arbitrary limits were set to the range of comparisons, both in respect to dysfunction and to clinical classification. Even with such limits, it would have been necessary to run representative samples of each diagnostic class through our many laboratory procedures. Though quite adequate in reporting clinical observations, the literature contains few data suitable for direct comparison with our experimental findings. It seemed to me that the best service I could render was to present an exhaustive inventory of the capacities of the patients I have studied, and make this information available to those who have comparable data about related diseases.

## Method

The research reported here spread over a period of 6 years. It started with individual interviews and with attempts at group discussions at the mental hospital, and the first few experimental sessions also took place there. Although from time to time the patients were re-examined by means of interviews and some portable experimental procedures at their hospital, most of the testing was done in my laboratory where some of the patients came as many as forty times. Patients examined in the early stage of the disease were investigated while in treatment at the Massachusetts General Hospital.

A nucleus of the principal experimental group of chronic Korsakoff patients remained constant during the research. Thus, it was possible to re-administer experimental procedures and interview questions to the same patients over a comparatively long stretch of time, and also to test certain hypotheses, as they were successively formulated, on a standard group of subjects who fluctuated little, and showed at best only slight progressive changes in performance over the years. Theoretical formulations about the processes that appear to be impaired in the amnesic syndrome developed apace with the research. As the pattern of function and dysfunction characteristic of this disease evolved, new hypotheses supplanted others tested earlier in the study, and these in turn were subjected to experimental tests, and retained, refined, or discarded in the light of the results.

The techniques of investigation reflected the dual purpose of the research, i.e., to determine capacities in, more or less, standard skills or operations, and to test the tenability of formulations about hypothetical neuropsychological processes. Several standard psychological tests were given to the patients, to determine their place in the general population or in relation to other classes of brain-damaged patients. Examples of this type of test are the Wechsler-Bellevue Intelligence Scale, Halstead's (1947) Battery of Neuropsychological Tests, or Benton's (1955) Visual Design Test. Other tests of capacity and skill were drawn from the experimental literature or designed for the purposes of the research, as were the procedures employed to test hypotheses. Some of the interviews contained set questions presented in a uniform manner.

*Individual Differences.* It could be argued that my concern about methodological considerations, in making descriptive statements or in drawing inferences from specific observations to general function, was indulged at the expense of potentially more profitable intuitive insights. More especially, it may be contended that reliance on group trends obscures individual deviations from central tendencies, and that these differences contain the more interesting information.

The characteristic behavior or derangement of individual patients undoubtedly provided some valuable material for the research. It was woven into the fabric of its design, though by setting limits and pointers rather than in the form of summary data. My purpose, however, was to survey a sufficiently large sample of amnesic patients to establish the range and distribution of their performance scores, and thus avoid unwarranted generalizations from single or a few instances. The analysis of data in group trends does not preclude their re-examination with a view to individual characteristics, and has not done so in this research. The design did, however, impose the restriction of uniformity. In a test situation, the relationship between experimenter and subject was deliberately impersonal; I was interested in performance according to prescribed rules of procedure. Any deviation or unscheduled occurrence, while discouraged, was nevertheless carefully noted for the hint it might provide toward a better understanding of the disorder under review and for its theoretical formulation. Between tests, and always prior to the laboratory session, experimenter and subject engaged in free and informal verbal exchanges, and with most of the patients, these gradually built up into a fairly stable relationship. These talks provided ample opportunity for picking up casually most of that information which may have been missed in the limited circumstances of the experiments.

*Motivation.* It seems reasonable to question whether the amnesic patients did in fact perform in ostensibly purposeless artificial experimental situations to the best of their abilities. My impression was always that they did; first because Korsakoff patients are unusually pliable and obliging. Furthermore, being institutionalized, they appear to nurture considerable respect for authority, particularly medical authority which, by association often mediated through a white coat, extends to the psychological experimenter and his assistants. At first most patients believed that the tests were in some way connected with their evaluation for discharge, and that successful performance would naturally help to promote that desired outcome. The experimenter neither abetted nor expressly disavowed this misconception. Most of the tasks, however, were inherently interesting and challenging, and the patients seemed to be as anxious to prove their worth in them as any college student. The occasion itself had its attraction for them, in that it offered a break in the monotony of the hospital routine. The patients were indeed motivated to come, to do as they were asked, and to perform as well as they could. The control subjects were volunteers who offered their time and services without remuneration for the sake of research that was fully explained to them. Those who failed to come a second time were automatically excluded from the analysis; if they returned they were presumed to be sufficiently motivated, and nothing in their conduct disavowed this assumption.

## Definition of the Amnesic Syndrome

Finally, a few words about the topic of the research. "Amnesic syndrome," like any alternative classificatory concept, is a term subject to criticism. No attempt will be made here to examine the universal criteria that must be satisfied in order to define a disease entity, or to argue for other than pragmatic considerations. To insist on an indissoluble association of a specific brain lesion with an invariant cluster of neurological and psychological signs would exclude most of the patients who have provided such interesting material toward the phenomenology of a remarkable disorder. Only a few of the brains of the men and women, who can be observed while performing tasks, will be available for pathological examination, and then only many years hence; in the meantime they are liable to undergo considerable changes.

The neurological signs characteristic of Wernicke's encephalopathy, although present in the patients studied in the acute phase, and also observed in most of our chronic Korsakoff patients in an earlier stage of their disease, are of no immediate significance for our psychological evaluation. At the time the amnesic syndrome is manifested in its purest form, i.e., relatively free from confusion, delirium, and severe affective involvement, the neurological signs are at most vestigial. Likewise, an insistence on confabulation would have eliminated quite a few of the patients studied, unless that term had been so broadly defined as to accommodate verbal behavior elicited with the express intent to demonstrate the presence of this anomaly.

Since the disease, psychosis, or syndrome attached to Korsakoff's name is often thought to imply either certain neurological symptoms or confabulatory behavior, or both, "amnesic syndrome" was preferred as a definition. The phenomena observed and problems discussed under this name, however, are the same as those dealt with in psychological analyses of the Korsakoff syndrome. None of these terms stands for a disease with a uniform etiology. The circumstance that this research was conducted almost entirely with patients who had a record of alcoholism might have justified the choice of "chronic alcoholic psychosis" or "chronic brain syndrome associated with alcoholic intoxication" as a term of reference. Since, however, there is evidence that the psychological as well as the neurological signs of the Wernicke-Korsakoff syndrome are attributable to nutritional deficiency rather than to toxic effects, this nomenclature would be misleading. Besides, it would have eliminated from consideration those amnesic patients, studied by me and by others, whose mental disturbances could in no way be traced to alcohol.

The topic of this report, the amnesic syndrome, is a psychological disturbance manifested primarily in a severe impairment of memory function, but affecting other aspects of behavior as well. Its characteristic attributes are that: (1) it is nonspecific, i.e., not limited to a certain class of events, experiences, or notions, or to a definite period in life history; (2) it affects memory for the recent past more severely than for the remote past, but always combines some retrograde effects—loss of memories previously available—with anterograde effects—an apparent inability to acquire new memories; (3) memory function is far more gravely damaged than other cognitive functions; (4) it is a relatively stable condition; and (5) patients afflicted with this derangement are either unaware of their incapacity or not fully aware of its extent.

*PART TWO*

# CLINICAL

## *Chapter 2*

# THE AMNESIC PATIENT

Confronted with a chronic Korsakoff patient, the observer may not find any obvious sign of a mental disorder for quite a while, even though they engage in conversation. If alerted, he will note a marked lack of initiative in the patient but, since interviews are often carried by the initiative of one party, this deficiency can easily pass unnoticed. However, as soon as the interview turns to questions about the patient's experiences, activities, or interests in the immediate past, his answers are certain to betray a characteristic derangement.

In the first place the content is extraordinarily slender; the paucity of information far exceeds the limits that could be attributed to the restrictive social setting of a mental hospital. Patients either profess to have done nothing at all over stretches of weeks, months, or even years; or they report their activities in general terms and are unable to name specific instances. If pressed, they are likely to present some information dating back to a time prior to their hospitalization. It seems that to the patient events that took place many years before appear as if they had occurred quite recently. Otherwise, his talk tends to be rational, sensible, and cautious; his demeanor courteous and placid. With a searching eye, one may find signs of vacuity in the patient's expression, more so if he has been left alone for a while. It appears as if he were sitting there without a thought crossing his mind, without registering any of his surroundings. Still, while sitting in a waiting room with magazines within his reach, he is more than likely to pick up one and look at the pages. He is not difficult to arouse: call his name softly, and he responds readily.

The first striking characteristic of Korsakoff patients is not their manner of response but their essentially respondent behavior. In an attempt to observe their social interaction, I formed them into groups of 4 or 5, encouraged them to engage in conversation, to talk about anything that might occur to them. All my efforts to form a discussion group from a sample of 20 patients, in various combinations of membership, ended in failure. In response to the first suggestion, one of the members may have commented on the weather or on the last meal he had eaten and, perhaps, elicited one more brief comment on that topic. That was all; the group then subsided into silence without any apparent sign of discomfort. Individual patients always readily answered questions addressed to one or another, but they neither elaborated beyond the barest reply nor raised new topics. Usually the answer was a statement of ignorance or lack of interest, and no one would break the silence that ensued, except for 2 patients who were ever ready to air their stock grievances in stereotyped phrases.

*Portrait of a Patient.* In face to face interview the patients tended to give brief and factual answers to questions, and only rarely expanded into a second informative or qualifying statement. This rule, however, was subject to at least one major exception, in the case of Larry who likes talking and carries on the conversation without prompting. He is also fond of wisecracks, and given the slightest pretext the joke will be sexually suggestive—between man and man or, for that matter, between old man and young woman experimenter. He speaks in short spurts, and his talk dies away with a giggle after each joke; he seems to have a good time. His pockets are full of odd things adolescents might hoard. Occasionally he carries a bunch of old periodicals, and sometimes reads for a stretch but never remembers what he has just read.

Larry, now in his 70th year, was admitted to the mental hospital at the age of 63. He has lived in Boston all his adult life, and talks with pride of his success in business, as a dealer in machine tools. He is no longer in business; some years ago he had to wind it up. His wife died, and that broke him up completely—"not physically, mentally you might say. I took it hard. Thank God I didn't go crazy." When did it happen? "It must have been several years ago, though it feels as if it had happened only yesterday." His memory, he says, is very good. In fact, he recounts in detail some trivial and other quite important incidents of the more remote past. As for the news in the world, he says he keeps posted, though sometimes he feels he is "still a bit in the fog."

Asked if he knows the word *sputnik,* Larry answers "it's a lot of bunk. The scientists have just invented it." What does it mean? He could not say, it is not the sort of thing he was ever interested in. Stalin? "Russian leader. They never were anybody; a very lethargic, ambitionless race. They never were in a war. More or less a nomadic race." Is Stalin still alive? "He might be, or is he dead?" Who is the head of Russia now? "The tsar. No, the tsar is not there any more, he's a goner. Haven't they tried to go in for a republican form of government? I think they did but I wouldn't know for sure. What happens there is not of much concern to us. Now take a leader in Europe, like Germany! But Russia, no. They are a nomadic people; lots of room, not a ferocious race. Now take the Germans. They took a good licking, but . . ." Yes, Larry knows there have been two world wars, both against Germany. Hitler? "The crazy guy, he engineered the war; the man chiefly responsible for the antisubmarine warfare." Who was he? "He was a crazy bastard. He was a man of Jewish origin, I believe—so they say. He was a bunkum man—not a soldier really." As for himself, Larry declares, "I was the best soldier you ever saw," though he never served in the army, just in some "left-foot, right-foot organization."

Larry is a short, chubby, smiling man, quick in movement and seldom at complete rest. He has been known to lose his temper in the experimental laboratory, flaring up for being asked to do things that are "fit only as games for children." But that was an exception; on countless other occasions he showed eagerness to do well in the various experimental tasks, and pride in his achievement. If they were or appeared to be easy, he would remark that any child could deal with such a simple problem. If the test proved to be difficult, he would work at it intently, exhorting himself with such phrases as "come along baby, let's get it into place." He cannot be beaten or be shaken in the position his age and achievement had established for him. If he fails in a task, and that happens often enough, he immediately becomes the detached observer, approving the test for its value in teaching others, for assessing the skills of others. His reasoning sounds confident rather than logical.

Clearly, Larry has little tolerance for any insult to his self-esteem, and he accepts his hospitalization only as a temporary measure to help him over the crisis that his wife's death has brought upon him. He is completely unaware that his wife had been dead for as long as sixteen years prior to his hospitalization, and seems to have no recollection of living as a widower with another woman—a fact entered on his case record. He talks with great affection of his dead wife and of their two daughters, always thinking of them at first as young girls in their teens. Then, reminded of his own age, he realizes they must be grown up now. Larry remembers that he married in his twenties; he also knows his present age, and speaks of it with as much pride as about any other achievement for which, rightly or wrongly, he claims credit. Are the girls married? He thinks one of them might be, but is vague on this topic, while affirming with apparent conviction that they regularly visit him at the hospital. "They are very good girls, very fond of me; they would not miss a chance to see me." In fact these women have long since ceased to take any interest in their father.

Ask him again a few minutes later about his daughters, and he will affirm with certitude now that one of them, at any rate, is married, though he does not know her husband's name or if she has children. He believes that they live at home, and a sister-in-law is minding house for him. He himself lives there too but, when asked whether he will go back home for the night, Larry answers no, that he sleeps in here. He is wrong; he has mistaken the laboratory for the mental hospital, even though the view through the windows should have helped to correct his error. When this is pointed out to him he pretends to recognize it, but does not change his local orientation. The time of the day he judges accurately, the time of the year too, by means of this reasoning. "It's raining, the hot weather has not started yet, it must be past April, not June yet. It must be May." What year? "1970, no 1960."

This is unquestionably the portrait of an amnesic patient, but how much of it is typical of the Korsakoff syndrome? Disorientation for time is a characteristic feature. In fact, Larry is not disoriented for time, but his circumstantial approximation to the correct answer is as typical of the syndrome as any gross error, and so is the readiness to turn the calendar 10 years ahead of time—although only for a moment in this instance. To think of his daughters as young children, while knowing at a level of reasoning that they must be adults now, is a very characteristic feature. The flow of time experienced stopped some years back; experientially nothing has happened, nothing has changed since. Looked at objectively, time has gone on through these years. The facts of experience and of certain notions are thus bound to clash, and no satisfactory resolution is possible. Therefore, the facts are presented within the setting in which they have been reached; either in the context of memories or of the calendar. It is doubtful whether Larry's remarks on Russia in 1960 were appropriate at any time of his life; those about Germany were only shifted from and confused within their historical context.

## Orientation in Space, in Time, and Towards Persons

But for the history of this disease, one might hesitate to cite Larry as an example of Korsakoff's psychosis. This patient illustrates more vividly than others much that is characteristic of the amnesic syndrome, but his ebullience and restlessness were entirely atypical. Even his incertitude and occasional confusion about the physical setting is exceptional in the chronic phase of the disease, and is not accidentally most apt to occur in patients of advanced years. Only one other of our Korsakoff patients, a man in his eighties, believed that he was living at home; all others knew it was a hospital. Most of them also realized it was a mental hospital, and could give its name correctly or with close approximation. Larry, however, was not the only member of this group who ignored the long drive through the city to the laboratory, and believed that this was part of their hospital. The latter consisted of a complex of buildings, somewhat baffling to a new visitor; yet in time the amnesic patients learned their way about there. Several of them also managed to find their bearings around the hospital in which our laboratory was situated, and to follow the labyrinthine path that led there from the entrance.

Few patients kept count of the passing years. Asked to name the year of their admission to the hospital, they usually gave the correct answer or missed it by a narrow margin; asked to name the number of years spent there, most of them grossly underestimated the span of time. None seemed to have an immediate awareness of its length, a few would try to figure it out by rapid calculation, and then utter their answer without much conviction. Four patients kept a fairly exact count of the years or months spent in the hospital; some others calculated it correctly on one occasion but contradicted themselves the next time.

A striking example of their unawareness of the passage of time was provided by Helen who had been hospitalized at the age of 63, and who always said that she had been admitted only the day before. One day I confronted her with the fact that she had been in the hospital for 4 years, and corroborated this information with her case record. She did not bother to glance at the notes, just looked at me for a moment with embarrassment, and then promptly answered: "Well, you are the doctor, you know better." A few seconds later, however, she added: "but it feels as if it was only yesterday."

*Knowledge of Own Age.* In spite of the immediate shock, this incident did not appear to have made any lasting impression on Helen, for on some 40 occasions during the subsequent 6 years she always maintained that she had come in yesterday and would be sent home today. Still, if questioned how she spent her days in the hospital, she would often describe her work in the sewing room, some of which manifestly spread over several days. If asked to talk about her daily routine, without specific reference to the hospital, her answer would be drawn from an earlier setting of her life.

Helen was the only patient who repeatedly failed to name the date of her birth. In earlier interviews this failure was not consistent, and even later it seemed doubtful that the information requested was beyond her reach of recovery. The indignant tone in which she professed her ignorance suggested refusal rather than an unsuccessful attempt at retrieval. All other patients named the date of their birth promptly and, as far as could be ascertained, accurately on most occasions. Some of them, however, gave conflicting reports in repeated interviews, and the same inconsistency characterized their statements about their ages. None of the patients could name his age both instantaneously and correctly. Prompt replies were invariably underestimations, except for the jocular answer of a woman in her sixties who, on one occasion, said "ninety-nine—that is what I feel." Ten patients were able, in at least one interview, to state their ages correctly after about a second's delay, during which presumably they performed some fairly rapid calculations.

Errors in judging age were not stable within the same patient from one interview to the next, and of course varied even more among patients. As a rule errors tended to increase with length of hospitalization, and frequently patients thought they were as old as they had been at the time of their admission, but usually such mistakes were easily corrected. Remarkably enough, some of the most severely amnesic patients stated their true age most readily, even though they had been in the hospital for several years. The same patients, however, were not the most accurate in naming the date of the day. As a rule, judgments of the season and of the time of the day tended to be accurate. Six patients named the day's date—day, month, and year—correctly on one occasion at least, but only one of them did so consistently in repeated interviews. Six more answered within 2 days' margin of error, and also knew the year and the season on other occasions. With the others, the errors were large, often amounting to several years, even decades. Larry's momentary slip by postdating the date 10 years was indicative of the lability of this information in amnesic patients. Considering their tendency to underestimate their age, however, it is remarkable that gross errors were comparatively rare. Many patients professed they had difficulties in remembering dates, and indeed it was astonishing how few knew the date of their marriage or of the births of their children. Several of them were able to give the month and day of their wedding, but not the year.

*Family and Friends.* Every patient could name and describe husband or wife and parents. Those who had no more than 2 children or siblings, referred to them with certitude, but larger numbers introduced some confusion. One woman consistently listed 6 grown children, but variously divided their numbers equally between the sexes, or claimed to have 4 sons and 2 daughters. A couple of patients had a clear recollection only of the oldest of their several children. Some kept in touch with their families and followed the events and changes that occurred there; others, like Larry, remembered their families as they had been at some point in the past, or cherished even more nebulous images. Several patients failed to register the occurrence of a death in the family either before or during their hospitalization, or took note of it on one occasion but not on another. If registered, the date of a death—as in Larry's example—was likely to be displaced in time.

Almost every one of the patients belonged to what are loosely described as broken families, or had been a solitary person. Judging by the patients' report, their families had split up—more often formally by divorce than otherwise—as a result of their own alcoholic and associated habits; in other instances the sequence and presumable causal relationship of these two circumstances seemed to be reversed.

Most of the patients lived without any close tie in the outside world, and neither expected visitors nor spent their Sundays in the family. A few kept in touch with their children or mothers but only one woman with her husband. The others had not one kind word to say about their husbands or the men they had last lived with, unless they happened to be dead. The men were all bachelors, widowers, or divorced. One of them was not sure whether his wife had divorced him; in fact, she had, 7 years before his hospitalization.

Only a few patients had retained friends outside the hospital, and even those ties were severed in the course of the years. None appeared to have established close friendships within the hospital. Roommates were typically discussed as generic examples rather than as individual persons. If asked whether they had any friends there, the patients would give one of four types of answer. Some felt nothing but contempt for their fellow inmates, and would not think of choosing them as friends; others just did not bother, or professed that everybody was their friend; still others had evidently selected a few comrades from the hospital population, but either could not name them or remembered their first names only. A few patients could list several friends by full name, but even they gave barely any indication of a significant personal relationship.

Apparently the effort involved in establishing such relationships proved to be out of proportion to the need the patients felt for them. If any carried over from their pre-morbid lives, they were quite able to maintain those. Most of the patients also managed to assume new roles and to note new characters in their environment. After two or three sessions every one of the patients recognized me, or professed to. Two of them clung to the mistaken belief that they had met me in a different social setting prior to their hospitalization; three repeatedly confused me with other doctors, and thus attributed to me medical examinations or the administration of procedures for which I was not responsible. Most of them, however, described my role accurately enough, even though with little precision. Eight patients regularly recalled my name promptly; 5 others habitually substituted for it a close enough alternative; 7 could never learn or retain it for 5 minutes.

*Encounters with the Experimenter.* After a few visits to the laboratory, none of the patients remembered that he had initially met me in the mental hospital. Several correctly named the hospital where our laboratory was situated—others did not realize that it was different from their own. After our laboratory had been transferred from an old building to a new part of the hospital, I asked the visiting patients whether they had been in the place before. This happened some 6 months after their last visit, yet none of the patients made a mistake. Some just answered negatively, others nicely explained that they had previously come to see me at the Massachusetts General Hospital, but in a different part of it. However, none of them remarked on the change spontaneously, even though they may have praised the view through the widows. Their identification of the laboratory assistants, who changed over the years, was unreliable; they were apt to recognize new and old faces alike, and both with considerable diffidence.

On two occasions, 18 patients were asked to say when they had last seen me, once after the lapse of 4 months or longer, the other time after an interval of 1 to 2 weeks. At the end of the longer period 15 patients thought they had been at the laboratory within the past month, 1 patient assessed the interval accurately, and 2 suggested that it must have been a year or so, indicating rather vaguely that it was a long time ago, much longer in fact than the actual distance in time. Their estimate of the shorter span was typically "last week" or "a month ago, or less"; in a few instances it was an indefinite "not so long ago." All the patients who underestimated the longer interval, as well as the one who judged it correctly, gave a more or less accurate estimate of the shorter period. The remaining 2, however, persisted in believing that about a year had elapsed since their last visit.

Asked how many times they had previously been at the place of the interview, none of the 20 patients questioned came close to the correct answer of 12 to 15. Three overestimated it, one of them clearly confused me with a doctor whom she remembered examining her weekly for over a year. Nine patients were under the impression that they had been there two, three or four times before, 8 believed it had been once only.

*Insight into Own Condition.* Few of the patients had a clear notion about the circumstance of their admission to the hospital. They might mention some accident, or one of the symptoms of Wernicke's disease, or quote some injury or ailment they had suffered at an earlier or later date. Asked the reason for their continued hospitalization, most of them referred to some physical ailment; only a few would consider the possibility of their being afflicted with a mental disease, and none would consistently regard this as his principal disabling condition. One can only guess about their insight into their condition, since most of them knew they were living in a mental hospital. None realized the full extent of his amnesic disability; some would admit to poor memory for names or dates, others denied any memory disturbance even in the face of the most striking evidence.

The majority staunchly denied ever having drunk excessively or even having cared for alcoholic beverages; several admitted it and also to neglecting their diet, and recognized the causal connection between their manner of life in the past and their current condition. One patient even attributed to alcohol the tuberculosis that laid her up during her hospitalization. Their recollection for details of illnesses and accidents, of medical and surgical treatments during their hospitalization, was often remarkably accurate.

Probably none of these patients was ever severely perturbed by his inability to recall information that would be expected to fall well within the reach of normal memory function. Their frequent evasion and caution in answering questions may reflect the difficulty they encountered in reaching the information required; it does not prove awareness of that difficulty. The amnesic defect, of course, impaired the efficiency of their reasoning but this limitation was not manifest when information and skills acquired prior to the disease were sufficient. Old established skills, such as are exercised in eating, dressing, or polite conversation, the patients had retained without apparent decrement.

## Mood, Affect

Apathetic though these patients appeared when left on their own, they were alert enough to react promptly to changes in their surroundings, to answer questions, and to respond to instructions. As subjects they were cooperative and even the few patients spirited enough to resist or rebel rarely refused to do as asked. In appearance they tended to be slovenly, like most of the mental hospital population; in body build they formed a very heterogeneous sample.

No attempt was made to determine the personality types of these patients, either by projective techniques widely used for this purpose or by means of objective tests. Observation in the interviews and in the experimental laboratory suggested a wide range of personality patterns. Blandness of affect appeared to be a common characteristic, and was most likely to be broken by short outbursts of anger. Other instances in which the patients clearly expressed affect were those of anxiety aroused by failure in a task, satisfaction with success, sorrow caused by the hopeless outlook of hospitalization, despair over finding no job outside when ready to be discharged, sympathy with sufferers. Their attitude toward other persons, particularly their family and the hospital staff, was typically that of detachment; but examples of resentment were common, and those of gratitude and warm affection also occurred. A few of the patients joyfully reported happy events—such as marriages or births in their families—others gave plaintive accounts of reversals in their fortunes.

In general, however, the mood of the patients was lethargic, far beyond a normal measure of stout detachment. Quite a few of them retained a sense of humor and, like Larry, were ever ready to crack a joke; most of these, however, were not spontaneous but given in response to a question or remark. Changes in the mood of certain patients could be noticed over the years. Three who were apt to flare up at first, later became quite placid and cooperative; one other became more irascible. The dominant trait of noninvolvement hardly changed with time, even though some of the patients distinctly improved in appearance, and perhaps also in intellectual efficiency. This gain may have reflected a genuine recovery of lost capacity, or alternately the acquisition of new skills in handling interviews and tests, a more efficient economy of available resources. In the course of the years a few patients had visibly risen from the deepest trough of degradation, while others improved but slightly and not consistently.

Because of the apparent indifference with which amnesic patients face events, several writers have attributed their failure to remember personal experiences to a lack of emotional involvement. The literature also lists some examples in which Korsakoff patients remembered episodes that had aroused their emotion, although even those were not instances of deliberate recall. This explanation, if confirmed, would still not account for retrograde amnesia or for the patients' incapacity to remember information that is normally not invested with affect. As it happened, my observations offered no solid support for this hypothesis; of the autobiographical data that the patients reported few seemed to be affect-laden or presented with any accompanying sign of emotion.

*Misfortunes.* Perhaps the fact that several patients tended to remember the circumstances of their medical histories in detail could be quoted in support of the argument. Still, even this rule was subject to exceptions, and most notably in the case of a woman in her late forties, whose anterograde amnesia was not particularly severe by the standards of the Korsakoff syndrome. In the third year of hospitalization she badly scalded her right leg, and had to wear a bandage over the open wound for several months. When asked about the circumstances of her injury, although in pain, she had only the vaguest recollection of how it had occurred, and at first could not remember any accident. Subsequently she accused a fellow patient of stabbing her with the sharp metal end of a pencil from which the eraser had been removed.

Three years later she hurt her other leg in a fall. Her account of the second accident was prompt, and exactly the same. She accused another patient of attacking her without provocation, and stabbing her with a pencil that had no eraser in it. Asked whether she had had any other injury on her legs, the patient recalled one a couple of years previously, and correctly said it had happened to her other leg, but remembered none of the circumstances. Her comments on the recent accident included complaints about the treatment given at the hospital and accusations that they wanted to get her sick again so that she could not be discharged. Asked to give her reasons and some details of how the accident occurred, she answered: "One gets callous about remembering names and events. You are not supposed to have any feelings."

Taken at face value, this comment could be quoted in support of the argument that amnesic patients forget their experiences for lack of emotional involvement. In fact it is unlikely that shock and pain were registered without their characteristic affective qualities. More probably they were thus experienced, but the affect remained as isolated as the cognitive content of the event, or, for that matter, the patient's delusional notion about a plot to keep her in the hospital. Suspicions of similar hostile intentions were uncommon among other patients, and their tendency to persist in complete independence of the patient's general thought processes or behavior is illustrated by another woman who habitually complained of having been deprived in the hospital of her spectacles, teeth, and money. She always voiced this grievance in a stereotyped phrase and a completely neutral tone, while her general manner in talking about her life was one of rather mischievous banter, tinged with mild nostalgia for the days of a far from respectable youth.

*Appeal by Interest and Emotional Arousal.* Obviously the patients' encounters with me did not provide for experiences of strong emotional coloring. Failures to answer interview questions did not seem to insult their self-esteem; failures in experimental tasks, if noticed, injured it little more or did so but fleetingly. Helen's response to the information given about the length of her past hospitalization was typical in its ephemeral effect. In formal tests the patients did not lack motivation, but after an hour's work they remembered at most two or three of the half dozen tasks they had performed, and their failures no better than their successes, largely because the first thing they forgot was whether they had succeeded or failed.

Neither did the appeal of a test to their interest or emotion help its retention. Larry, when asked to read and retain a fairly platitudinous sentence, exclaimed, "how true it is!" A moment later he could not recall it, and explained that he had not realized he was to memorize it. He was shown the sentence again, with careful instructions to remember it. Again he commented on the wisdom of the statement, and again he forgot it in 5 seconds. It was hardly surprising that at the end of a morning, much of which was spent waiting and resting, the patients often gave blank answers when asked what they had been doing, or recalled in rather general terms that they had been given some tests.

One of the younger patients always seemed more concerned about her success in tests than the others. She once tried to relearn a nursery rhyme of four lines that she remembered having known as a child. She worked at it for a week and felt certain she had mastered the verse, yet utterly failed in the test. Again and again she tried, without ever managing to recite more than the first few words. For some weeks she remembered her failure somewhat shamefacedly; then she would refer to it occasionally, but without any apparent emotional disturbance, and finally she forgot the incident altogether.

Life in a mental hospital does not provide for many experiences of intense affective impact; it is monotonous and devoid of landmarks. One woman patient who tried to leave without permission on repeated occasions, following a somewhat violent escapade, talked about that adventure with malicious glee but the incidents she reported were confused and vague. Another, after being formally discharged, was subsequently brought back by the police who had picked her up in a fight. She remembered clearly enough how she had got drunk and mixed up in a brawl, and at that time readily admitted that this presented a perpetual danger, so that it was in her own best interest to stay in the hospital. Three years later, however, she denied having been involved in that incident, and affirmed that alcohol was out of her system for good, that she despised the stuff.

The patients usually registered accurately their transfer from one hospital building to another—events marking a step in their slow progress. Those who were given regular work could describe their activities, though in very broad outlines; the others who had no occupation—more than half of our group—hardly ever managed even a simple statement about their daily routine. Their replies to quite specific questions, however, indicated an awareness of the circumstances in which they lived, e.g., about washing facilities and the rules concerning their use. A common remark was that in the hospital one day was the same as another, so what can one tell about it? One man said he regularly went out to see sports matches but could not recall a concrete example; another who watched fights on television seemed equally unable to name the contestants of the previous day. Those who viewed other programs never reported anything more specific than "stories" or "shows." Most of the patients who had permission to leave the hospital grounds for the day took no advantage of it, possibly because of lack of funds to benefit from the opportunity, but more characteristically for lack of incentive.

Visits to or from their families may have furnished emotionally tinged experiences as well as some variety to those patients who maintained such contacts. Little evidence of it emerged in our interviews; reports of those events were as vague and inconclusive as any other. One woman knew that her twin daughters had married since her hospitalization, and remembered the name of one son-in-law, but not of the other. Two patients regularly met their grandchildren, without apparently making their acquaintance as distinct persons.

The most remarkable example of delayed recall of an emotionally charged incident occurred when the affect was vicariously experienced. The patients travelled in pairs from their hospital to the laboratory. On one occasion the partners were Minnie, a patient atypical on account of her stable delusions, and another woman who was generally depressed in mood and who had at times protested with considerable agitation and anger about being prevented from rejoining her son. That day too she began with vehement complaints and had evidently voiced her grievances on the way, for as soon as Minnie followed her in the laboratory she too appealed to the experimenter on behalf of "that unhappy woman who would die of grief or do away with herself unless allowed to leave the hospital." This in itself was not particularly striking, for Minnie was also exceptional in persistently initiating conversations with me—usually remonstrating over some imaginary neglect and demanding attention—and barely half an hour had elapsed since her arrival. It was not to be expected though that 2 weeks later, when she came accompanied by a different patient, the first thing she would do was to ask: "Doctor, have you done anything about that poor woman? You know she will die if you don't let her go!" Of course, Minnie's motivation to tell the doctors their business was unusually keen, and the problem in the amnesic syndrome is not so much whether memories recur spontaneously but that they cannot be evoked deliberately.

*Retrograde Amnesia.* Many memories that date back before the onset of the illness can be retrieved with no apparent difficulty. Patients varied considerably in the extent of their retrograde amnesia. For some of them spans of many years were lost without a trace; this happened to Larry and to an older man who was oblivious of everything since the time he had run a farm, long before his admission to the hospital at the age of 78. One woman in her seventies remembered in considerable detail the circumstances of her life in the parental home and the family business, but apparently knew nothing about the several decades that had since elapsed, although they included her marriage and the death of her husband. So little did she take cognizance of the passage of years, of the wizened old woman bent in body she had become that, once asked what she would like to do if and when she left the hospital, she answered "to go out to dances on Saturday nights."

Another woman in her seventies had no apparent recollection at all of the last three decades of her life, and remembered only a few landmarks of her youth. She believed her hospitalization followed an automobile accident in which her husband had been killed. He in fact had died only a couple of years prior to the interview, in ripe old age and many years after the patient's admission to the hospital. Their oldest child, whom the patient thought of as aged 24, was in her fifties.

These patients, like Helen, were extreme examples, and all

over 70 years old; the contributions of the damage specific to the Korsakoff syndrome and of possibly more diffuse senile deterioration to their retrograde amnesia cannot be sharply allocated. The other patients could trace their past fairly closely to the time of their hospitalization, though none without serious gaps, more or less confusion, and considerable vagueness. They remembered their childhood and adult life less completely and accurately than do men and women of normal intelligence. Their ideas about the future were less bizarre than the old woman's but also less colorful. Asked what they would like to do after leaving the hospital, every one of the patients answered with some hope about a job. Even when encouraged to discuss another topic, few of them could think of anything but work; a couple of men might look forward to watching a sports match, a woman or two to being back home. Of rejoining members of the family or friends, or resuming some interest or hobby of the past there was no mention at all.

## Information on Public Events

All the patients had reached adulthood before the Second World War, and with one exception had lived what was for each his or her normal life through those years, i.e., outside the constraints of an institution. Most of them had grown up before the First World War. In 1960, 16 patients were systematically interviewed about those two events, the Great Depression, and some of the famous or notorious names in recent history: Roosevelt, Eisenhower, Hitler, Stalin, Mussolini. One of them with complete and extensive retrograde amnesia, of course, gave blank answers to every question. All the others could describe the Depression fairly accurately—no jobs, no money, shortage of food, public relief, etc.—and most of them placed it correctly in the early thirties. Eight clearly distinguished the two World Wars, and two spontaneously mentioned the Korean War. Five gave 1914, 1917, or 1918 as the date of the First World War, but only one of those placed the Second with approximate accuracy in the years 1940-1942. Six had no idea when the latter took place, the others listed the following dates in chronological order: 1919, 1920, 1932–1933, 1932–1935, 1940, 1941, 1945, and "it ended a couple of years ago."

Confusions between the two wars and their prominent figures tended to occur particularly with the older patients; all of them had hazy notions about the major parties involved. Everybody knew, or at least asserted with confidence, that the United States had won the war; most of the patients also recalled Germany as the enemy. Russia and Japan stood about an even chance of being placed on either side or in the neutral camp. Britain, Canada, and France were no more likely to be listed as allies than Italy, Belgium, or neutral Sweden and Ireland. If any image stood out with clarity, it was that of a single combat between the United States and Germany, and a composite of the two world wars.

Eisenhower's name was known to most patients, although some only remembered him as a senior officer in the army, others only as the President. Hitler, Stalin, and to a lesser extent Mussolini, were meaningful names, and assigned in most instances to their proper nations. Most patients thought Hitler was dead, several also cited speculative reports about his disappearance or escape to South America. Only a few of them registered the death of Stalin and Mussolini; most of the patients thought that Franklin D. Roosevelt was dead, but in many cases by wrong inference, since he no longer was President. Often the replies to questions about world events or statesmen, while not incorrect, were just too terse and stereotyped to be accepted as normal. An example would be this: "Stalin—leader of Russia. Hitler—leader of the Germans. Churchill—leader of England." Undoubtedly, most of the patients had been unsophisticated and indifferent observers of world events long before their psychotic breakdown; nevertheless, talking leisurely, they would have been expected to say something more colorful about these three "leaders."

While the positive replies are of the greatest interest, it should be noted that the most frequent response to questions of this type was an instant admission of ignorance, occasionally strung to an excuse that the patient had a poor memory for names or dates, or had known the answer but no longer remembered it. Even positive answers were typically given in a diffident, often questioning tone, as if prepared to be rejected or corrected. Much the same was true about the patients' replies to questions on current public events. Though quite a few of them professed to be interested in these and to be regular readers of news or to watch it on television, when asked specific questions they hastily found a reason for their inability to give an answer. Some professed to be too busy to follow the events or just did not care about that sort of news; they could not afford to buy papers, or the television in the hospital had broken down. One patient even dragged in the temporary absence of the superintendent owing to illness, and attributed the delay in repairing the instrument to that circumstance.

*Current Affairs.* Toward the end of 1956 the presidential elections in the United States were preceded by two major events farther afield, both of which received considerable publicity here. One was the ill-fated Hungarian revolution, the other the abortive Franco-British expedition to the Suez Canal. All 20 patients interviewed about these three events, mentioned Eisenhower's name in connection with the election, although 2 would not credit him with the victory he had just won. These gave the prize to Roosevelt or Truman, one of them conceding victory to Eisenhower too—but on a previous occasion. The other names prominent in that electoral campaign were virtually unknown to the patients who mentioned them less frequently than those of several local politicians or of the two ex-Presidents. Helen, who never could retain a new name for as long as 3 minutes, was the only one to list both principal contestants correctly.

Fifteen patients knew nothing about the two recent crises in world affairs, but 2 were fairly well informed about events in Hungary and in Suez. The answers of 3 others may have been based on facts, but in their generality could equally well have come from some other source, e.g., "disaster," "starvation," "perhaps revolution" in Hungary. Although starvation was not among the many misfortunes that had befallen that country, the information may have been based on factual foundations, for the patient elaborated it by saying that "the Hungarian people are starving to death; they cannot get them any food by air or sea, because of the war." It so happened that relief shipments of medical supplies had actually been halted at the Austro-Hungarian frontier. The same patient was also right in reporting that at "Suez a ship blew up a few weeks ago," even though this was but a very minor episode in the chain of events there. The substitution of a true but minor incident for the complexity of events is characteristic of amnesic patients. Naming Poland as the only ally, or thus summarizing the Second World War are typical examples: "The Germans fought the Italians, and the Americans went in."

*Errors and Nonsense.* Displacement in time and condensation of two events, the characteristic features of the autobiographical report of amnesic patients, also occur in their recall of world affairs. Their frequent failure to distinguish the two World Wars was a typical example of this tendency. The opposite type of error, analogous to Pick's (1903) description of reduplicative paramnesia, occurred when a patient, asked to name some outstanding generals of the last war, said "Cushing, Eisenhower. I don't mean the President; someone of the same name. But he spells it different." The first name is that of the Cardinal Archbishop of Boston, and was presumably given instead of Pershing's. The same patient, though quite well oriented about her own life in the hospital, described Stalin as "a spokesman of Germany," thought in 1960 that both he and Mussolini were still alive, and gave the following answer when asked who was at the head of England: "I was going to say Churchill but he isn't any more." I tried to help by asking whether it was a king or a queen. "No, hasn't England gone like America?"—was her comment. "You mean a republic"—I suggested. "Yes, that's it. There is a queen."

Here is a patient who, although she always talked sensibly about her own life, uttered in one breath two mutually exclusive statements, and thus furnished some evidence for Pick's (1915) later formula of confabulation. As a rule the amnesic patients were willing enough to admit their ignorance about public affairs, but at times they answered with a meaningless statement or an evasive generalization. An example of the latter is this comment on President Eisenhower's widely publicized travels to foreign capitals: "He travels quite a bit. He goes all over. Every time you pick up a newpaper you read Eisenhower is in this place or that place. I suppose he has to; it's his job." Nevertheless, I would not subscribe to the thesis that talking nonsense and, by inference, defective reasoning is a characteristic feature of the amnesic syndrome. Korsakoff patients often contradict their own previous statements in a short space of time, and do so with equanimity, and two mutually exclusive statements do indeed make nonsense; but deranged reasoning is not its only possible cause. The manner in which these contradictions arise will be considered next.

*Chapter 3*

# CONFABULATION

The psychopathology of Korsakoff's disease is frequently referred to as the "amnestic-confabulatory syndrome." This nomenclature proposes amnesia and confabulation as joint defining attributes of the syndrome and, by implication, excludes from its nosological class any disorder characterized by only one of these two anomalies. The rigor of this logic, however, is considerably softened in practice by the loose definition of confabulation. The term often seems to be treated so comprehensively as to include any palpably false statement. Thus undoubtedly it is applicable to every amnesic patient but hardly valuable for differential diagnosis. The utility of loose, global concepts is rapidly exhausted, and at that point they need refinement.

Bender and her associates (1938) had some reason for presenting as an example of confabulation the pictorial reproductions of their patients who distorted meaningless patterns so as to make them look like familiar designs. Did they intend to convey to their reader that confabulation is a falsification by which the sense or form of a raw model is improved? That would be a meaningful proposition but not one by which confabulation—a pathological type of behavior—could be distinguished from the normal processes of mnemonic reproduction. Wyke and Warrington (1960) proceeded in the same direction when they showed a Korsakoff patient a series of ambiguous figures, and presented her attempts at elaboration and completion as examples of confabulation, and moreover as evidence of its being a primary symptom.

Customarily confabulation refers to a certain class of verbal statements, and there seems to be no compelling reason for stretching the application of the term beyond the confines of verbal behavior; its meaning is confusing enough within that area. In its widest sense it may only suggest a readiness to talk without regard to factual accuracy. Even within these broad limits, the term should not be applied without first weighing the patient's readiness to talk against his apparent lack of factual knowledge; it does not mean simply ease of engaging in and sustaining general conversation. Textbook definitions are usually narrower, restricting the term to "pseudoreminiscence which involves fabrication" (Henderson and Gillespie, 1937); "making up a likely story" (Cameron and Magaret, 1951); or "free inventions taken as experiences" (Bleuler, 1924).

From these definitions it would appear that the content of confabulation is gratuitously invented, fabricated rather than erroneously reproduced or reconstructed from actual data. Yet, the clinical examples quoted in the literature are almost exclusively of the latter type. Korsakoff (1892) traced the pseudoreminiscences of his patients quite explicitly to true memories; others (e.g., (Clarke, 1912; Régis, 1913) indiscriminately bracketed under confabulation the distortion of true events and the invention of those that never took place. Surveying the many uses to which confabulation has been put in the literature, one will find that it refers to anything from a deliberate lie or a product of creative imagination (neither of which is characteristic of amnesic patients) to rounding out the memory of something experienced, learned, or casually observed—in fact normal remembering.

*Purposive Confabulation.* Patients with Wernicke's disease often sound as if they were spinning a yarn, and were rather clumsy at it to boot. Do they tell lies deliberately, and fail to convince the listener only because of their poor intellectual skills? The question is seldom put in quite so drastic terms, but something of the sort was implied in Bonhöffer's (1901) concept of confabulation of exigency, in the suggestion that patients confabulate in order to oblige the listener, or to fill in gaps in their knowledge of facts. Pick (1905), who held that suggestibility played an important part in confabulation, made much of this argument and so have other writers. Janet (1928), for example, distinguished confabulation from fabulation—an uncritical construction of memories without reference to the present—in attributing to the former a purpose to impose some order on one's discourse.

Although it may be useful to distinguish confabulation of exigency from spontaneous tales of adventure, it does not follow that patients confabulate to escape the embarrassment of their ignorance. Because telling an untruth can serve a purpose, it has been argued that amnesic patients invent information in order to please the interviewer or to fill gaps in their memory. The reasoning is plausible enough, and amnesic patients are not all paragons of virtue. They are as apt as others to tell a deliberate lie, although I cannot recall many instances. They would be more likely to evade an answer with a remark that appeared to be a crudely contrived lie, e.g., when asked about a magazine he has ostensibly been reading, a patient replies "I wouldn't know, I am not interested in that sort of thing." Probably the transparent falsity of this remark was not apparent to him; he might have been interested in going through the motions of reading the magazine one moment, yet uninterested in its name and contents the next. In any case, the chronic patients' typical response, when they are unable to furnish the information requested, is to admit ignorance. They resort to this on uncountably more occasions than they do to evasion or substitution, let alone to fabrication.

Wernicke patients, on the contrary, rarely admit ignorance, and freely invent answers on the spur of the moment. Do they invent answers in order to avoid embarrassment, to satisfy a need, to resolve a tension? Possibly so, even though a patently absurd reply would hardly serve that purpose in normal conversation, and can satisfy them only because they are unaware of its inadequacy. It certainly does not sound like a contrived fabrication or distortion of a true event. Neither is it done to humor the interviewer or to bolster their own self-esteem. Those patients are too apathetic or agitated to care about either.

In one sense the suggestion that confabulation fills gaps is quite correct. It is incontrovertible because it explains nothing beyond the fact that the information required is missing. There is a gap in the patient's memory, and whatever he supplies in the place of the correct answer fills that gap. However, if the proposition is meant to be more than loosely descriptive, it suffers from ambiguity on several scores. It is misleading as an analogy, because confabulation is not a process of interpolation, the fitting of some appropriate content between two or more firmly established landmarks. Rather is it in the nature of extrapolation that takes place when information at only one end of a series is available. As an explanation it is incorrect because the substitution is not deliberate; when aware of a gap in his knowledge the amnesic patient usually pleads ignorance. If meant to refer to some unconscious process of substitution, it is an untestable proposition and, moreover, the point of interest would then be why substitution should occur rather than straight admission of ignorance.

*Confabulation from Disorientation.* Whichever way one looks at confabulation it would not occur but for the amnesic defect; the unavailability of some previously acquired information, and the patient's unawareness of this deficit. Is the amnesic defect a sufficient explanation for the occurrence of confabulation? Clearly not, and for two reasons at least. First, confabulation tends to disappear as patients progress from the confusional to the chronic phase, while the amnesic disturbance remains constant or changes only slightly. Second, some chronic patients confabulate more, others less or not at all, and there is no discernible correlation between their propensity to confabulate and the gravity of their amnesia. These considerations point to two factors that determine the occurrence of confabulation, one of which is independent, the other involved in the amnesic disturbance. The latter is the patient's disorientation, and particularly his labile temporal anchorage. The other factor is his personality structure, his traits evolved in dealing with the environment and in maintaining his self image. These, like other overlearned skills, are barely, if at all, modified by the amnesic disorder.

Although the total disorientation characteristic of Wernicke's disease gradually improves, the patients' unstable temporal anchorage persists into the chronic phase. It also forms part of the Korsakoff syndrome when this has not evolved from Wernicke's disease. The conclusion indicated by these observations is not that disorientation for time and disorientation for places or persons are caused by the disturbance of different mechanisms, but that the former is more closely involved in the amnesic derangement than the others. Amnesic patients are capable of some new learning; many become more or less familiar with their surroundings in the hospital and with a few new faces, but none is securely set in the objective present. Even if he does know the date shown by the calendar, today for him is not at one extreme of a firm structure built on the preceding days or months. At its simplest, the effect of this temporal discontinuity is a gap extending from the onset of the patient's disease to the present. In fact, the derangement is more complex; the gap is not complete, and it stretches back to the time before the onset of the disease. The ways in which the temporal relations of past events can be distorted in the patient's memory will be discussed in greater detail in a later section. All that need be considered here is that these temporal placements are erratic, and that consequently dislocations and recombinations of past events are liable to occur even in the chronic phase of the amnesic syndrome, and to that extent confabulation too may continue.

## The Acute Phase of the "Amnestic-Confabulatory" Syndrome

In the early stages of the amnesic syndrome the patient is severely confused and disoriented. He does not know or only gradually realizes that he is in a hospital and he has no recollection of the events that resulted in his transfer to the ward. Probably because of this break in the continuity of his self record, he seems unable to accept his new condition with the same conviction of reality as other patients show in registering their hospitalization. If asked where he is, he may indeed correctly state it is a hospital and even name it, yet a minute later his answer to the same question could be that of an entirely different place. Perhaps at first he took note of the interviewer's white coat and the row of beds, but not the second time. If transferred from one wing of the hospital to another, he will refer to either the former or the latter as some place outside; he recognizes the difference but misjudges the transition. Certitude in identifying a place bears no relation to its accuracy. The notion that it is a hospital can be entertained very tentatively or fleetingly; the delusion that it is some rooming house or "The Eagle which used to be Mrs. Porter's tavern," can be held firmly day after day, or discarded at the first intimation of doubt.

*Disorientation in Time.* Errors in recognizing the surroundings are paralleled by misjudgments of time and persons. Typically the patient believes the date is the same as that which just preceded his hospitalization; his time errors therefore are usually slight at first, a matter of a few weeks or months. Visible evidence to the contrary is unlikely to change his judgment: although the trees outside his window may be in bloom, for him it still seems to be December, just before Christmas. Judgments about the time of the day are rarely better than a guess.

Even though a patient may know the calendar year, he is unlikely to be equally accurate about his age; that may be given as 50 at one moment and 26 the next. If his answer is right, he probably arrived at it by subtracting from the current year that of his birth, a datum often available even to the confused patient. In this manner one of our patients correctly calculated that he must be about 60 but soon afterward thought he was a young man and that we were in 1928. I reminded him that the current year was 1959. To this piece of information the patient's immediate reaction was one of indignant rejection, but a few moments later he grudgingly accepted it, and to be quite certain he asked explicitly: "Did you say we are in 1959?" Then, in reply to the affirmative nod, he commented: "Oh, I thought it was more than that." It would appear that, having first slipped back 31 years in his frame of reference, the patient quickly resumed that of the calendar year, but an impression that he had just lost count of the years still persisted.

*Misidentification of Persons and Events.* Few patients in the acute phase learn their doctor's name sufficiently well to reproduce it on demand, or even to decide with confidence whether the white-coated man facing the bed is Dr. X or Dr. Y. A new name may be registered, though, so that it re-emerges in a story about recent events, the substance of which, however, is drawn from an earlier setting. One patient, while admitting one moment that he had been in the ward for the past 2 weeks, in the next gave a lively account of his outing the previous Sunday, when he "remembered" having been taken to church in a car, and to dinner afterward. The person who accompanied him in repeated versions of the story was alternately his brother and one of his doctors. When asked whether he has seen the interviewer before, the patient's typical answer is that of tentative assent, hardly ever a firm denial. *Déjà vu* is quite common, and is often treated as one aspect of confabulation. Furthermore, in the acute phase patients do not simply remark on the questioner's familiarity; they tend to identify him as a particular person, one whom they know well enough, though not by name—"the man who sold me the insurance"; "the guy I often meet at the bar."

Whether misidentification of the environment is the substance of confabulation or not, it is the product of the same circumstances from which emerge the logically consistent stories that fully qualify for this description. The classic example is the patient's reply to questions relating to his activities earlier in the day or the previous day. He almost never answers that he had been lying in the same bed, been in the same spot where he is at the moment. Typically, he gives a coherent report of his activities at work, a day in the home, a meeting with a friend, a visit to the doctor. A report of what the patient did at the shop in the morning, or whom he met the previous evening is confabulatory because it is given in relation to a time when we know he was laid up in the hospital. He does not know; that time does not exist for him phenomenally. There is nothing in his cognitive system to provide the appropriate temporal context, and thus lead to the correct answer or inhibit an incorrect one.

One man interviewed had a single child, a grown woman who was the mother of a young boy. When asked whether he had any children, the patient replied he had a young son. Faced outright with a question about his daughter's age, only a few minutes later, he said: "My daughter? Well, one of them is 21 . . . the other may be 20; one may be 52." This lability of reference at one extreme, and the perseveration of the same theme at the other, both agree with Grünthal's (1924) explanation that amnesic patients confabulate because they are set on the wrong track and cannot get away from it. The track can follow a mood as well as a topic of content. The man quoted was interviewed on 3 consecutive days; the first time he responded to every question in a querulous, suspicious manner. The second day he confided in me, and almost all he said concerned the ingratitude and intrigues of various undefined persons. The third day he talked effusively and with tears in his eyes about the kindness of all manner of people toward him.

A similar observation was made with Rose who was also interviewed 3 days running, shortly after hospitalization. On the first occasion she brought her uncle into almost every answer she gave about her circumstances, and that included the hospital, for she was dimly aware of her surroundings. Next day her mother occupied the same central position, referred to as if alive, although in fact she had been dead for some years. The patient did not mention her husband until the third day, but then everything she talked about led to him.

In the second interview, when asked about her husband, Rose at first denied that she was married. Whereupon I pointed to her wedding ring, and asked why she wore one. Having convinced herself of its presence on her left ring finger, Rose named in close succession three imaginary husbands, none of whose name she bore. She also provided some background for these fictitious marriages, involving parental opposition and a few other plausible circumstances. Withal, she denied ever having lived with a man, or having lived outside her mother's house. Her story was confused, yet much of it could have been based on facts, on events dating back over 10 years, the time before she had married.

Nothing in this situation or in the subsequent interview suggested that the patient had invented the three husbands in order to fill a gap in memory, or to please me. She was too deeply absorbed in herself to take any but the most superficial notice of me, too strained to piece together an account of herself to spare any resources for the invention of fictitious information. A brief moment of insight into her condition produced no words, only a visible emotional shock and tears of distress and bewilderment. Confabulation was resumed a minute or two later, by which time the cognitive as well as the affective registration of her disability had vanished to all appearances. On each of the 3 days, the patient structured her fragmentary but fluent talk around a different person, molded her physical surroundings so as to accommodate the visible sights and audible sounds of the ward as well as the characters of her phenomenal environment. This endeavor one day placed the uncle in the hospital for blood transfusion, on the third it converted the hospital into the shop where her husband was working.

On the surface, all the attributes of creative imagination, instantaneous invention, and denial of memory gaps were present in these interviews with Rose. Nevertheless, to account for her behavior in terms of those constructs would gratuitously involve cognitive processes that neither possess much explanatory value, nor strike the eye witness as convincing in that setting. Rose's fabrications could be taken to justify Bleuler's definition of confabulation as "free inventions taken as experiences"; but most other examples provided by amnesic patients would fail to fit the formula. They involve no invention, only gross transposition in context. Even the patient quoted, unaware as she was of her inability to give the right answer, did not confabulate to conceal her ignorance. Her stories were not inventions mistaken for truth, they were involved and visibly desperate attempts to escape perplexity.

*Definition.* In contrast with Bleuler's definition, but in agreement with many other students of the problem, it is proposed that in the early phase of the Wernicke-Korsakoff syndrome confabulation is: (a) typically, but not exclusively, an account, more or less coherent and internally consistent, concerning the patient. (b) This account is false in the context named and often false in details within its own context. (c) Its content is drawn fully or principally from the patient's recollection of his actual experiences, including his thoughts in the past. (d) Confabulation reconstructs this content, modifies and recombines its elements, employing the mechanisms of normal remembering. (e) This material is presented without awareness of its distortions or of its inappropriateness, and (f) serves no other purpose, is motivated in no other way than factual information based on genuine data.

## The Chronic State of Korsakoff's Psychosis

After the peripheral signs of Wernicke's encephalopathy and the confusional state improve, the amnesic impairment becomes more prominent. A certain measure of disorientation and possibly also of confabulation is likely to continue in some patients, but none in others. Reports about the presence of confabulation in chronic Korsakoff patients differ; many treat it as a typical sign, while others have remarked on its absence. Even though they may not make the point explicitly, few observers would dispute Kräpelin's (1900) comment that a marked drop occurs in the elaboration and falsification of memories as the patients pass from the acute to the later phase of the disease.

If confabulation were indeed the product of creative fantasy, it would be somewhat paradoxical that, as the patient improves, he should also lapse from a condition of lively productivity into a state of psychotic apathy. Williams and Rupp (1938) stated the more convincing case that confabulation stops as insight appears. Insight, of course, is itself determined by such clues as the patient's awareness of his surroundings, the referral of his recent experiences to the hospital environment, by his recognition and admission that he lacks the information requested, i.e., by his avoidance of the traps of confabulation. To this extent Williams and Rupp's thesis is unassailable, but there is no evidence that the cessation of confabulation is conditional on the patient's insight into his memory disturbance, or into the gravity and duration of his disease. It is doubtful if any Korsakoff patient ever gains complete insight into his condition in this sense of the term, and some certainly do not. Nevertheless, their tendency to confabulate diminishes quite considerably, and may indeed completely vanish.

*Individual Differences.* In this respect there is considerable intra-individual consistency; some patients carefully refuse to speak when in doubt, others—only a few in my experience—freely advance incorrect information, usually in a limited area of reference. It is therefore reasonable to trace persistent confabulatory tendencies to the basic personality, as Williams and Rupp have done. Since, however, rarely is enough known about the patient's pre-morbid behavior, the evidence must be inferential. To me the argument seemed most convincing when I witnessed the obvious attempts of a few patients to present their past in a light more favorable than a truthful account would, or when listening to a delusional theme.

Among the former the most remarkable case was that of Helen (see p. 24), who after many years of hospitalization maintained with imperturbable consistency that she had been admitted only the day before. She comported and presented herself as a lady of leisure who was living in one of the better residential hotels of the town, where she always expected to return the same day. Her highly stereotyped account of her past was probably true, but she seemed unaware that the conditions of that very agreeable life had long since ceased.

It was difficult to believe that this woman was so completely unaware of her present circumstances as she appeared to be, so majestically indifferent to the contradictions and sheer nonsense of the remarks with which she tried to parry the unwelcome effects of her amnesia. When asked to give the name of a person she had just been introduced to or talk about a book she had been carrying under her arm day after day, or to report what she knew about events in the world, she would brush aside the question with some such comment as, "I'm too busy to care about those things." Yet she tried to keep up a pretense of the woman of the world, in spite of her evident ignorance of current events. Her attempts at evasion were not very subtle, amounting to such retorts as "just events"; "just happenings of the day"; "I never remember wars. They don't mean a thing to me. Who cares about wars? I like to think about pleasant things . . . The Depression?—who wants to know about that! I like all the best places: The Ritz-Carlton. New York is the only place to live. I was there a month ago . . .".

She never voiced a complaint, and judged by her account the food she received was always excellent, and often included dishes more luxurious than are served in a hospital. Her reason for drinking only tea with those meals was her purported indifference to alcoholic beverages other than champagne. While so careful to maintain the illusion of her privileged position, Helen in her many interviews never spoke disparagingly or resentfully about life in the mental hospital or about her fellow inmates. All that barely existed for her.

One would think that an elaborate facade such as hers could not be maintained without immense effort and something very much like rigorous mental drill, for she did not once betray her disbelief in anything she pretended. Helen was our one Korsakoff patient who responded to hypnosis[1] but repeated attempts with that technique produced absolutely no new material of recall, nor an admission of an awareness of her condition. Motivational influences undoubtedly played their part in furnishing her with glib evasive answers and in her obstinate adherence to a past image of herself. These, however, would hardly have resulted in her characteristic behavior, unless they had been superimposed on her amnesic derangement.

Helen was one of the 5 chronic amnesic patients who had no stable and clear notion about their condition, the fact of their hospitalization, or of its approximate duration. In her

[1]We were interested in testing the hypothesis that memories would be available to Korsakoff patients but for their inability to initiate the process of recall, and hoped to elicit some more information about their past. Two colleagues trained and experienced in hypnosis repeatedly failed with all our patients, excepting Helen.

case, though, there was reason to suspect that she knew better than she would admit. Our most thoroughly disoriented patient was a man in his eighties who on repeated occasion firmly believed that he had just driven over in a horse-drawn wagon from the family farm. He knew his own age, yet thought both his parents were still alive and depended on his work for support. He seemed to have forgotten everything that had happened during the last few years prior to his hospitalization at the age of 78, and appeared to be completely unfamiliar with his surroundings. His confabulation, however, extended beyond errors attributable to a gap in a phase of life remembered. He reported that he had served in the army during the World War—presumably the First—had seen battle and fought the Germans. Withal he affirmed that he had never left Canada. Had he then fought the Germans in Canada? Indeed, that is what he said he had done "when they came over—though not in full force."

It has already been stressed that disorientation for the surroundings occurred in the oldest members of our patient group, and this under the pressure of questions or even without prompting easily led to confabulation. Another source of confabulation, an attempt to embellish the dull autobiographic records, I spotted in 4 patients. Of these Larry and Helen have been discussed at some length; the other two were middle-aged women who, talking about the past, consistently omitted some discreditable details noted on their charts, but nevertheless so described their lives as to make it appear adventurous as well as respectable. It is quite likely that in these instances the predisposition to improve on the facts was independent of the amnesic disturbance which only added confusion and contradictions to those attempts at fiction. Similarly, the delusional themes of two patients seemed unrelated to the Korsakoff syndrome, and cannot be properly listed as instances of confabulation.

*Delusions.* Larry's delusions rarely intruded into his grasp of the world around him, and neither did seriously those of the middle-aged woman who twice believed she had been stabbed in the leg by a fellow patient. She had in fact been twice attacked by another patient but on neither occasion sustained an injury to her legs; she had also gotten into trouble in the work room for spreading false rumors about fellow patients. There seemed to be even less substance to her other delusional topic that concerned her husband's schemes to keep her in the hospital, so that he can live with another woman and spend without hindrance the money he had drawn from her savings. She often described in the same details and much the same phrases an occasion when he had unjustly accused her of infidelity, and a later incident when he had her arrested on a bench in the park. According to her file the patient had indeed been arrested, in fact three times, but always for drunkenness; she herself had withdrawn her bank balance, and her husband was in a sanatorium at the time of her hospitalization.

Another woman, diagnosed as having Korsakoff's psychosis following Wernicke's encephalopathy, but also with a record of paranoid behavior, alternated her interminable talk between involved conspiracies against her financial interests and confidential complaints about her health and its culpable neglect by the medical profession. With her the delusional content almost monopolized every communication. She was always clearly aware of her surroundings, and had an uncommonly exact memory for incidents that could be woven into her distorted image of the world. This was an entirely atypical patient in our group, and therefore she did not take part in the experiments; the amnesic syndrome, complex though it be, formed only a part of the total pattern of her psychosis.

No evidence was found in our Korsakoff patients of hallucinations or other abnormal perceptual experiences. Half the members of a group of 20 interviewed said they never dreamed; 8 professed to having dreams rarely, 2 more regularly. Most of these had no memory of their dreams or recalled but the vaguest incidents.

*Residual Defect.* Apart from the exceptions quoted, the analysis of the interviews with 28 Korsakoff patients showed: (a) that they reliably knew the fact of their hospitalization and related their reports to that setting; (b) gave accounts of their past that did not conflict with the known facts, with common sense, or their own previous statements. The latter proposition should be qualified on two scores: (1) Inaccuracies and inconsistencies in details did occur (e.g., the number of sons and daughters); (2) events were liable to be grossly displaced in their temporal context, and less often in their social-geographic environment. An example of the latter type of confusion was one patient's stubborn assertion that she knew me from many years back when she used to visit my neighbors, a statement that she reaffirmed in spite of my repeated denials. Various instances have been cited to illustrate the patients' confusion in the temporal placement and ordering of their memories. This is the disorder to which should be attributed most, if not all, occurrences of confabulation in Korsakoff's syndrome.

In this respect, the origins of confabulation are much the same in Wernicke's disease and in the chronic amnesic syndrome, though in the latter phase it contains far less delusional material or patent nonsense, and no gibberish. Rose, the young woman whose voluble and chaotic talk in the near-delirious state of Wernicke's disease was quoted earlier, came to be interviewed again 2 and 3 years later. Then she described the conditions of her home and work prior to hospitalization quite accurately and in fair detail, although she could not say much about life in the hospital. She talked slowly, appeared rather apathetic, diffident, and easily given to tears. She did not confabulate any more but at times would declaim without an apparent clue in the context of the interview: "I am an American citizen fighting for freedom." Since on one occasion she added: "I want to stand on my own feet, to be a housewife," it is not improbable that her patriotic testimony was an appeal for discharge from the hospital. Overtly she never protested against her hospitalization, and indeed frequently expressed gratitude for the care she had received as a tuberculotic patient. She was also apt to "Thank God" for any small success, be it but a correct answer to my question.

It mattered to Rose, as it did to the other patients, that they should be able to handle problems set to them, whether these were questions to be answered or tasks to be performed. Yet they did not resort freely to specious answers when in doubt about the proper response. Several experiments allowed two alternatives to the correct response: either an incorrect answer or admission of ignorance. The preference for the latter was very notable in the Korsakoff patients, and often stronger than in the control group; so little did they fill in gaps of memory arbitrarily and without regard to the truth.

At one time I tested 20 patients with the familiar catch question: "Now didn't we meet over a drink last night?" Although I put it as jovially and convincingly as I could, all the responses were denials. Some of the patients took the question for a joke, others more earnestly pointed out that last night as every other night they had been in the hospital where no drinks are served. Perhaps the monotony of hospital life and its sober diet drain that cheerful spirit from which spring the carefree tales of the newly admitted patient; moreover, in its stable environment much of his initial disorientation recedes. Neither in interviews, nor in an experiment designed for the purpose, and ostensibly testing olfactory acuity, did the Korsakoff patients show any higher degree of suggestibility than men and women who have no amnesic troubles.

## Summary

Defined as a factually incorrect verbal statement—other than intentional deception, fantastic fabrication, wild guess, gibberish, or delusion—confabulation occurs frequently in many, possibly all, patients with Wernicke's disease. Its content is typically, but not exclusively, autobiographical; its source is predominantly that of the patient's actual experiences in an earlier phase of his life. It seems to arise from the disruption of his temporal frame of reference, so that true statements become displaced in their chronological setting, those drawn from different periods become fused. Typically, a memory of the more remote past re-emerges as an event in the present or immediate past. Confusion between memories of actual experiences and second-hand information or mere ideas also occurs. A dominant theme or affect of the hour may violently distort the content of confabulation into a forcibly uniform pattern.

In the chronic phase of the amnesic syndrome confabulation is much less common, and may not be detected at all in the discourse of many patients. The patient's insight into his condition is neither a necessary nor a sufficient condition for the absence of confabulation. Personality traits developed before the psychotic break are quite likely to account for a tendency to confabulate. Most of the 28 patients interviewed always understood their circumstances, and realistically discussed the events of their lives within the setting of the mental hospital. Their answers to questions relating to world events as well as to their personal experiences were factual, usually correct or plausible, even though extraordinarily sparse and subject to certain characteristic distortions. As a rule they were quite ready to admit ignorance, and gave their answers with an inflection of diffidence. No one instance of fantastic fabrication was observed in this group of patients.

Confabulation as a sign in the Korsakoff syndrome can properly be regarded as secondary to the amnesic derangement. It occurs within contexts that, lacking adequately structured memories, are diffuse and devoid of points of anchorage. The patient himself is almost certainly not aware of the gaps in his knowledge when he confabulates; he transposes information from an earlier period in his life, condenses or distorts material without consciousness of his deficit or of the confabulatory process, and hence without intent. Even under these circumstances confabulation may only be elicited by leading questions. The amnesic deficit creates an occasion for its occurrence, and dispositions characteristic of the individual patient determine its presence, rate, and quality.

*PART THREE*

# HISTORICAL

*Chapter 4*

# THE LITERATURE OF THE AMNESIC SYNDROME

A survey of the literature of the amnesic syndrome could be guided by several principles of selection and organization. For the writer, no doubt, none would be simpler than the adoption of a chronological canon: to discuss the reports as they appeared in print over the past seven decades. For the reader, a more attractive alternative might be to pursue each of the controversies about one or another aspect of the amnesic syndrome, as it emerged and has developed. In fact, however, the latter would be a most unrewarding enterprise, for the several strands of the controversies have become thoroughly entangled in the course of the years, and entangled in different patterns with different authors. Many an argument marshalled by a writer on one of the issues would appear rather insubstantial out of the context of his observations on some other issues pertaining to the amnesic syndrome.

The compromise solution chosen combines a fairly close chronological order with a classification according to a few major divisions in interest and point of view. These two principles, of course, are not entirely independent, since the focus of interest and theoretical bias in psychology have shifted gradually with the years. On the other hand, the problems presented by the amnesic syndrome have remained constant and largely unresolved. The subheadings of this chapter should, therefore, not be taken as representing exclusive categories. The dividing line between affective and conative functions has never been clearly drawn; an interest in the neurological model of the amnesic psychopathology was not exclusive to those listed under that heading; and the cognitive dysfunction has served as a focus for most of the reports, from the earliest to the present day.

The bulk of the work describing the amnesic syndrome and analyzing its disturbed processes has been done by clinicians. Their first problem was to recognize the identity of the disease and to distinguish it from other confusional states, i.e., diagnosis. Having defined the syndrome, with boundaries necessarily not too tightly closed, its students had to face some paradoxes of its psychopathology. Two major questions were raised, and, in one form or another, most investigators of the amnesic syndrome have had to contend with these: (1) Does it present simply a degradation of the memory function, and (2) what processes in memory are affected by it, and to what extent. The answer given to the first question has been virtually unanimous; the disturbance is not simply or exclusively one of memory. In attempting to solve the second problem there has been more controversy. Many psychological analyses have suffered from being tied to conceptual systems that offer no ready answer, and more particularly to crude models of brain function. Certain constructs proposed by more recent neurophysiological theory may fit the amnesic syndrome better than the older ones.

## Nosological Determination

The earliest phase in the literature of the amnesic syndrome was marked by an endeavor to classify the clinical material and to define the syndrome as a nosological class. The principal issues of the early studies were, first, the establishment of the conditional relationship between peripheral neuropathology and the mental derangement and, second, the etiology of both sets of symptoms. They also attempted to define the psychological deficit and debated the possibility of complete recovery.

Korsakoff (1889, 1890) claimed to have first shown that the psychological signs were not simply superimposed on the neurological disease, as virtually independent effects of chronic alcoholic intoxication. Central and peripheral signs formed a unitary syndrome, though either could occur independently of the other. Alcohol, he declared, was not a necessary etiological factor, though some poisoning was always involved. In view of these considerations, Korsakoff suggested that the mental disorder be known as *psycho-toxemic cerebropathy* or *polyneuritic psychosis.* Many of the patients he observed had died in the early stage of the illness, which was most often characterized by stupor or by delirium tremens. Those who survived regained their lost functions slowly, and in some instances listed by Korsakoff recovered them completely.

Because he studied most of his patients during the acute phase of the disease, in describing their mental state, Korsakoff laid considerable stress on affective disorders. With excessive irritability as a basic symptom, these include the whole gamut from anxiety and phobias to compulsive thoughts and depression. He reasoned that the patients' incapacity to concentrate prevents them from efficient thinking; failure to connect ideas results in confusion. Later this general mental disturbance may clear up, and it is then that the memory derangement becomes prominent. The patients take in accurately enough that which is in their surroundings, and their reasoning appears to be intact. Still, even this impression is deceptive, since the patients rely entirely on routines acquired prior to their illness, and apply those in a stereotyped fashion.

Events experienced during their illness leave no trace in their consciousness; no new learning occurs. Yet, it would be incorrect to assume that those events pass without making any impression. Korsakoff inferred from some observations of his patients' behavior that such impressions must have been made on them unconsciously. The memory defect, consequently, is in the process of recall, not in registration. As for content, the patients illustrate Ribot's (1881) laws of regression: recent memories are lost before distant ones, habits are the last to go, language is affected only in exceptionally severe cases. The extent of the amnesic deficit varies widely among and within patients. In mild cases even recent events can be recalled, in very severe ones memory for the remotest past can be destroyed. Memories are often placed outside their proper temporal context. Korsakoff believed that the patient's capacity to make an effort to remember was a decisive factor, and also suggested that favorable conditions could make a considerable difference, but did not specify these conditions. He was certainly aware of the importance of his patients' unusual lack of vitality and the need of constant external stimulation to elicit their activity.

Korsakoff's careful and extensive reports of a series of cases certainly deserve the respect vouchsafed for pioneer studies, even though he was not the first to describe the peripheral neuropathy in chronic alcoholism, or to remark on the accompanying confusional symptoms and memory disturbance. He himself quoted Magnus Huss (1852) as a forerunner; French authorities refer back to Lancereaux (1864). Moeli (1883), Strümpell (1883), and Charcot (1884) had also remarked incidentally that such anomalies as memory loss, confusion, contradictions, denial of drinking, tend to occur with peripheral neuritis, but they had paid attention almost exclusively to the neurological signs. Babilée's (1886) dissertation, however, anticipated many of Korsakoff's observations on the psychological disturbance in the chronic alcoholic syndrome. Contemporaneously with Korsakoff, Ross (1890) and Tiling (1890) reported on clinical observations that suggested a pattern of psychological disorders associated with peripheral neuritis of diverse etiology. Tiling (1892), who had read Korsakoff's Russian publications, held that the amnesic syndrome occurred regularly in alcoholic neuritis and only rarely with neuritis of another etiology.

*Colella* (1894) should be credited with writing the first monograph on the syndrome, even though it was divided into three separate articles. The case material of 32 patients for his survey of the polyneuritic psychosis included 20 that Korsakoff had reported on in his various articles and 8 whom the author had studied personally, under Charcot in Paris, and at Hitzig's clinic in Halle. All but one of these 8 patients had been heavy drinkers. Colella's chapter on the psychopathology of the disease is a thoughtful statement of the associationist position of his time, and thus reproduces many of Korsakoff's arguments. He, too, favored an explanation in terms of defective recall rather than damaged registration, because after some measure of recovery several patients could remember events they had been unable to recall consciously during their illness. Colella emphasized the importance of attention and volition as being the functions which, when regained, enable the patients to recover memories at will. He confirmed the opinion of Ross and Bury (1893) that amnesia often did, but need not invariably, accompany peripheral neuropathy due to alcoholic paralysis. Since the amnesic symptoms were found to be coexistent neither with peripheral neuritis nor with toxemias, Jolly (1897) concluded that they ought to be entered into the clinical nomenclature under their own name, and suggested that this be *Korsakoff syndrome* or symptom complex.

*Mönkemöller.* A number of Korsakoff's patients died during the early phase of their illness, several others advanced into a chronic state of "apathetic confusion," and still others seemed to achieve complete recovery. Tiling (1892) and Mönkemöller (1898) disputed that full remission of the psychological damage ever occurs in the amnesic syndrome; most subsequent students of the disease subscribed to this opinion.[1] These authors concluded from their clinical observations that the amnesic psychosis never cleared up without leaving some residual memory impairment and a general curtailment of mental function. Their case suffers from the weakness of an inductive conclusion based on an inevitably limited sample of observations; the opposite argument, however, also founders

---

[1]For example, Bonhöffer (1901); Meyer and Raecke (1903); Clarke (1912); Kauffmann (1913); Moll (1915); Steinthal (1921). Lückerath (1900) limited his adverse prognosis to Korsakoff's psychosis of alcoholic origin. More recently Victor and Adams (1953) arrived at a more hopeful conclusion but noted that "complete restoration of memory . . . is unusual" when the defect is severe. Wernicke (1900) wrote that most patients recover from polyneuritic psychosis but, no doubt, he only referred to the neurological symptoms of the early phase of the disease. He called the chronic condition inanition psychosis, equated it with presbyophrenia, and admitted the possibility that it was the same disease as Korsakoff's psychosis. Applying the term "Korsakoff syndrome" to the acute stage of the illness, Rosenbaum and Merritt (1939) reported a fair percentage of complete recovery, as did Williams and Smith (1954) on amnesic disturbance with tuberculous meningitis.

because none of the amnesic patients who were thought to have made a full recovery had been thoroughly examined prior to their illness.

Mönkemöller based his report on observations of 20 odd patients whose disease fitted the description of polyneuritic psychosis of alcoholic origin. He attributed Korsakoff's unduly optimistic prognosis to the fact that the Russian psychiatrist had had no first-hand impression, nor reliable clinical reports on his patients as they progressed beyond the acute phase of the illness. Mönkemöller himself followed a number of patients whose neurological symptoms had appeared several months prior to the psychological, and their improvement in the two areas hardly progressed apace. Physical recovery could be complete while the mental deficit remained virtually unchanged. He never saw an instance of complete remission from the psychological impairment; some loss of memory function, heightened fatiguability, a narrowing of interest, and listlessness were the mildest residual effects. In the chronic state of the disease, apart from the amnesic anomalies, the patients—with one euphoric exception—showed dull affect and a lack of interest in others or in events around them, but no disorder in perception or judgment, and they often filled memory gaps with humorous remarks. Without exception, the effects of the disease are so severe that "the patients can no longer play their parts in the affairs of the world, their self is lost."

*Bonhöffer's* (1901) monograph on the acute alcoholic psychosis devoted one of its three sections to chronic alcoholic delirium or Korsakoff's psychosis. He distinguished four principal psychological signs of this disease: (1) defective registration of new impressions; (2) loss of memory for temporal succession; (3) retrograde amnesia; and (4) a tendency to confabulate. All these signs, however, can also be detected in the incipient delirious phase of the disease. Disputing Korsakoff's observations, Bonhöffer stated that he had never noticed any evidence of memory traces in the absence of registration, i.e., of delayed recollection when immediate recall could not be elicited. Therefore, he attributed the amnesic disorder to a derangement in registration rather than in recall. Nevertheless, Bonhöffer also stressed that the capacity to register new impressions was never completely destroyed in amnesic patients, that it could be limited to the visual modality, and was likely to be quite efficient for matters of especial interest. Moreover, Bonhöffer suggested that defective registration itself was partly due to impaired perception.

In a later discussion, Bonhöffer (1904) examined the clinical standing of the amnesic syndrome. He argued in favor of distinguishing Korsakoff's psychosis, which is commonly of an alcoholic or infectious etiology, and involves peripheral neuropathy as well as the oculomotor symptoms described by Wernicke, from the amnesic symptom complex. The former he admitted to be a disease *sui generis*. To the amnesic symptom-complex Bonhöffer refused to accord the status of a nosological class, but at the same time acknowledged its phenomenal affinity with Korsakoff's psychosis, and proposed that it be known as either the Korsakoff syndrome or the amnesic syndrome.[2] He also argued for a more rigorous definition, i.e., that all four psychological signs be found in conjunction, and that the rate of forgetting be extremely steep. Contemporaneously, Stransky (1905) proposed an alternate principle of classification, distinguishing first the instances of alcoholic origin from all the rest, and second those of toxic-infectious origin and accompanied by peripheral neuropathy from others that affected cerebral function only.

The opinion that Korsakoff's syndrome should not be treated as a clinical entity was widely accepted in France, where psychiatrists—e.g., Dupré (1906)—tended to classify it with confusional states. Angelergues (1958) credits Chaslin (1912) with the first statement in the French literature that attributed to this derangement the status of an autonomous mental syndrome, defining it by the familiar triad of amnesia, fabulation, and disorientation. In fact, Sollier (1895) reported,

---

[2]Later Steinthal (1921) and more recently Flament (1957) recommended the same distinction, the latter between the "psycho-polyneuritic syndrome" and the "mental syndrome" of Korsakoff.

within a decade of Korsakoff, a case of psychosis with polyneuritis, in which amnesia persisted long after the peripheral neuropathy.

## Studies in Registration and Recall

By the beginning of the present century the clinical description of the amnesic syndrome was fairly complete. But no agreement had been reached on whether it should be treated as a distinct and unitary clinical class. The usual emphasis on confabulation and disorientation, as derangements of equal significance to the amnesic, suggests that the reports were based principally on patients in the early phase of the disorder. Several students of the amnesic syndrome held that, contrary to appearance, it did not present an example of memory disturbance. The function damaged was registration, in the sense of Wernicke's *Merkfähigkeit,* i.e., the capacity to absorb new impressions, as distinct from mere attention on the one hand, or the availability of old memories, on the other. With this statement of the problem the time had arrived for experimental investigations, and most of these were done at first in Germany, under the influence of Ebbinghaus (1885), the founder of laboratory studies of memory.

The dominant psychological theory at the time was a structural associationism, that conceived of learning and remembering in terms of more passively mechanical processes than is common nowadays. Memory was visualized as consisting of inert neural traces, that were first registered, then retained as more or less stable impressions, and finally revived in recall or recognition. The most widely accepted paradigm of forgetting was the fading of traces, and an incapacity to acquire new learning was attributed to some condition that prevented the formation of associations. Experimenters, therefore, saw their first task in determining the rate and extent of acquisition of new associations, and of their decay in amnesic patients.

*Kräpelin* (1896) was one of the earliest champions of experimental studies in psychopathology. The description of Korsakoff's syndrome in his textbook was influenced by the first experiments with amnesic patients. Finzi's (1901) tachistoscopic studies having established some norms about the span of perception, two other members of Kräpelin's school applied the technique to amnesic patients: H. Schneider (1901), in presbyophrenia, and R. Krauss (1904) in polyneuritic psychosis. Both found a twofold impairment: an abnormally restricted span of perception and very rapid decay of memories.

Kräpelin (1900) attributed the perceptual defect to the unavailability of memory images. He also noted that longer delay before testing both reduced the number of items correctly recalled and increased incorrect report. He thought this was a remarkable combination of errors, for a patient who registers so little should retain that much quite easily. Registration was obviously not the only process damaged in the amnesic syndrome; in his textbook, Kräpelin stated that, in addition to memory, reasoning too was usually affected, a view that markedly differed from Bonhöffer's.

*Brodmann* (1902, 1904) tested 2 patients for recall of nonsense syllables, read aloud repeatedly in lists of 8 or 12. No learning took place in the acute phase, but the patient who could be retested 5 to 7 months later showed some learning by the savings method. The data also reveal that the ratio of incorrect responses to no response also increased in the chronic phase, and both effects were much more marked with the shorter list. Errors tended to perseverate, and interpolation of a brief verbal task abolished such learning as could be detected after a free interval. Brodmann found no perceptual deficit, but the capacity to register new impressions remained deficient even after a prolonged period of clinical recovery. Defective registration, nevertheless, could not be the only cause of the amnesic disorder, since the effects of certain impressions could be demonstrated later, though not in immediate testing. Furthermore, even in the period of recovery some newly acquired information would be rapidly forgotten.

*Ranschburg* (1911), another pioneer of experimental research in neurological diseases, leaned heavily on Brodmann's findings in his treatise on diseased memory. He attempted a systematic investigation of the various processes of learning in the Korsakoff syndrome, and found them all impaired, though not in the same degree. New associations, for example, can be formed, but the capacity to break through the ring of immediate or conventional associations is lacking. Ranschburg has been credited with distinguishing *anterograde* and *retrograde* amnesia, and he certainly made the point that information acquired before the illness, unlike new information, could be relearned with comparative ease, even though it appeared to be lost. At the same time, he was another proponent of the view that the effects of certain current impressions, while undetectable by immediate tests, can be demonstrated later. This opinion Ranschburg (1939) reaffirmed after many years, in a report on 2 patients, one of whom had developed the Korsakoff syndrome as a result of gas poisoning and the other from a midbrain tumor. Isolating the functional damage from his clinical and experimental observations, Ranschburg presented these patients as illustrating the Jacksonian thesis that in the decomposition of the mind the superior, complex functions are the first to suffer, particularly those that depend on volition.

*Gregor,* with Römer (1907), first reported on 2 alcoholic patients, and (1909) subsequently doubled his sample. He employed the savings method exclusively, i.e., he measured the effects of learning by the reduction of repeated presentations required for correct reproduction. His material included meaningful coherent texts—prose and poetry— and meaningful discontinuous words as well as syllables. Success in learning, of course, differed with the types of material. Acquisition was the slowest and retention the shortest with the meaningless; the continuous text stood at the opposite end on both criteria. Gregor also noted that, in contrast with normal persons, spacing made for less efficient learning in his patients.

In analyzing his findings, Gregor stated quite explicitly that the psychopathology under examination was not one of memory impairment, that the patients studied were capable of forming new associations, i.e., of new learning, but only under favorable conditions. Their defect was a diminished capacity of attention; at best they noticed that which seemed essential, and entirely ignored that which appeared to be of secondary importance. This would account for their errors in placing events in their temporal context or sequence. Registration was indeed the process affected in amesic patients, but not in the sense of an incapacity to absorb new impressions; they seem to lack interest for anticipating new impressions. Although Gregor did not elaborate this hypothesis or extend it to the phenomena of retrograde amnesia, he intimated that the basic dysfunction in the amnesic syndrome might be attitudinal.

*Schneider.* Some evidence that memories unavailable for voluntary reproduction nevertheless persisted latently in amnesic patients could be found in a number of reports on the Korsakoff syndrome. Schneider (1912) demonstrated this experimentally in 3 Korsakoff patients, and others representing different clinical classes. The tasks he set his subject were: (1) naming complex pictures; (2) recognition, by naming, of drawings of simple objects displayed gradually by the slow removal of a covering paper; (3) object assembly; (4) filling gaps in a text. In all, the Korsakoff patients tended to perseverate with errors, were also slower, and in (4) made many more errors by omission than the other groups of patients. Concerning their formal thought processes, Schneider agreed with Bonhöffer that these were undamaged. Their memory defect he attributed principally to faulty recall, and later (1928) reaffirmed this opinion. The opposite view, i.e., that the source of the disorder is in registration, or impressionability, was put forward most forcibly by Moll (1915) whose clinical report from Pretoria is notable for an attempt to classify the varieties of fabrication.

*Kohnstamm.* The casualties of the First World War provided Kohnstamm (1917) with an interesting case of amnesic disorder, as those of the Franco-Prussian War had done for Liepmann. Liepmann's (1910) patient exemplified retrograde amnesia in its almost complete form, as he could voluntarily remember nothing that had occurred after 1871; yet he performed difficult arithmetical tasks and played chess with considerable accomplishment. Kohnstamm's patient was thought to have suffered brain damage as a result of carbon monoxide poisoning while buried in a shell crater. He too could calculate and play cards without apparent loss of skill, while incapacitated by severe retrograde amnesia. Although a teacher by training, he was unable to recall historical dates, identify the names of important public figures of even the very recent past, or reproduce geographical data. His amnesia included memories of personal experience as well. He did, however, recognize some historical information as being false. He could play, on the piano, music he had known prior to his illness and, moreover, was capable of learning new pieces; yet he could not name the music he was playing, nor did he remember the following morning a concert of the previous day in which he had accompanied a singer.

Tests showed no deficit outside memory function; reaction time and verbal facility were normal, and there was no confabulation. Kohnstamm found evidence of latent memories but hypnosis elicited no new memory content. Generalizing from this patient, Kohnstamm proposed a new subdivision of memory functions. First, he reiterated Bergson's distinction and observation that sensorimotor memories are less vulnerable to brain damage than inert memories. Second, he differentiated spontaneously acquired from learned, i.e., deliberately acquired information. Although his patient's retrograde amnesia affected both types of knowledge alike, Kohnstamm believed that the anterograde disability was more pronounced for spontaneous acquisition. Deficient attention may indeed have accounted for the patient's impaired registration but hardly for his faulty retention, since he forgot rapidly that which he had been able to reproduce on instant testing.

*Claparède.* The distinction between the two modes of registration had been made implicitly by Gregor, and Claparède (1911) applied it to the process of recall. His interest was prompted by the observation that amnesic patients, although they behave quite appropriately to the hospital setting, when answering questions often appear to believe that they are in some different surroundings. Tests of recall of short stories demonstrated the same apparent paradox: the patients correctly answered prompting questions about details of the stories, yet could not reproduce them spontaneously. Claparède sought an explanation in a theory expounded by Katzaroff (1911), that recognition is always preceded by an affective response, by a feeling of familiarity. The amnesic disorder of Korsakoff patients may be rooted in an inadequacy of the affective function.

In order to test the hypothesis that affect, such as that aroused by pain, would establish more lasting memories, Claparède tried the following experiment. He hid a pin between his fingers and, while shaking hands with a woman patient, jabbed hers. Within a few minutes the patient was unable to recall the incident, yet she refused to shake hands with him again, and pulled hers back as he approached her. In an attempt to explain her conduct, the patient admitted her fear lest she be pricked with a pin, though ostensibly unaware of the fact that precisely that had happened to her earlier. All she would admit in justification of her suspicion was that the thought this might happen had crossed her mind, for people sometimes do hide pins in their hands. Claparède discussed this incident and other instances of memory failure in this amnesic patient, as illustrating a fundamental derangement in establishing links between impressions and the self.[3] More generally, he stressed the importance of affective and attitudinal factors in recall, and suggested that his patient was deficient in the process of conscious and voluntary remembering rather than in that of forming new associations. MacCurdy (1928) who followed Claparède quite closely, however, had to modify this conclusion in the face of Wechsler's (1917) results. MacCurdy's own contribution to the theory of the Korsakoff syndrome was in such vague terms as a defective image function and lack of conscious awareness.

*Wechsler* (1917) studied 5 alcoholic Korsakoff patients to test four hypotheses about the amnesic syndrome. These were:

---

[3]Claparède's term was "moiïté," MacCurdy (1928) and Rapaport (1951) translated it as "me-ness." MacCurdy also qualified it so as to refer to the past as well as to the self.

(1) defective perception; (2) failure to link new associations with old ones; (3) rapid fading of newly formed associations; (4) inability of reproduction. He found the immediate memory span normal in all but one of the patients, and the tests of paired associate learning impressed Wechsler with the following findings. Increasing repetitions in the acquisition phase, or shortening the list had little effect on recall; incorrect reproductions predominated over errors by failure to report items, and they also tended to perseverate; the least familiar or conventional associations proved the most resistant to learning. Wechsler's conclusion, based on clinical observation as well as on the experimental results, was that Korsakoff patients were unable to form new associations; this was their fundamental disorder that accounted also for such other of their symptoms as, e.g., confabulation.

*Nyssen* is one of two Belgian investigators who have continued to the present with experimental studies of the memory disturbance in the Korsakoff syndrome. As far back as 1926, Nyssen pointed out the striking contrast between a severe learning defect and a virtually intact retention of other intellectual functions in a Korsakoff patient. In 1956, he demonstrated the same deficit in an area that is barely affected in the amnesic syndrome, i.e., vocabulary. He tested 39 alcoholic Korsakoff patients on a list of words that had gained currency during the decade preceding their illness and on a control list of long-established words. They defined the latter quite adequately, but the former less accurately than several control groups, and in recall the difference was wider still. Comparing the rate of forgetting of verbal and visual material between 17 alcoholic Korsakoff patients and two control groups, Nyssen (1957) found that the advantage of recognition over recall was greater for the former. The correlation between retention by the two methods was positive but not high. Recognition tests showed some retention after as long as 5 months in 12 patients, and this led Nyssen to the conclusion that the capacity to learn and to retain new information is not completely lost in the Korsakoff syndrome.

*Crahay* (1957) tested immediate and delayed recall in 15

alcoholic Korsakoff patients, to resolve the old controversy about registration or recall as the site of the impairment. Like Nyssen, Crahay also found that immediate recall gave better results with verbal than with visual material; in fact it showed no deficit at all, but some loss occurred after the shortest delay. Crahay concluded that no general statement can be made about apprehension or registration in Korsakoff patients, for this function may be intact or defective, all according to the type of material presented for learning. He also distinguished two independent mechanisms; one involved in the establishment of memories, or immediate apprehension, and a secondary process of integration or retention. Crahay presented his findings as evidence for this distinction, and in support of the view that in the amnesic syndrome registration is impaired less than recall. Beyond a relatively low level of complexity, however, the patients' registration is very weak and may fail completely.

## Theories of Cognitive Derangement

During the three decades that began with Korsakoff's reports, attempts to account for the puzzling and often contradictory symptoms of the amnesic syndrome were made within the framework of a structural associationist theory of mental function. A new approach had been foreshadowed by Gregor, and was further inspired by the Würzburg school.

*Pick.* Influenced chiefly by Selz (1913), Pick was the first student of the amnesic syndrome explicitly to reject the assosiationist, and more especially Bönhoffer's, interpretation. Prior to his paper (1915) on the pathological thought processes in Korsakoff's psychosis, Pick (1903, 1905) had already written on two aspects of its psychopathology. One was the phenomenon of reduplicative paramnesia, or the splitting of a continuous series of events in memory into isolated events. The second topic that brought Pick to the amnesic syndrome was confabulation, and in that connection he stressed the patients' inordinate suggestibility.

Pick's principal contribution to the Korsakoff syndrome was based on a single patient who owed his disability to tubercular meningitis. Pick thought that the anomalies observed in this patient, though possibly more pronounced, were typical of the Korsakoff syndrome in general. He paid particular attention to certain contradictions in statements that are indeed common with amnesic patients. Pick took verbatim records, and could thus document numerous examples of contradiction; they almost all concerned irreconcilable answers about the patient's own age, the place of the interview, or his age in relation to that of his children, his marriage, his school, or his past military service. For example, in reply to a question about his age, the patient stated that he was 14 or 15, and then said he was married and had several children. Inconsistencies of this kind allow for a variety of interpretations, and probably the most obvious one is that the patient reported on himself within a different context on each occasion. Pick, however, discovered in his behavior an illustration of Selz's principle that problem solving proceeds through phases of doubt and phases of testing tentative solutions. Amnesic patients have lost their aptitude to doubt, the need to correct contradictions; and even when the need is present, it does not give rise to the process of correction. According to Pick, it is in their thinking processes that amnesic patients are basically disturbed, and this the associationist theory of their dysfunction fails to take into account.

*Grünthal.* One contribution of the Würzburg School to psychological thought was the principle that associations between items of content or processes do not happen randomly according to proximity, similarity, or contrast; that it is necessary to hypothesize an additional process that directs and determines the relationship between discrete events. This process, the adoption of a set or attitude, was allotted a central position in Grünthal's (1923, 1924) theory about the amnesic syndrome. Grünthal first evolved his theory from information provided by a single patient—an alcoholic man hospitalized following concussion—and in this instance, perhaps more than in any other, the small size of the sample seriously limited and possibly distorted the conclusions. It so happened that the experimental tests employed by Grünthal, word association and tachistoscopic perception, produced no evidence of the anomalies detected by clinical techniques. Furthermore, directive questions never failed to elicit the correct information. Confronted with the patient's contrasting behavior in the two types of situation, Grünthal resolved the dilemma with the conclusion that given a proper task set (*Einstellung*) he showed no impairment of mental function.

That a disturbance in orientation or set is the central derangement in the amnesic syndrome was the thesis of Grünthal's subsequent report on 10 patients with "exogenous psychosis," most of whom he presented as examples of Korsakoff's psychosis. According to this theory an amnesic patient cannot depart from the trend of thought he has been following, and therefore is virtually unable to place ideas within another context. Impressions gained at any one moment thus fail to be set in relation to the patient's total experience, and so remain disordered. Because the patient's thought proceeds along a single track, alternate points of view are not available to him to provide bases for comparison, criticism, and correction. This latter formulation is akin to Pick's; otherwise Grünthal's theory was not necessarily confined to the thought processes, even though he himself placed the derangement at that level. Concerning the controversy about the disturbance in retention and recall, Grünthal's position was quite unambiguous. In pure examples of the syndrome that, of course, are rarely seen, no forgetting occurs at all in the sense that mental contents fade and become unavailable. The apparent loss of memories results from an interference with the process of reproduction, and that can be removed by restoring the appropriate mental set.

*Störring.* Grünthal later turned his attention to the neuropathology of the Korsakoff syndrome, but reverted to its psychopathology in one more instance, reporting on a patient with gas poisoning who seemed to present "the first pure case of a man with complete and isolated loss of the capacity to register" (Grünthal and Störring, 1930a). The case was discussed in greater detail by Störring (1931). As described in these reports, this patient was indeed remarkable for having a memory for new impressions limited to a fleeting moment, while functioning without serious impairment when he was not dependent on information received in the course of the immediately preceding events. Unlike other amnesic patients, this man showed no diminution of spontaneity and, far from being apathetic, appeared to be extraordinarily emotional. Störring scrupulously disclaimed the diagnosis of Korsakoff psychosis for this case, but suggested that the amnesic derangement, which occurred here in isolation, might throw valuable light on how a similar disability would affect Korsakoff patients. His report was certainly interesting enough for Purdy (1934) to quote it in support of Jenkins and Dallenbach's (1924) theory of forgetting, i.e., that this occurs as a result of interaction between one memory trace and another.

In spite of his crippling disability, B, the name under which this patient was to gain notoriety as the subject of a remarkable controversy, survived the turmoils of the thirties and forties. While B lived in the obscurity of a Bavarian village, Scheller (1950) brought him to the attention of a new generation of clinicians. Scheller's criticism was based on the persuasive argument that a function as complex as is the registration or acquisition of impressions can hardly be lost in complete isolation from other mental functions. He attributed most of B's pathological behavior to psychogenic, more especially to hysterical causes, drawing a sharp division between disorders typical of the latter and those caused by cerebral damage. Conrad (1953b) then pointed out that the striking feature of B's disorder was its constancy over time and, excepting schizophrenia, only behavior disturbance associated with brain damage could remain unchanged for 26 years.

Further evidence in support of the original description and diagnosis of B's disease followed from Scheele (1951), Heimann and Heimann (1952), and Grünthal and Störring (1954), while Lotmar (1954) in a lengthy review reinforced Scheller's thesis. The controversy, at this point, instigated a field study in psychopathology, when two of Störring's assistants arrived in B's village to study the case on the site. Although they had entered the fray on behalf of their teacher, Völkel and Stolze (1956) had to admit that much of B's behavior revealed unmistakable features of hysteria and simulation. In a final review of the case, Grünthal and Störring (1956) attempted a resolution of the controversy, proposing —contrary to Conrad—that over the years B's condition had changed quite radically; the effects of carbon monoxide poisoning may have cleared up gradually, giving way to the traits noted by the patient's recent observers. This graceful, if not quite convincing, gesture of compromise failed to bring the debate to a close. Lotmar (1958) reaffirmed his criticism, and probably the last interpretation of B's case has not been published yet.

*Lidz's* (1942) report on 3 patients with the amnesic syndrome, afforded him an opportunity to review some of the German literature on the subject for the English reading public, and to make a constructive as well as critical contribution to theory. The 3 patients each represented a different degree in severity of the amnesic syndrome. At the one end was a case of virtually pure amnesic disorder following carbon monoxide poisoning; at the other extreme an alcoholic patient disoriented and confabulating as well as severely deranged in his memory function. The intermediate example was another alcoholic patient, but not disoriented.

With his least defective patient, Lidz demonstrated again, in this instance for visual test material, that memories although they appear to be blotted out, can be recalled with some prompting. The most striking defect in the amnesic syndrome, therefore, is constructive recall. This in turn results in the patient's inability to follow the sequence of events that lead up to any one moment, and to his consequent isolation in his surrounding. His personality disorder and loss of spontaneity are a consequence, not a cause, of the disruption of integrated behavior due to defective recall, "for spontaneity depends on the welling up of material from within." Lidz traced the additional defects of his other patients, notably confabulation and disorientation, to the same source of impairment. He did not treat the distorted temporal judgments independently of the memory impairment, for his examples supported the argument that the more gravely the capacity of recall is damaged, the more disturbed will be the patient's sense of time. In contrast to several other students of the amnesic syndrome, Lidz stated that the memory of post-traumatic events could never be recovered, for they had not been completely perceived and integrated. Lidz provided no empirical data of a perceptual defect, but implied its occurrence in his model of integration, and also by extending Bartlett's (1932) theory of remembering to the amnesic syndrome. Accordingly, the failure in recall occurs because the amnesic patient is unable to place himself in the setting by which material from the past becomes available. Lidz made a point of distinguishing this formula from Grünthal's, that amnesic patients cannot change their orientative sets, for those he had studied were all able to do this.

*Van der Horst.* An entirely novel theory of cognitive dysfunction was expounded by van der Horst (1932)[4] that attributed all the characteristic features of the amnesic syndrome to a breakdown in the function by which temporal signs are attached to experiences. Van der Horst's theory was undoubtedly influenced by Bergson's (1896) concept of "durée toute pure," and also by his fellow countrymen, Bouman and Grünbaum (1929), who distinguished a subjective time sense, *chronognosy,* from the objective function of *chronology* and the mensuration of the latter, *chronometry.* Van der Horst too postulated a sense for the immediate apprehension of the flow of time or continuity as the source of temporal order in memory, and held that in amnesic patients this sense was disturbed.

Discussing 6 amnesic patients, drawn from as many etiological classes, van der Horst confirmed the proposition of several previous observers that the disorder was not simply one of retention. He pointed out that such memories as amnesic

---

[4]It was known before that date; van der Horst had published a paper on the topic in a Dutch Journal (*Psychiat. en Neurolbl.,* 32: 217-235) as far back as 1928.

patients were able to evoke usually emerged out of their sequential order, and that their errors were more marked in judging time spans and the recurrence of events than in recalling or recognizing the same events. His theoretical formulation fitted these anomalies much more neatly than it did other signs typical of the Korsakoff syndrome. Still, he was prepared to derive them all, retrograde and anterograde amnesia, confabulation, paramnesia, and disorientation from the same root disturbance in temporal marking.

Contending that the apparent memory disorder of amnesic patients was the effect of the unavailability of temporal signs rather than their cause, van der Horst imposed on himself the burden of proof. He had noted, and quoted similar observations made by others, that amnesic patients performed better in experimental tests of memory than in clinical situations. His explanation was that patients are more likely to forget events impregnated with temporal signs, i.e., personal experiences than impersonal information imparted to them. This conclusion was almost the exact opposite of Kohnstamm's and, although revived by others from time to time, has not been sufficiently supported by empirical evidence. Neither has the other corollary of van der Horst's theory, that Korsakoff patients are incapable of registering the sequence of events (see Chapter 11).

*Ehrenwald.* Van der Horst's principal thesis defied direct testing. Ehrenwald (1931), who proposed to interpret the Korsakoff syndrome in terms very similar to van der Horst's, readily admitted that Bergson had excluded the possibility of applying scientific tests to his theory of time. Ehrenwald tried to investigate the existence of a primitive sense of time by means of hypnotic experiments and obtained encouraging results with normal subjects. His work with amnesic patients, however, proved less successful, since most of them either resisted hypnosis or failed to wake up after the interval appointed in their instruction. Three Korsakoff patients did obey Ehrenwald's suggestion, and such evidence as they provided indicated to him that their time judgment was disturbed at a higher level of cognition rather than at the primitive level of immediate experience.

*Williams.* Van der Horst's theory has exercised considerable influence, and has re-emerged in the work of such diverse neurologists and psychiatrists as Kleist (1934), Gillespie (1937), Delay and Brion (1954), Mouren and Felician (1958). Williams and Zangwill (1950) considered it in relation to their own observations about the disturbed temporal judgments of three brain-damaged patients with severe memory disorder, including one with Korsakoff's psychosis. The patients tended to antedate events, and to displace the serial order of successive items. These defects suggested a general disturbance in the apprehension of sequence, for which the authors coined the term "agnosia of succession." Although this concept is reminiscent of van der Horst, and although the patients pointed to much the same derangement as that proposed by the Dutch psychiatrist—inability to date events and a propensity to isolate them—Williams and Zangwill elected to regard these anomalies as an effect rather than the cause of the memory impairment. A more categoric rejection of van der Horst's thesis came from Gál (1955), for being incompatible alike with materialist philosophy and with the evidence of conditioning experiments.

*Zangwill's* (1941) first report on the Korsakoff syndrome revealed an anomaly in recognition. On repeated presentation of the same material, 2 alcoholic Korsakoff patients tended to recognize it only in part, and therefore regarded it as a modified version of the original picture, text, object, or environment. Zangwill saw in this failure to respond to identity a variety of reduplicative paramnesia that could be attributed alike to differential forgetting, transformation in recall, or a depersonalized mode of recognition. Still another explanation might be the patients' lack of confidence in their memory performance.

Further material from one of these patients came 6 months after her discharge from the hospital, while she was still subject to retrograde amnesia for events of the preceding 10 years. Zangwill (1950) asked her to draw sketches of a woman and a bus. Both drawings were remarkable for the accuracy with which they reproduced the fashion and model current 10 years earlier, so much so that Zangwill was tempted to stress the positive aspects of amnesia, but for which a reconstruction of generic images in a style of the past would have been less successful.

Two Korsakoff patients, who provided material for another report by Zangwill (1953), underestimated their ages by a wide margin and, moreover, clung to these errors with unwonted tenacity. In view of their extensive retrograde amnesia the magnitude of their errors would hardly pose special theoretical questions; their staunch resistance to corrections, however, raised the possibility of motivational factors superimposed on the amnesic disorder.

*Bernard.* Perhaps the most uncompromising restatement of the cognitive interpretation of the Korsakoff syndrome in recent years was Bernard's (1951), a theoretical examination of negative and positive—i.e., confabulatory—symptoms, without new experimental or clinical data. Bernard squarely attributed the disorder to defective registration, the process that integrates percepts with preceding and subsequent experiences. This process he distinguished from fixation which he regarded as a lower level operation of trace formation without contextual synthesis, and a function undamaged in amnesic patients.

It follows from Bernard's definition of the root derangement that a deficiency in the temporal ordering of events accounts for much of the Korsakoff patient's psychopathology. This he presented as a cognitive disorder in the strictest sense of the term, namely, as the effect of disintegration in thinking along the temporal dimension. Generally the amnesic patient has not lost his intuition for the concrete flow of time, but is impaired in the rhythmic organization of phases.

Although Bernard's short essay does not pretend to arrive at a theoretical formulation of the amnesic syndrome, it is notable for its categoric dismissal, not only of memory disorder as an explanation, but of memory as a special function. Memory is an operation functionally integral with thought, and its determining process is in the phase of registration, which Bernard in fact equates with perception. Recall is a constructive synthesis at the original perceptual phase. Bernard's interpretation of the psychopathology in the Korsakoff syndrome might have been strengthened in its explanatory power if he had considered retrograde amnesia, and had treated the patients' failure to recognize events or to date them chronologically as a relative impairment rather than an absolute disability. His purpose, however, was the less ambitious one to illustrate mental confusion at the level of dissolution of the thought process characteristic of the Korsakoff syndrome.

## Affective Inhibition of Recall

As evidence was accumulating that the amnesic syndrome may exemplify a disturbance in recall rather than in registration or retention, its analysis in terms of psychoanalytic constructs seemed indicated to some students. Psychoanalytic theory has a very powerful explanation of forgetting, i.e., repression or the motivated inhibition of remembering. The occasions to which the model of repression is applicable are limited and certainly do not extend as widely and indiscriminately as the examples of amnesia in the Korsakoff syndrome. Attempts to account for its psychopathology by means of motivated forgetting therefore appear to be tentative, and to be advanced as partial rather than exclusive explanations.

*Schilder,* in his work with epileptic patients (1924, 1925), discovered an affinity between twilight states and amnesia. He was also impressed by Righetti's (1920) report of a patient who recovered from a prolonged amnesia after recalling in a dream the circumstances of the trauma that had caused his disability 3 years before. Schilder's several attempts to elucidate the problems of amnesic disturbances formed part of his more extensive program to arrive at unitary concepts applicable alike to psychological and neurological disorders. His formulation of the process of recognition at that time was reminiscent of Katzaroff's: "an impression first arouses a quality of familiarity." Recognition fails because of some inhibitory process that is "organic" in origin. The fact that its psychological representation is unknown as yet does not exclude psychological causation. For Schilder a distinction between the mechanisms responsible for forgetting in, e.g., hysteria and brain damage appeared to be entirely unncessary. Much later, in a posthumous book, Schilder (1942) once more turned his attention to the Korsakoff syndrome. By that time gestalt theoretical formulations and certain neuropathological findings had also influenced his formulations. He reasoned, on *a priori* grounds, that a cortical as well as midbrain lesion must be associated with the Korsakoff syndrome, the one to account for the cognitive, the other for the affective disturbance, neither of which is secondary to the other.

*Hartmann.* Betlheim and Hartmann's (1924) experimental study with 3 amnesic patients served Schilder well in documenting his early thesis. The evidence was a tendency toward symbolic distortion in the patients' reproduction of stories with obscene or blasphemous content. Parapraxes of this "vertical" type, that occurred alongside examples of "coordinate displacement," were of interest to the authors since they demonstrated the applicability of the psychoanalytic theory of dream symbolism to neurological disorders.

Hartmann and Schilder (1925) returned to the controversy in the following year, discussing 3 cases of post-traumatic amnesia, a woman who had suffered concussion in a bicycle accident, and more briefly 2 cases of attempted suicide with gunshot wounds. Perceptual or memory defects could not account for the amnesic symptoms; neither could the mechanisms of denial or displacement, though both appeared to be active. The authors' formulation of the neural damage nicely demolished the barrier between psychogenic and organic amnesias, and explained how, for example, displacement could occur as a result of physical injury. Memories, they argued, are differentiated stepwise in the process of remembering, and organic trauma destroys the content of memory no more than does a psychological disturbance; both derange the process of differentiation.

In a later publication, Hartmann (1927) declared that registration was the function that was most severely impaired in amnesic patients, rather than retention. His own experimental results, obtained by means of hypnosis from 2 patients, however, again pointed to recall as the phase at which the failure occurs. In this and in a subsequent paper, Hartmann (1930) held up Schilder's challenge of the conventional distinction between an organic-biological and a primarily psychological causation in psychopathology, and also disputed another popular tenet, i.e., that memories of events personally experienced are better retained than those of impersonally learned facts. He subjected to experimental test the hypothesis that their affective significance helps to preserve memories in an amnesic patient. Hartmann tested 6 patients, 4 of whom were genuine examples of Korsakoff's syndrome—which those investigated jointly with Betlheim hardly had been—and a fifth who also had a history of alcoholism. He repeatedly read them two stories, one containing something of affective significance to each patient and another which was relatively neutral in content; then he tested the patients on immediate reproduction. The results showed that the affect-laden material was retained no better than the neutral, but that disagreeable content tended to be omitted or distorted, "repressed" in the psychoanalytical nomenclature. By pointing out that Korsakoff patients, when given a story to learn, tend to assume the role of the active character in reproducing it, Hartmann (1935) at least obliquely exploded another favorite hypothesis about the amnesic syndrome, i.e., that its basic disturbance is a failure to relate events to the self.

*Rapaport's* contribution to the theory of the Korsakoff syndrome was embedded in two selective surveys of the preceding literature. The first (1942) formed a small section in a monograph written to demonstrate the influence of emotions on remembering. At that time Rapaport was attracted by the formulations of Pick and Grünthal, which he reinterpreted so as to equate lack of orientation with Bleuler's (1922) concept of autistic thinking; the cognitive disorders of amnesic patients exemplified the operations of the psychoanalytic construct of the unconscious. For a later book of readings (1951), Rapaport selected the papers of Claparède, Betlheim, and

Hartmann, and Bürger-Prinz and Kaila, all pointing to emotional or motivational influences in the psychopathology of the Korsakoff syndrome. Rapaport himself concluded his survey of the literature with this surprisingly firm statement: "It is now beyond doubt that the Korsakoff syndrome, which originally was considered to be registration and retention loss due to organic lesions, has proved to imply important emotional components which affect the appearance of such losses" (Rapaport, 1942, p. 231).

*Davidson.* The boldest case for a psychodynamic explanation of the Korsakoff syndrome has been made by Davidson (1948) who interviewed 8 patients under sodium amytal. He reported that under this treatment a "reversal of the clinical syndrome" occurred in 5 cases, and attributed especial significance to changes in mood and disposition thus accomplished. Interpreting these findings, Davidson attempted a new formulation of the oft-reaffirmed proposition about affective factors in the amnesic syndrome. He suggested that in this condition "affectivity is expressed as euphoria. Along with it inner actualization ceases. When reversed under sodium amytal, euphoria changes to irritability and aggression; inner actualization is revived; and patients become spontaneously productive." Davidson did not provide any definition of inner actualization beyond assigning it an intervening function between affectivity and the integration of the present—presumably with consciousness, for he also omitted to indicate the context of integration. Although sketchily drawn, Davidson's model served the purpose of deriving the Korsakoff patients' cognitive disorders from an affective derangement; and all that was known about the anatomical pathology of the syndrome fitted that derivation to his satisfaction.

*Lindberg.* Further evidence of affective repression in the amnesic syndrome was marshalled by Lindberg (1946) in a report of a longitudinal study. His patient was taken ill after he had drastically stepped up his ever liberal intake of alcohol. This heavy drinking spell ensued as a reaction to the man's grief over his fiancée's death. Lindberg attributed considerable etiological significance to the affective disturbance caused by that loss. In view of the patient's alcoholic record, the author's interpretation is by no means obvious; furthermore, Lindberg could not elicit any confirmatory evidence from his interviews. The patient seemed indolent and showed no affective reactions. Support for the thesis came from repeated tests of word association; the patient's reaction to emotionally charged stimuli exceeded the critical limit of 4 seconds more frequently than it did to neutral words. Lindberg also noted that in three tests, and over a period of 2 years, his patient responded with the same word to more than half of the set list. He attributed this perseveration to affective repression, and was thus further encouraged to present his Korsakoff patient as exemplifying "the double effect of lesional cerebral disturbance and psychological factors due to the situation." His report is notable for its nice description of the progressive improvement of the confusional and other gross mental disorders over the years, while the amnesic derangement and emotional blandness remained unchanged.

## Insufficiency of Conative Function

*Gamper.* The main line of reaction to the various cognitive analyses of the amnesic syndrome developed from a neuropathological study of the disease. Gamper's influential reports (1928, 1929) on the Korsakoff syndrome marshalled evidence for locating the lesion in the midbrain, more particularly in the mammillary bodies, and they also contained an outline of its psychopathology. The title of the latter paper—"Sleep, delirium tremens, Korsakoff's psychosis"—offered a theme for elaboration to several subsequent students of the syndrome, and probably none pursued it as far as Bessière (1948) who proclaimed the basic identity of the Korsakoff syndrome and presbyophrenia with hypnotic and manic states, confusion, delirium, and dreams, each representing a grade on a continuous scale of psychic dissolution.

A lesion in the vegetative center of the brain called for a psychological explanation of the Korsakoff syndrome in terms other than cognitive dysfunction. Although superficially Gamper's formulation of the amnesic psychopathology reduces to a disturbance in registration, he regarded this as an insufficient explanation. According to Gamper, the derangement involves a cessation of further personality development, in that the patient is unable to relate new impressions to his self. Gamper's restatement of the psychological disorder in Korsakoff's disease was reminiscent of but also more obscure and more influential than Claparède's: "a deficit in the construction of a spatio-temporal background which in normal persons is continuously apprehended in passive attention," and that also subserves the serial ordering of experiences. Such a derangement could account for retrograde as well as for anterograde amnesia but not for the frequent examples of accurate recall, unless they are conveniently credited to the intact higher brain centers, as some theorists were later tempted to do. Even though the finding that the lesion in the amnesic syndrome is close to the centers that control wakefulness and consciousness does not explain anything, it does fit in rather nicely with the generally listless behavior of the patients, and suggests that the source of their disturbance may be in conative function.

*S. Krauss.* Gamper's re-evaluation of the Korsakoff syndrome occurred at a time when Goldstein's (1934) organismic theory and Lewin's (1935) novel formulations of concepts and methods in psychology were gaining influence in Germany, complementing gestalt theory in the area of motivation and action. Lewin's theoretical constructions were patterned on physical models of tension systems, and thus seemed apposite for defining the characteristic symptoms of the Korsakoff syndrome. Examining the amnesic symptom complex from a Lewinian point of view, S. Krauss (1930) traced it to a basic impairment in the patient's affective function which in its diffuseness fails to sustain mental processes sufficiently for them to achieve completion.[5] As a consequence of this disability, the patient is unable to anticipate events, and thus to interact with others. In addition to this doubtfully correct ob-

[5]Literally: "an amorphous feeling life prevails which makes it more difficult for articulate totalities *(gestaltete Ganzheiten)* to develop."

servation, Krauss also reiterated the familiar remarks about the patients' deficiency in the temporal marking of experiences and their failure to correct errors and thus avoid contradictions, in spite of their undamaged intelligence. He attributed both these defects to an attitudinal disturbance.

*Bürger-Prinz and Kaila.* An emphasis on inadequate motivation, low states of tension, rapid satiation, which loomed so large in Krauss's analysis, also characterize Bürger-Prinz and Kaila's paper of the same year. These authors set out to demonstrate that, notwithstanding the variety in the range and pattern of its signs, the amnesic syndrome could be explained by a unitary dysfunction. This, of course, had been the goal of all major studies of the disorder prior to 1930, and has been since. Bürger-Prinz and Kaila clearly meant to offer something different from their precursors, and quite definitely something contrary to theories of memory disturbance. Their investigation was designed on a large scale, including several experimental procedures as well as clinical observations, and their explanatory concept became a broadly conceived and somewhat loose cluster of functions. The authors' decision to base their report on 4 patients selected from a large sample in no way altered this outcome.

Bürger-Prinz and Kaila were impressed with the apathy amnesic patients manifest in their overt behavior and report on introspectively. A derangement in their affective and attitudinal functions seemed to explain the patients' diverse abnormalities more adequately than a memory disturbance. Their lack of initiative, yet normal promptitude in responding to external stimulation, struck the authors as no less characteristic a trait of the syndrome than the amnesic signs proper. Bürger-Prinz and Kaila admitted that amnesic patients were capable of emotional reaction, but this did not last beyond the duration of the event that had aroused it. Errors in recall occur because the patient feels no need to correct them. The authors, who thus revived Pick's theory, adopted a seemingly critical position toward Grünthal. In fact, much of their own contribution was an extension of Grünthal's formulation. Their remark about the amnesic patient's narrow experiential horizon was certainly reminiscent of Grünthal's isolated track in the realm of thoughts. They too commented on the patient's single orientation and his virtual inability to shift sets; though given help, they thought, he could change his set. His trouble, therefore, originated from an incapacity to set himself points of orientation; yet this deficiency could itself be an effect of his fluctuating fund of memories.

Although Bürger-Prinz and Kaila emphasized such loosely defined factors in the amnesic patients' psychopathology as difficulty in gestalt formation, dedifferentiation, weakening of the sensory content of ideas, etc., they also determined operationally some parameters of perception that showed a marked deficit in amnesic patients. Much of their theoretical analysis elaborated Bürger's (1927) earlier findings based on perceptual experiments. Their final formulation of the psychopathology in the amnesic syndrome, however, was not presented within the frame of gestalt principles; instead they traced it to a vital layer of the organism, to the patients' "personal sphere."

Several years later, Bürger-Prinz and Büssow (1943) reverted to the problem to refute Störring's case for a pure example of registration impairment. They pointed out that a complete loss of memory would reduce a person to a much more primitive level of functioning than that which Störring had described in his patient. They again affirmed that lack of initiative was the most pronounced defect in amnesic patients, though not exclusive to their diagnostic class. Arguing from the absence of affective attitudes and the similarities between this syndrome and pathological sleep states, they advocated that it be regarded as an example of disturbed consciousness. The paradox that impressed them was that the minds of amnesic patients were not devoid of all content, yet they acted as if there were complete emptiness, nothing to drawn on.

Bürger-Prinz had also spurred Körner (1935) to re-evaluate the confabulatory behavior of amnesic patients and to propose that it also originated in passivity, suggestibility, and an "impersonal existence." Körner also tried to blend a personality-oriented and a gestalt-theoretical approach to the amnesic syndrome, and furthermore to graft on it van der Horst's concept of temporal organization as well.

Three reports from independent sources, each about a single patient and none a typical example of the Korsakoff syndrome, proved the appeal of the formulation proposed by Gamper and by Bürger-Prinz and Kaila.

*Scheid's* (1934) patient was remarkable for his lack of subjective certainty about the reality of the events he recalled. This suggested to Scheid that the cognitive functions were not affected, but that there was a derangement in the patient's deeper layers of vital drives. His memories in waking life were like those normal persons have in dreams. This apparent similarity between the Korsakoff patient's memories and dream experiences led Scheid to propose an obscure modification of van der Horst's theory, i.e., that the impairment of temporal ordering applies only to the experiential quality of events remembered.

*Horányi's* (1946) case of vascular etiology also exemplified a combination of intact comprehension and reasoning with retrograde amnesia for 15 years, severely impaired retention, and a total lack of initiative and of affective responsiveness. The patient repeatedly described her condition as one of complete emptiness as well as of confusion. Horányi was particularly impressed with her disorientation in the temporal dimension, for she had lost the capacity to perceive the biological phases of the day as well as to order events in time. Following Bürger-Prinz and Kaila, Horányi recognized in these defects signs of a disturbance at a deep instinctive layer of the personality and also the root of the amnesic syndrome. He also quoted the patient's paranoid delusions in support of this thesis, though the latter are hardly a characteristic sign. Autopsy demonstrated lesions in the mammillary bodies, as expected. In another patient with a similar psychopathology, however, Horányi found these anatomical areas intact.

*Kerschbaum's* (1953) patient, with a shell splinter lesion close to the mammillary bodies,[6] was atypical in that he dis-

[6]The neuropathology of this case was reported in detail by Czechmanek (1954).

played much spontaneity in conversation. Although apparently an active young man, he became fatigued rapidly, seemed to be completely devoid of sexual drive, instantly forgot anything he had said, and was unaware of this disability. In contrast, he could learn and memorize fairly exacting test materials and showed no sign of agnosia or apraxia. Kerschbaum repeatedly stressed the patient's egocentric attitude, and attributed this to his frontal lobe injury, but treated the patient's reluctance to adopt an objective attitude as characteristic of the amnesic syndrome. By the evidence of this case, the amnesic syndrome could not be explained in terms of restricted capacity in performance. Kerschbaum found the formulations of Gamper, Bürger-Prinz, and Scheid the most illuminating; the patient could not establish connections between discrete experiences of the present and his total experience; his sensory needs were rapidly satiated; and his memories were as diffuse as are dream contents. Claparède too might have been quoted, since Kerschbaum identified the disorder, which reflects a disturbance of vital regulations following brain damage, as one in "ego resonance," in the relationship to the self.

*Freund and Srnec* (1956) reported an experimental test of the hypothesis that diffuse amnesias were caused entirely or largely by a disturbance in spontaneity. Since they studied electric shock patients, their findings are relevant here only by analogy. They asked their patients to reproduce two stories before and two after ECT, one with the help of prompting questions, the other unaided. ECT achieved its therapeutic goal by reducing the patients' apathy; it also reduced their capacity to memorize stories, under both conditions of recall. The authors therefore concluded that, while there might be some relationship between memory loss and apathy, amnesia was not a simple function of the latter.

## Defective Field Structure

The model of psychic field forces was employed by gestalt psychologists chiefly to account for certain phenomena of perception, and less directly also for the processes of memory.

It is, however, meant to comprehend all aspects of behavior and experience, and therefore analyses of the amnesic syndrome in terms of gestalt theory are neither primarily cognitive, affective, nor conative. In fact, of course, with its emphasis on formal attributes of behavioral and experiential processes, gestalt psychology leans in the direction of cognitive primacy.

*Bender.* Bürger-Prinz and Kaila had worked within the framework of gestalt psychology, but their principal conclusions were derived from a different theoretical system. Bender *et al.* (1938) advanced an undiluted gestalt interpretation of their amnesic patients' drawings. In these, the authors recognized the influence of field forces that are manifested in primitive organization, comparable to the drawings of children. Since the anomalies emerge in perception, the amnesic derangement cannot be adequately explained by fading memory traces. This view has been reiterated by subsequent gestalt analyses of the amnesic syndrome.

*Müller-Suur* (1949) studied a patient whose amnesic syndrome of traumatic origin was complicated by ideational apraxia. For example, when asked to sit down, she would make several preparatory moves and verbally affirm her intention to comply, but could not accomplish the feat of seating herself. The case belongs within the present survey only because Müller-Suur elaborated it into a comprehensive theory of "amnesic dementia," in which he distinguished three basic components. From ideational apraxia follow disturbances in set and in the sense of time; these constitute the cognitive deficit. The second component accounts for aspontaneity and poor affect, the third for the lack of personal memories.

All three components could be attributed to inadequate differentiation between personality and environment. This consideration brought Müller-Suur close to Bürger-Prinz and Kaila, but he disputed that it amounted to a loss of personality, for he could recognize faint traces of his patient's pre-morbid personality in her demented state. He also rejected Ewald's (see p. 100) distinction between amnesic syndromes associated with cortical and with brain-stem lesions. His theoretical analysis relied heavily on such gestalt concepts as the establishment of relations, tensions, differentiation, and articulate structures, though it also strayed into some recondite German philosophies. These metaphysical entanglements and the emphasis on the entirely atypical symptom of ideational apraxia vitiate Müller-Suur's constructive contribution to the amnesic syndrome, which places the basic impairment squarely at the noetic level: the "vital person" is constrained by derangements in the cognitive superstructure.

*Conrad* examined the psychopathology of the amnesic syndrome in three papers, each dealing with a single patient. The first (Conrad and Ule, 1951) was a rebuttal of Grünthal's (1947) thesis that bilateral destruction of Ammon's horn results in complete intellectual disintegration. Conrad's (1953a) analysis of the amnesic syndrome in terms of gestalt principles was based on observations made on a severely deranged alcoholic Korsakoff patient, in clinical interviews and simple performance tests. He advocated that clinical syndromes be traced to basic functions, but also warned against equating function with performance such as remembering, for example. Functions are inferred within a theoretical system. Gestalt theory eschews such functional concepts as the formation of isolated engrams; instead, it offers the constructs of an autochthonous trend toward better form, of psychic tensions, of figure-ground relations, of relations between momentary processes and the subject's field of traces, and more generally of differential and integral functions. The Korsakoff patient's confabulation exemplifies in reverse the trend toward tighter, more articulate patterns within memory traces. His failure to avoid contradictions or to correct errors arises from an insufficiency of psychic tension. Such corrections always involve the replacement of one reference system by another, and are therefore undertaken only under sufficient pressure. Both disorientation and defective registration can be explained by a failure in the integral function, i.e., in relating details to the total field, the unique event to the background of previous experience that invests it with meaning. A breakdown in the differential function prevents ordering the "total field," from which unique items must be sorted out for the purpose of reproduction.

In another paper Conrad (1953b) discussed a patient with virus encephalitis, under the title of "minute memory," which just about summarizes the report, and provides an apt generic term for the cases described by Mabille and Pitres (1913), Syz (1936), and Grünthal and Störring (cf. pp. 77-79). Conrad took exception to the latter's definition of "complete and isolated loss of the capacity to register," only to the extent that the defect was not isolated. In his own patient it may not even have been complete, since he had a digit span of 6. He also displayed other cognitive anomalies, in that he could grasp complex percepts only summatively, e.g., he was unable to name a room, and could only list its contents. Otherwise, Conrad sided with Grünthal and Störring, in the face of Scheller's attack, arguing that complete incapacity of registration can indeed occur, but only as part of a radical change in the total personality and "as a result of the degradation of the integral processes in the temporal dimension."

*Ploog's* (1955) gestalt analysis of the amnesic syndrome attempted to subject several of Conrad's hypotheses to experimental tests. He too presented data obtained from a single patient, a woman whose amnesic disorder barely less grave than Conrad's case of a minute-memory was attributed to general cerebral atrophy. Ploog employed a series of very simple experiments in learning, arithmetic, and motor performance, each designed to test some principle of gestalt theory. His hypothesis was that the patient would demonstrate the principles of normal function in a simplified version; that given favorable conditions, she would perform no differently from normal men and women. The conditions included the selection of appropriate material, the length of retention period, the subject's attitude, and—in accordance with Conrad's principle of the refractory phase—the degree of satiation.

Ploog held that forgetting is a process of levelling, and this explains why amnesic patients remember the unstructured material better than the structured, since the latter allows for more levelling. Integrative processes do occur in amnesic patients, though they rapidly give way to decomposition. Impressions, if uninterrupted by interference, can become organized in the field of traces; thus, by returning to the field of the task, the patients can also recover latent memories. Remembering fails because the patient has left that field. Ploog's theoretical formula is, at any rate, consistent with two of his experimental findings, i.e., that practice had no effect, and that his patient was unable to order the sequence of even the simplest acts. Ploog attributed her lack of spontaneity to this, basically perceptual, defect in ordering.

## Neurological Theories

Most students of the Korsakoff syndrome have confronted it as a medical problem and have been concerned with its neuropathology as well as its psychiatric symptoms. The present monograph is restricted to the psychology of the amnesic syndrome; nevertheless, it cannot entirely ignore the neuroanatomical and neurophysiological theories of the disease, so many of which influence the psychological formulations.

The principal and most controversial question of the relevant neurological literature has been the location of the brain lesion that is both necessary and sufficient for the emergence of the several characteristic signs of the Korsakoff snydrome. No definite answer has been pronounced yet, but there is almost complete unanimity about placing it in the region occupied by the hypothalamus, thalamus, the walls of the third ventricle, and the aqueduct. This is a relatively large area involved in many diverse functions of the organism, and most writers have narrowed the site of the lesion within the diencephalon.

The majority of the reports, starting with Gudden's in 1896, connect the syndrome with damage in the mammillary bodies.[7]

---

[7]In disease attributed to chronic alcoholism: Gamper (1928); Ohkuma (1930); Neubürger (1931); Kant (1933); Környey and Saethre (1937); Remy (1942); Delay and Brion (1954); Malamud and Skillicorn (1956);

Indeed, Orthner (1957) declared that "bilateral damage of the mammillary bodies has never been observed without some memory disorder, therefore one must conclude that registration *(Merkfähigkeit)* depends on the intactness of these areas." Ule (1958) and Delay *et al.* (1958) expressed the same opinion, but more recently Collins, Victor, and Adams (1961) reported on several patients with Wernicke's disease, one of whom had been under observation right up to death, who had lesions in the mammillary bodies but no noticeable memory disorder. These authors have concluded that the amnesic symptoms of the Korsakoff syndrome are most consistently associated with a lesion in the medial dorsal nucleus of the thalamus.

Other writers, as well as some of those listed in the footnote, including Gamper (1929), found that the same effects can occur with lesions in different rhinencephalic structures as well: anterior thalamus (Benedek and Juba, 1941), walls of the third ventricle (Williams and Pennybacker, 1954; Victor and Yakovlev, 1955), Ammon's horn (Grünthal, 1947; Conrad and Ule, 1951; Glees and Griffith, 1952).[8] Derangements similar to those characteristic of the Korsakoff syndrome were also found in neurosurgical patients after bilateral transection of the fornix (Sweet, Talland, and Ervin, 1960) and of the hippocampus including uncus and amygdala (Milner and Penfield, 1956; Scoville and Milner, 1957). It is noteworthy that all these areas mentioned in connection with the amnesic syndrome form a closely connected anatomical system, to which a functional unity has repeatedly been attributed (e.g., by Papez, 1937).

---

Gruner (1956); Orthner (1957); Delay, Brion and Elissalde (1958); Delay *et al.* (1958); Adams (1959). In Korsakoff's syndrome caused by tumor: Förster and Gagel (1934); Lhermitte *et al.* (1937); Grünthal, (1939); Benedek and Juba (1941); Sprofkin and Sciarra (1952); Ajuriaguerra, Hécaen, and Sadoun (1954); Rizzo (1955); Ule (1958), etc.

[8]Walker's (1957) report and Grünthal's (1959) review paper, however, stress the contingent association between temporal lobe damage and the amnesic syndrome, as well as the likelihood that the latter occurs as part of a diffuse dementia.

Cortical damage has been reported in several pathological reports of the Korsakoff syndrome, and this has led a few writers to dispute the hypothalamic theory of its locus (Carmichael and Stern, 1931; Marcus, 1932; Walton, 1953). Kleist and Ewald proposed a dual brain pathology, cortical and diencephalic, and corresponding to this a psychological theory that will be briefly summarized below. The other two neurological models that have been repeatedly used for the foundation of a psychological theory of the amnesic syndrome are independent of considerations about the site of the lesion: Hughlings Jackson's (1884) general principles concerning the decomposition of function and Pavlov's (1927) conditioning paradigm.

*Kleist* (1934) interpreted the amnesic syndrome in much the same manner as had van der Horst; he saw it as a derangement in the temporal recording of experiences and memories, not as a memory disturbance. What he observed in the patients was not a loss of ideas, but only their uncertain, inexact, unclear, or faulty temporal assignment and ordering. Gamper's evidence for the site of the lesion in the vegetative centers of the brain suggested to Kleist that the time sense may be connected with the mechanisms controlling such periodic organic functions as the heart beat, visceral mechanisms, and sleep cycle. He admitted that patients disturbed in their sleep rhythm have not shown defects in the registration of temporal signs and sequences, and neither are amnesic patients troubled with sleeplessness.[9] Possibly, therefore, the two functions are controlled from different centers, the mammillary bodies serving as "vegetative time markers." New experiences would, accordingly, leave their impressions first in the diencephalon

[9]Fraisse (1963, p. 165), nevertheless, reaffirms Kleist's argument, developing a plausible allusion to a functional relationship from the structural proximity of the mammillary bodies and the "vegetative nuclei which play an important part in setting . . . in motion: hunger, thirst, sleep, sex needs." Apart from the occasional instance in which an amnesic patient asks for food immediately after a meal, there is no evidence of any serious anomaly in these vegetative functions in the Korsakoff syndrome.

before they reach the cortex. Thus, old memories stored in the cortex should not be affected by midbrain lesions, and if they are in Korsakoff patients that indicates some additional damage at the cortical level.

*Ewald* (1940) advanced a similar explanation, divorcing the amnesic syndrome from the Korsakoff syndrome. Bland affect, lack of initiative, confused temporal ordering—all characteristics of the latter—were attributed to a lesion in the brain stem; but Ewald would not concede that a derangement in registering new experiences could occur below the cortex. Having thus neatly paired off anatomical and behavioral functions, Ewald did not exclude the possibility that the two types of lesion occur jointly and produce combined effects.

*Barbizet* (1963) quite recently proposed a threefold division of amnesic disorders that accords better with current notions about neural systems transcending the boundary between cortical and subcortical regions. According to Barbizet, the Korsakoff syndrome, no matter what its etiology, is characterized by an inability to establish new memories and by a lesion in the hippocampo-mammillary system, in other words, in the Papez circuit. Amnesia of cortical origin which, however, may also implicate subcortical areas, is notable for slow learning and complications of the aphasic-apraxic-agnosic type. Some old established aptitudes, such as language or arithmetic, may be impaired; the electroencephalogram (EEG) is abnormal; and in contrast with the other type of amnesia, the digit span is narrowed. Finally, there is global amnesia that combines an inability to acquire new memories, with partial or complete obliteration of old memories. Global amnesias result from diffuse brain damage, typically atrophic. Like so many French theorists, Barbizet cherishes a classificatory system that is too neat to accommodate the varieties of am-

---

I have recently studied three young men who developed an amnesic syndrome without any record of alcoholism, and who were also notable for a complete or almost complete loss of sex drive. (cf. Kerschbaum, 1953). This defect, however, did not seem to result from a loss of the rhythmicity of the vegetative functions. They all retained their normal appetites for food, sleep and—mostly nonalcoholic—drinks.

nesic patients, and certainly needs considerable stretching to admit those with Korsakoff's disease into the box reserved for them. Although Barbizet underrates the retrograde component of their amnesic syndrome, his essay is valuable for an up-to-date summary of the relevant anatomical pathology.

*Delay's* two monographs (1942a, b) on the dissolution and diseases of memory exemplify the grand schemes by which the varieties of disordered memory function are classified, and each is assigned its position in a hierarchical structure. Starting with a definition of the varieties of normal memory, Delay proposed a threefold classification. First, there is sensorimotor memory which, shared by man and beast, manifests itself in habits and in still simpler automatic acts. Second comes social memory which, in contrast, is the sole property of man who lives in a social system, and which is also linked to his use of language. Finally, Delay followed Bergson in distinguishing a third type, i.e., autistic memory that appears in dreams and also in dementia and delirium. Defined as desocialized memory, autistic memory could be treated as a subdivision of social memory. The principal distinction between the two is that social memory always implies a knowledge of its reference to the past, while memories revived in dreams and in delirium are experienced as events of the present. Delay's distinction between the first two classes of memory is even more ambiguous if based on his statement that "sensorimotor memory is closely dependent on the brain, social memory is equally dependent but less closely" (Delay, 1942a, p. 32). Presumably, this loose definition only amounts to a reaffirmation of the fact that the cerebral localization of sensorimotor patterns has been more fully mapped than that of more complex memories.

In accordance with the division of sensorimotor and social memories, Delay distinguished between two types of amnesia: the neurological and the psychiatric. To the former he allocated all the varieties of specific dysfunction, to the latter every instance of diffuse memory impairment. His distinction did not imply a contrast between organic and psychogenic causation, a dichotomy Delay combated with an appeal to

Hughlings Jackson whose law of dissolution determines the content of amnesia, no matter what its etiology. The Korsakoff syndrome, being an example of general amnesia, belongs to the psychiatric derangements. This classificatory assignment in no way diminishes the significance of its neuropathology. In fact, Delay's interest in this syndrome has been principally in its anatomy. Regarding its psychiatric status, Delay reverted to the opinion of the earlier French clinicians; the Korsakoff syndrome is but a variant of mental confusion, it entails a deficit in mental synthesis and, consequently, in retention.

Although Delay categorically dismissed the hypothesis that the amnesic syndrome was a disorder of registration, it is not entirely certain that his own explanation in fact contradicts that view. His definition of registration is barely meaningful and certainly not clear. He distinguished the fixation of things from the fixation of the present, and then equated fixation—presumably, though not explicitly, of things—with perception and registration (Delay, 1942b, p. 61). In the same book Delay also proposed this somewhat idiosyncratic definition of registration, in the operational sense of immediate recall: "It appears to be common to perception and to memory, perception in the process of being formed into an image" (p. 121). One trouble with Delay's constructs is that they correspond to definitions in experimental psychology only "to a certain degree." The defect to which he traced anterograde amnesia, and which he vaguely attributed to a disorder in brain metabolism, is impaired retention. Delay explicitly excluded the possibility that this impairment might originate in perception or registration, in the sense of immediate memory. He implicitly excluded the alternative explanation that the derangement occurred in recall, for it is a defect in mental synthesis, in integration.

*Gantt and Muncie.* An early application of the Pavlovian technique to the amnesic syndrome was the conditioning experiment of Gantt and Muncie (1942) with 3 chronic Korsakoff patients. Their method was avoidance conditioning, varying both conditional stimulus and response, but using the same unconditional stimulus throughout: electric shock applied to the subject's hand. The conclusions these experimenters drew from their subjects' failure to condition, and from their differential performance when required and when not asked to verbalize the appropriate sequence of responses, can be divided into two classes. Some confirmed several well-established observations about the amnesic patient's learning: poor retention, difficulty of absorbing new information, failure to achieve fixation by repetition. Others, while also reaffirming previous formulations of the amnesic disorders, attempted this at a level of complexity that conditioning experiments are not commonly considered as suitable to probe. Moreover, several of these propositions are a great deal more controversial than those about the learning defects. For example, Gantt and Muncie discovered some evidence in their data for van der Horst's "time factor"; for a disorder in formal thinking; for greater difficulty presented by experiential than by more impersonal data, new or old; and for the tendency of amnesic patients to adopt sets in accordance with verbal formulations or instructions. In summary, the deficit in the amnesic syndrome derives from an inability to analyze events for their meaning, and to synthesize the facts of analysis into a plan of action.

*Popov* (1954), who is presumably an authoritative spokesman of the Pavlovian School, sees in the Korsakoff syndrome an example of excessive inhibitory function, more especially of external inhibition. The effect is a lowered energetic level in the cerebral cortex, and consequently associations between memories are difficult to condition. Negative induction is probably the crucial mechanism in the Korsakoff syndrome. Angelergues (1958), whose summary of Popov's theory is quoted above, pointed out that reduction of cortical activity could hardly affect memory without also impairing other complex intellectual functions that remain intact in amnesic patients.

*Russell* (1959), best known for his work on post-traumatic amnesias, regards a dissociation between memory and remembering as the characteristic derangement in the Korsakoff syndrome. A distinction between learning and remembering would be more accurate, since Russell attributes the disorder to damage in a mechanism that adds memories, records events. He contrasts the effects of its dysfunction with the relatively efficient retention of memories acquired by the patient at a time when this mechanism was still functioning. While emphasizing this contrast, Russell notes that Korsakoff patients, no less than those suffering from the effects of concussion, are subject to retrograde amnesia, and locates the neurological source of both anterograde and retrograde amnesia in the hippocampal system.

*Kral.* The new era in neuropsychological theory, which began with Moruzzi and Magoun's (1949) and Jasper's (1949) studies of the activating and integrating functions of subcortical systems, will undoubtedly lead to a reinterpretation of the amnesic syndrome. The first hint in that direction, at any rate in print, came from Kral (1956) who had a notable record of research in various amnesic disorders (Klein and Kral, 1933; Kral and Durost, 1953). His attack on so broad a front impressed Kral with the variability both of the etiology of the amnesic syndrome and of the courses it can take. Consequently he took care to formulate a behavioral definition of the disorder, that distinguishes it from amnesia, or "unselective memory loss for a limited period of time." According to Kral, the characteristic features of the amnesic syndrome arise from its being a selective "memory dysfunction whereby present personal memories cannot be recalled."

Kral's definition of the amnesic syndrome is too narrow even to accommodate his own clinical material which includes loss of remote memory, and which does not restrict loss of recent memories to those with a personal reference. He also proposes a second distinction in terms of perceptual awareness: amnesia follows from unconsciousness, but in the amnesic syndrome the patient completes the sensory process of perception quite adequately, yet cannot invest it with a personal meaning. He fails to integrate the sensory and affective components of perception. Kral's formulation of the amnesic syndrome in terms of impaired integrative functions restates

Gamper's theory, taking into account neurophysiological principles prominent in the intervening years.

*Pribram.* Theoretical models of the functions subserved by the limbic system, though based chiefly on the effects of surgical lesions, are nonetheless relevant to the Korsakoff syndrome. Pribram (1960) in a recent review of the literature outlined a neuropsychological paradigm that accommodates the observations of several earlier students of the amnesic syndrome to current neuropsychological thinking, and with his co-authors (Miller, Galanter, and Pribram, 1960) subsequently incorporated it into a general psychological theory modelled on information processing machines. Their theory distinguishes two major sets of cognitive function, discrimination or imaging and planning or sequential ordering. This distinction corresponds to Pribram's division of the brain into two major systems, of which the limbic is concerned with sequencing, including the various homeostatic or self-correcting operations of the organism.

Damage in this sequencing mechanism does not interfere with the capacity to register memories but it does affect spontaneous recall as well as appetitive behavior. That a disturbance in homeostatic regulation should derange the motivational-emotional aspects of behavior is immediately obvious, but recall also involves programming, setting up and executing a sequence of acts. Patients with lesions in the limbic system fail to get such a program under way, or to correct mistakes if they get going, for with external help they are able to initiate and even execute the necessary sequences. The fact that disorders in motivation and in memory do not always occur in the same patients can be explained by attributing different functional properties to different sites in a neural system.

It should be noted that Pribram makes no specific reference to the Korsakoff syndrome or to lesions in the sites customarily associated with this disease, and therefore cannot be criticized for not taking into account its full psychopathology. His model tentatively attributes to the hippocampus a gating function by which the brain is kept at work on the successive stages of ongoing plans and is protected from distracting environmental signals, and this implicates a neural system that in the Korsakoff syndrome is almost certainly diseased at some point. It is also worth noting that Pribram's speculative attribution of a protective or inhibitory function to the hippocampus has been confirmed experimentally by Grastyán (1959, p. 148).

## Summary

The boundaries of the amnesic syndrome are not rigorously delineated. Some of the observations made on amnesic patients are typical of a variety of brain lesions. Certain anomalies of function, however, appear to be more closely associated with the gross amnesic impairment of Korsakoff's disease than are others. This pattern of derangements is the more remarkable since it occurs in diseases of diverse origin. The patterns may vary in one detail or another, but none appears to be specific to a definite etiology.

Some principal themes emerge from this review of the literature; the same formula appeared at different times, in different parts of the world of scholarship, and often without any apparent communication among its advocates. A failure to establish connections between impressions and the self, dreamlike registration of events, omission of temporal signs, the absence of a critical attitude, an inhibition to utilizing stored information, are characteristic examples of formulae unrelated to a particular general theory of psychology. They are also typical of those explanations advanced for the amnesic syndrome that virtually preclude translation into testable operations.

Other explanatory formulae can be, and have been tested. Examples in point are the influence of the affective or experiential quality of an event on recall in contrast to formal acquisition; the sequential ordering of memories; errors in judging time spans; voluntary versus automatic recall; the presence and properties of confabulations. On some of these points there is considerable consensus, on others the authorities disagree. Certain differences of opinion are undoubtedly due to the premature generalization of an observation, others are primarily semantic. Few of the writers listed took the trouble to define exactly the terms they employed, let alone to specify operations for that purpose. Theoretical systems as different as the structural-associationist and gestalt, the psychoanalytic and Jacksonian necessarily lead to conclusions that, even though based on similar observations, can only be reconciled by elaborate reformulation. No doubt, there have also been true discrepancies in clinical observation, and they have led to genuine controversies through generalizations based on too few or on unrepresentative instances.

In all the literature surveyed there is no systematic examination of the patients' capacities over a wide spectrum of skills and mental function. About their motor skills virtually nothing has been reported. Their perceptual function has been investigated chiefly by gestalt psychologists who drew global conclusions about certain highly inferential processes. These experiments were done with a few very severely impaired patients, and therefore convey no information about the perceptual capacities of those who are less gravely disabled. Several other investigators failed to notice perceptual anomalies or, if they found experimental proof as did Kräpelin, tended to regard these as defects secondary to the memory impairment. Regarding the higher intellectual functions, the views expressed clash quite sharply.

Although opinions about the patients' perceptual function form only a minor theme in the literature of the amnesic syndrome, the conflicting views point to some of the more fundamental issues raised. If perception is regarded as an integrative mental function that places new information in some ordered relationship with certain pre-established categories or reference systems of the organism, then indeed it is more likely to show defects in the amnesic patient than it is with a more limited definition of the term. Most of the authors reviewed did not burden perception or, for that matter, registration with this function of ordering. Those who went furthest in this direction pointed to difficulties amnesic patients show in switching sets, a construct that is not exclusively perceptual. Others postulated certain additional functions that invest the perceptual input with personal significance, or with a feeling of familiarity, or merely prevent its isolation and fragmentation.

Some of these functions might indeed be classed outside the domain of cognition but hardly under the heading of personality, as that term is currently used in psychology. The Korsakoff patients' conspicuous lack of spontaneity has served as a constant reminder that their disturbance extends into the conative-affective processes. The impact of that derangement on memory function is typically expressed in such terms as insufficient capacity to bring ideas into consciousness. Explanations originally couched in terms of volition and attention have re-emerged in one form or another, and most recently in the shape of faulty programming or sequencing mechanisms. This reformulation of the theory should help to lift the problem of the amnesic syndrome from the rut of psychophysical interactionism. Lewis (1961) may have been unduly skeptical when, in a survey of the literature, he intimated that not much progress has been made in this area since Descartes envisaged recall as a searching operation impelled by volition and mediated by the flexion of the pineal gland toward discrete traces in the brain.

At any rate, there is now fairly general agreement that the amnesic syndrome does not present simply a derangement in memory. Nevertheless, the patients' memory function is clearly impaired, and the source of this impairment has not been spotted with certainty. In the days when memory was equated with associations impressed on a passive organism, the issue was simply whether Korsakoff patients were capable of forming new associations. Most of the evidence suggested that they were, although their capacity was very limited. A decision to attribute their amnesic defects to faulty recall seemed therefore preferable. The alternative explanations rested on the concept of an active process of registration that could involve all those processes of volition, attention, anticipation, and set flexibility that were considered above in relation to perception. The amnesic patient, so conspicuous for his lack of initiative, could reasonably be presumed to be lacking in these. A compromise solution postulated two stages in association: a passive process of fixation elaborated by a more constructive process of registration.

Memory is no longer, and indeed may never have been, thought of as the storage of information acquired by the organism in the course of undirected responses to its environment. There is evidence that certain psychological and neurological processes, other than a state of undifferentiated receptiveness, are necessary for the acquisition or registration of information. The disability that undoubtedly affects the amnesic patient's recall may indeed derange his registration of information as well. Neither those studies that concluded with a registration defect, nor the others that demonstrated impaired recall need be rejected. There remains, however, a third possibility that the trouble is in retention. Insofar as retention is a distinct memory function, it implies the existence of hypothetical or biologically identifiable traces. The literature surveyed has presented explanations of the amnesic syndrome in terms of rapidly fading traces, both hypothetical and biological. They were few and all untested either against the alternative hypothesis of forgetting by interference or against such empirical evidence of lasting memories as Nyssen has demonstrated.

Two conclusions can be drawn from a survey of the literature with considerable confidence. Notwithstanding the categoric statements that summarize so many reports, it is apparent that the amnesic syndrome does not necessarily involve the complete loss of a capacity. Certain mental functions are drastically reduced but at times even they can approximate their normal levels. The conditions under which this happens, however, have not been reliably determined. The second conclusion concerns the inadequate definition of these functions, despite much ingenious reasoning to fit clinical observations into one or another psychological theory. The functions that are impaired cut across the boundaries of all established classificatory systems. The problem the amnesic syndrome poses to the psychologist is not simply that of determining which functions are damaged and the extent of the damage, though this too needs doing. He must also consider certain hypothetical mechanisms that, if disturbed, could account for the diverse and at times unpredictable manifestations of the amnesic syndrome.

*PART FOUR*

# EXPERIMENTAL

# PREFATORY NOTE

Some implications of the problems presented by the amnesic syndrome were reformulated into hypotheses and subjected to experimental tests. The following chapters describe the procedures employed and summarize the results in tabular or graphic form. Little space will be allotted to a theoretical discussion of the results, since that is the subject of the final section.

Since the majority of the experiments compared performance between two groups, the results are typically shown as mean performance scores, and a measure of their scatter is indicated by standard deviations (SD). The experimental group was always drawn from the standard sample of chronic Korsakoff patients, control groups from the sources described on pp. 8-10. The latter are identified by code letters: A, for ambulatory patients in the Alcohol Clinic; H, for patients hospitalized with a peripheral neurological disease; X, for members of a recreational club; P, for a mixed group of psychiatric and orthopedic in-patients.

While it is often feasible to draw conclusions from measures of performance levels without reference to control data or statistical operations, differences between group means cannot be reliably evaluated by a simple comparison of the numerical values. Therefore, statistical tests of significance were calculated, and their results are given. Significance, unless otherwise qualified, means a difference expected to occur by chance less than once in 100 instances. A difference stated to be not significant indicates a probability of over 5 in 100. Whenever appropriate, the test employed was Student's $t$-ratio, and this if higher than 2.75 gives a $p < .01$ with samples of the size tested in our study. Probability levels are indicated when other tests of significance were used, e.g., *chi* square, Wilcoxon's (1949) $T$ for unpaired replicates, the Mann-Whitney (1947) test which gives normal deviates $(z)$, or analysis of variance.

*Chapter 5*

# VERBAL AND MOTOR SKILLS: ACTIVITY RATE

Apathy, indifference, lassitude, listlessness are all attributes properly descriptive of Korsakoff patients, yet misleading too. In so far as these terms refer to a lack of initiative, an abnormal tolerance of inactivity, an apparent vacuity of drive, of goal directedness, they are apposite, but let them not imply also reluctance to proceed with a task given, or its lethargic pursuit, or an excessive urge to stop and relax into torpor. Indeed, deficient as these patients are in the incentive to start something, they seem to be equally wanting in the impulse to stop once they have got going. Those I have studied, faithfully observed their instructions over experiments that lasted 20 minutes or longer, even while isolated in vigilance tests with only a few intermittent events (cf., p. 204). On one occasion, several Korsakoff patients were asked to draw circles on paper for as long as they wanted to. They kept at the job until I decided to call a halt, when after 5 minutes they still had not laid down their pencils.

In clinical descriptions of Korsakoff patients an abnormal measure of inertness and the absence of spontaneity have been regularly associated with the amnesic anomalies. Although lack of initiative does not necessarily involve a halting rate in execution once action is under way, reports often include the latter. Sluggishness is hardly a trait specific to the Korsakoff syndrome, but could be linked to residual signs of the ataxia characteristic of Wernicke's disease, and to a shuffling gait. Most of our patients, indeed, moved and talked rather slowly, but others seemed to be quite agile, spoke at a brisk pace, and habitually reacted with alacrity. Many appeared to be chronically depressed in mood, but even they were more notable for their lack of drive and affect.

## Speech and Reading

*Fluency.* Only 2 of our Korsakoff patients were remarkable for their halting speech, and even they never seemed to be at a loss for the right word or phrase. The group mean score on Wechsler's Vocabulary test, 10.0 (SD 2.3), was above the population norm for their age.

Two tests of verbal fluency were given to 16 Korsakoff patients and a control group (A)[1] of the same size. First they were to name as many different things one is likely to see in the street as they could in 60 seconds, and next to list different animals for 30 seconds.

Several Korsakoff patients could think of no more than 4 things that can be seen in the street. Their mean list of 8.8 (SD 3.8) items per 60 seconds was significantly shorter ($t$=4.20) than the control group's 15.7 (SD 4.9). The more definite directive to name animals increased fluency in both groups, but with much greater effect on the Korsakoff patients. In 30 seconds they named an average of 9.1 animals, compared with 5.6 things in the street, a statistically significant ($t$=4.96) increment, while that of the control group from 10.3 to 12.5 was not. Neither did the two groups differ significantly in the mean number of animal names listed. A tendency to tighten the loose boundaries of the instruction was also apparent in the responses of those Korsakoff patients who listed various types of vehicles or stores in succession, or named a store with an inventory of its contents—an attempt that gained them no extra credit.

A second test of verbal fluency presented six unfinished sentences for completion, e.g., "People are praised when . . ." Here again the choice was fairly narrowly defined, since one or two words were sufficient to round off each sentence, and few subjects attempted to make it longer. A qualitative analysis of the responses might have shown the inferiority of the Korsakoff patients' performance, but they were scored for speed only. With a mean of 23.8 seconds (SD 21.8) for the six

[1]For identification of code letters A, H, X, and P used in conjunction with control groups see "Prefatory Note" at the beginning of this Part.

sentences, against the control group's 25.0 seconds (SD 20.2), their responses came slightly but not significantly faster.

*Word Association.* The same two groups were also tested for speed of response in word association on three lists. List A consisted of words that have no logical opposites, while $B_1$ and $B_2$ were composed of words that do, e.g., dry, pull, top. The subject's initial instruction was to call out any word in response, as fast as he could think of one, "e.g., in answer to black, it could be shoe or white or dark or color." Lists A, and alternately $B_1$ or $B_2$, were presented with this instruction. Then following a new instruction, i.e., to respond with the opposites of the words presented, the remaining list was read out and immediately followed by the first B list. Each list consisted of ten words, but since it was arbitrarily decided that responses in excess of 10 seconds should be ignored, several substitute words were also provided. Latencies of 10 seconds or longer were rare; except for one patient, they occurred not more than once in any one list, and about equally often under the different instructions.

The effect of a definite set on the Korsakoff patients' speed of response was again apparent. Their mean association time (per word) was 3.1 seconds (SD 1.0) for list A and 2.4 seconds (SD 0.7) for list B; the corresponding control means were 2.5 (SD 0.8) and 2.5 seconds (SD 1.5). None of the four tests yielded statistically reliable intergroup differences, but while the directive to respond with opposites reduced the Korsakoff patients' association lag to 1.5 (SD 1.1) for the new and to 1.6 seconds (SD 0.5) for the familiar word list, that of the control group slightly increased to 2.6 (SD 0.9) for new words, and was reduced by no more than .2 seconds on list B. In contrast to the control group, for the Korsakoff patients the differences between latencies on list B under the two instructions, and between lists A and the first B were both statistically significant ($t=4.64$ and 3.2). Practice would hardly account for this; it seems more likely that the mere possibility of following a directive, i.e., to name opposites, helped in establishing a set, and that speeded up the responses.

*Reading; Stroop Test.* Almost all our Korsakoff patients

read slowly, haltingly, and with errors, even though they wore glasses and the print was in large (1 inch) type. Faced with print, be it but a sentence of three words, they usually held back before starting to read. It appeared as if a perceptual impediment prevented them from immediately grasping the letters or words as a whole.

Fluency of reading was tested incidentally with the Stroop cards which, in our experiment with 15 Korsakoff patients and 16 control (X) subjects, each presented ten rows of five items. Card A had the following color names printed in black type on white: blue, green, red, yellow. Card B was identical with A, except that the words were printed in colored ink, in the same tints that were used for naming, but in no instance were the name of a color and the color of its print identical. Card C presented the same array of colors as B, but the figures were round dots, not words. First, the subject read card A, word after word; next card B with the instruction to read the type and ignore the colors. Third, he had to name the colors shown on card C. Last, he was given card B again, but that time his task was to name the colors of the print and ignore the type. In all four trials he was instructed to proceed line by line from left to right as fast as he could without making errors.

**TABLE 1**

STROOP TEST: MEAN READING TIME AND SIGNIFICANCE OF DIFFERENCES BETWEEN KORSAKOFF AND CONTROL GROUPS

| | *Time in Seconds* | | | | |
|---|---|---|---|---|---|
| | *Korsakoff (N=15)* | | *Control (N=16)* | | |
| | *Mean* | *SD* | *Mean* | *SD* | *t-Ratio* |
| Trial I: black print | 30.3 | 7.3 | 24.7 | 8.7 | 1.87 |
| Trial II: read colored print | 39.7 | 13.5 | 32.9 | 12.6 | 1.40 |
| Trial III: name colored dots | 42.1 | 9.3 | 40.9 | 8.1 | .37 |
| Trial IV: name color of print | 94.8 | 25.4 | 71.8 | 19.4 | 2.76 |
| Trial IV–Trial III | 52.7 | 23.8 | 30.9 | 17.7 | 2.90 |
| Trial IV–Trial II | 55.1 | 23.9 | 38.9 | 20.1 | 1.97 |
| Trial IV–Trial I | 64.5 | 23.6 | 47.1 | 20.5 | 2.12 |
| Trial III–Trial II | 2.4 | 8.9 | 8.0 | 7.5 | 1.83 |
| Trial II–Trial I | 9.4 | 8.9 | 8.2 | 6.2 | .42 |

Mean reading time and difference between tests are given in Table 1. Errors averaged below 1 in 50 on the first three trials for both groups, and rose to 2.93 and 2.31 in the fourth. In this respect the two groups did not differ significantly, and in rate of reading they did only on the fourth trial. The Korsakoff patients were slower, but not significantly, in reading black or colored print, and in naming the colors of dots. The experimental instruction to maintain a naming set in conflict with their habitual reading set, however, slowed them down to a greater extent than it did the control group.

*Cancellation tests* of work rate involve some visual operations employed in reading, but not the formation of words or phrases. Three tasks were set, each consisting of five consecutive 60-second work periods. Task A was to cross out all capital letters found on a page with letters printed in unsystematic order, 40 to a line, 14 of which were capitals randomly distributed in each line. The work sheet of the other two tasks differed from the first in that each line was interrupted by six gaps of two spaces at irregular intervals. The instruction for Task B was to "cross out every capital letter and every letter, large or small, that is preceded by a gap"; for Task C "to cross out every capital letter and every letter, small or large, that is just before or just after a gap." These instructions were printed on top of each page, followed by examples. Each test began with pilot trials until the subject clearly understood his task. Twenty Korsakoff patients managed to grasp the instructions, and had sufficiently sharp eyesight to pass the trials, as did 20 control (A) subjects. Raw scores were obtained for each 60-second period for: (a) number of letters surveyed; (b) correct cancellation; (c) error by omission; and (d) incorrect cancellation. From these, two additional scores were derived: ratio of correct cancellation to all letters surveyed; and ratio of total errors (c plus d) to correct cancellation.

In addition to the data of Table 2, the following points are worth noting. (1) Differential scores between task A on the one hand, tasks B and C on the other, were significant in the Korsakoff but not in the control group for correct can-

TABLE 2
CANCELLATION: MEAN GROUP SCORES PER 60 SECONDS

| | *Korsakoff* | | *Control* | | | |
|---|---|---|---|---|---|---|
| | *Mean* | *SD* | *Mean* | *SD* | *t-Ratio* | *Wilcoxon's T* |
| Correct cancellation: raw score | | | | | | |
| Task A | 26.3 | 13.7 | 49.8 | 13.4 | 5.34[a] | |
| Task B | 29.4 | 14.2 | 52.4 | 13.5 | 5.11[a] | |
| Task C | 30.9 | 15.6 | 54.5 | 13.2 | 5.02[a] | |
| Total Error: raw score | | | | | | |
| Task A | 10.6 | 11.5 | 3.9 | 4.9 | | 284.5[a] |
| Task B | 20.5 | 20.3 | 4.6 | 6.5 | | 253.5[a] |
| Task C | 28.4 | 10.9 | 6.8 | 11.2 | | 264 [a] |
| Correct cancellation: ratio | | | | | | |
| Task A | 0.83 | 0.20 | 0.95 | 0.05 | | 344 |
| Task B | 0.69 | 0.26 | 0.94 | 0.07 | | 274.5[a] |
| Task C | 0.64 | 0.27 | 0.83 | 0.10 | | 257.5[a] |
| Error: ratio | | | | | | |
| Task A | 0.62 | 0.67 | 0.09 | 0.32 | | 318.5 |
| Task B | 1.39 | 2.24 | 0.07 | 0.18 | | 237 [a] |
| Task C | 1.53 | 3.14 | 0.15 | 0.82 | | 254 [a] |

[a] $p<.01$

cellation, ratio of correct cancellation, and total error. (2) Only in task A did the control group survey significantly more letters than the Korsakoff patients, with group means per 60 seconds of 52.4 against 31.9 ($t$=4.10). (3) Taking total cancellation as a measure of activity rate, the control group worked significantly faster in all three tasks. (4) Neither group fluctuated much across the five 60-second periods. (5) In both groups, the higher a subject's ratio score was for correct cancellation, the lower tended to be his ratio score for errors, as shown by *rho*=.76 for the Korsakoff and .95 for the control group. (6) Of the two types of error, those by omission were the more numerous, forming 64, 78, and 83 percent of the total error in the Korsakoff, as compared with 51, 77, and 83 percent in the control group in the three tasks.

## Visual-Motor Skills

*Finger Reaction.* Speed of response to discrete signals was tested on an apparatus that showed three 1-inch round lights in the vertical midline of an upright panel: red, yellow, and green from top to bottom; on either side of the panel a bell and a buzzer were mounted. The subject, comfortably seated and leaning with his hands on a table, operated one or two horizontal bars supported on springs, by pressing them down with one or several fingers. Response signals automatically started an electric clock; pressure on the bar stopped it.

Two experiments were conducted 3 years apart. Experiment I probed simple reaction time (RT) with 20 consecutive green light signals, choice RT with 20 green and 20 red signals shown in a standard randomized order, and alerted simple RT. In all three tests the response was with the right hand to green. In disjunctive tests latency of RT with left hand to red light was not recorded. In alerted RT the subject was told that he would be shown all three lights but that he was to respond to green only, with his right hand as before. One hundred sequences of 2 or 3 signals were presented, the first 8 and another 55 RYG, 18 RG, 9 YG, and 10 RYR, giving the initial letters of the three lights. Each light but G was on for about 1 second. RYR called for no response and probed the interference of an anticipatory set, the other signals tested the effect of anticipatory set—complete or partial—on speeding up RT. Experiment II consisted of seven tests: *i* and *v* were identical with simple RT and choice RT in Experiment I; *ii, iv,* and *vii* presented three more disjunctive tasks—green light and buzzer—bell and buzzer—both lights and both sound sources; *iii* tested simple RT to the bell; *vi* a cross modal alerted RT—yellow light followed by bell.

Table 3 lists the results of both experiments, even though they are not directly comparable because the Korsakoff patients' RT was consistently slower in the second. The probable reason for this change is their higher mean age which exceeds 3 years. Of the 14 patients who took part in both experiments all but 1 had lost speed in both duplicated tests. The two control groups, (A) in the first, and (X) in the second experiment, performed at much the same level.

In Experiment I, RT to simple chained signals did not differ between the two groups; latencies were more variable among

Table 3

FINGER RESPONSE: MEAN REACTION TIME (IN MILLISECONDS)

| | | | *Experiment I* | | | | | *Experiment II* | | | | |
|---|---|---|---|---|---|---|---|---|---|---|---|---|
| | | | *Control (N-15)* | | *Korsakoff (N-15)* | | | *Control (N-15)* | | *Korsakoff (N-15)* | | |
| *Test* | *Signal* | *Hand* | *Mean* | *SD* | *Mean* | *SD* | *t-Ratio* | *Mean* | *SD* | *Mean* | *SD* | *t-Ratio* |
| Simple | Green | R | 374 | 70 | 375 | 126 | — | 378 | 152 | 481 | 130 | 1.89 |
| | Bell | R | — | — | — | — | — | 402 | 198 | 497 | 216 | 1.21 |
| Disjunctive | | | | | | | | | | | | |
| Visual | Green | R | 486 | 74 | 538 | 198 | — | 498 | 163 | 614 | 206 | 1.66 |
| | Red | L | — | — | — | — | — | 566 | 171 | 692 | 192 | 1.85 |
| Auditory | Bell | R | — | — | — | — | — | 580 | 194 | 684 | 204 | 1.38 |
| | Buzzer | L | — | — | — | — | — | 624 | 188 | 698 | 218 | 0.96 |
| Cross modal | Green | R | — | — | — | — | — | 483 | 179 | 619 | 215 | $3.16^b$ |
| | Buzzer | L | — | — | — | — | — | 569 | 180 | 755 | 224 | $2.42^a$ |
| Four-Choice | — | R/L | — | — | — | — | — | 780 | 311 | 1123 | 531 | $T=169^b$ |
| Alerted | | | | | | | | | | | | |
| Visual | R-Y-G | R | 381 | 76 | 490 | 161 | $2.29^a$ | — | — | — | — | — |
| | R-G | R | 480 | 78 | 602 | 184 | $2.28^a$ | — | — | — | — | — |
| | Y-G | R | 423 | 107 | 567 | 221 | $2.19^a$ | — | — | — | — | — |
| Cross modal | Y-Bell | R | — | — | — | — | — | 405 | 138 | 518 | 123 | $2.27^a$ |

$^a p < .05$; $^b p < .01$.

the Korsakoff patients but not significantly so. In every test of both experiments between-subject variances were significantly larger than within-subject variances, but in two instances the former were not homogeneous for the two groups. This happened with disjunctive RT in Experiment I, but the scores of the two groups overlapped sufficiently so that the nonparametric test showed no reliable difference. The groups did differ in alerted RT. While the control subjects merely failed to benefit from a complete warning signal, the Korsakoff patients were in fact slowed down by it ($t=3.45$). The differential effect of partial as against complete alerting signals was about the same in the two groups, as was the incidence of errors by incorrect choice or by premature response.

Experiment II showed that in simple RT the two groups were again about equal, and that the Korsakoff patients responded as promptly to auditory as to visual signals. Warning signals also had the same effect as in Experiment I, in that they did not speed up the control group, but slowed down the patients. Analysis of variance, calculated on the six arrays of scores in two-choice tests, showed a significant difference between the two groups but no significant difference between other experimental variables or interaction effects between the latter and group membership.

A choice task that still presented only two alternatives for response, but demanded the processing of four different signals, increased latencies in both groups. This effect was more pronounced on the Korsakoff patients both in absolute and in proportionate terms. Their mean ratio score (four-choice ÷ two choice), .61 (SD .64) was significantly lower ($t=2.95$) than the control group's .74 (SD .60). Errors by anticipation were negligibly few; incorrect choices occurred more often in the four than in the two-choice test, but since a handful of subjects were responsible for them, they did not differentiate the two groups.

*Work rate and manual dexterity* were tested by two tasks performed separately and in combination. One required the continuous and repetitive operation of a manual tally counter with the thumb, first held in the left, then in the right hand, each for 5 minutes. Scores were read every 30 seconds, and variance in work rate was calculated over the 10 consecutive half minutes, while decrement over time was measured by comparing performance during the first and last minute, as listed in Table 4.

**Table 4**

CONTINUOUS MOTOR TASK: TALLY SCORES

| | *Mean Score per 30 sec.* | | | | *Mean variance over 10 periods* | | *First minute-fifth minute* | | | |
|---|---|---|---|---|---|---|---|---|---|---|
| | *Right* | | *Left* | | *Right* | *Left* | *Right* | | *Left* | |
| | *Mean* | *SD* | *Mean* | *SD* | *Mean* | *Mean* | *Mean* | *SD* | *Mean* | *SD* |
| Korsakoff ($N=15$) | 88.2 | 15.9 | 79.7 | 13.7 | 118.8 | 108.1 | 9.5 | 27.4 | 17.9 | 25.3 |
| Control ($N=15$A) | 86.9 | 15.6 | 78.7 | 15.4 | 139.8 | 170.5 | 0.8 | 21.4 | 12.8 | 23.9 |

Tallying was performed on another occasion with the non-dominant hand only, in a series of several tests, each lasting 1 minute. First, following a trial period, small steel balls were moved with a pair of tweezers held in the dominant hand, from one bowl to another, 6 inches away. They were placed within comfortable reach, the one about one-third full to the right of right-handed subjects. Second came tallying, third working the counter as before, and simultaneously picking up steel balls with the other hand. The fourth task was to move blue beads, as before, from a bowl in which these were mixed with an equal number of yellow beads. Next, this task was combined with tallying, and then all five tests were repeated in this order: 4, 5, 2, 3, 1. Mean scores are set out in Table 5.

**Table 5**

SINGLE AND COMBINED MANUAL TASKS: MEAN SCORES PER 60 SECONDS

| | *Tallying* | | | *Metal balls* | | *Blue beads* | |
|---|---|---|---|---|---|---|---|
| | *Alone* | *With metal ball* | *With blue beads* | *Alone* | *With tallying* | *Alone* | *With tallying* |
| Korsakoff ($N=16$) | | | | | | | |
| Mean | 163.7 | 83.6 | 81.4 | 30.6 | 29.1 | 21.7 | 22.8 |
| SD | 35.6 | 44.7 | 43.1 | 10.2 | 7.3 | 8.5 | 5.7 |
| Control ($N=16$A) | | | | | | | |
| Mean | 182.5 | 124.6 | 122.1 | 32.0 | 27.7 | 27.3 | 26.6 |
| SD | 33.9 | 55.0 | 150.7 | 12.9 | 10.7 | 8.8 | 9.7 |
| $t$-Ratio | 1.48 | 2.24[a] | — | 0.32 | 0.41 | 1.84 | 1.30 |
| Wilcoxon's $T$ | — | — | 206.5[a] | — | — | — | — |

[a] $p < .05$

It appears from Table 4 that the difference between the mean tally scores of the two groups was very slight with either hand. The Korsakoff patients performed more steadily over the 5-minute period, but the difference between the mean variances of the two groups was not significant, neither was that between mean decrement from the first to the fifth minute. Table 5 shows that the two groups did not differ significantly in the other manual skill tests, except that the Korsakoff patients were slower with the counter while engaged in moving beads. Divided attention resulted in a lower rate of counter pressing in both groups, while performance with the beads was unaffected. A further complication of the instruction, i.e., to select blue beads only, significantly reduced the efficiency of the Korsakoff patients ($t=4.94$ and 3.94) but not of the control group ($t=1.96$ and .44).

Three years later, the experiment was repeated with a group of 16 Korsakoff patients, but that time five periods of 60 seconds were allowed each for selecting blue beads, doing the same while working the counter, and picking beads from a homogeneous stock. Mean scores were overall somewhat lower than in the first experiment, again suggesting that the patients' motor efficiency may have deteriorated in the intervening years. It was certainly not due to fatigue effects, for the trend on all three tests was a gradual improvement from first to fifth trial.

*Tracking.* Rate of performance in a task demanding finer visual-motor coordination and tactical decisions was tested on a tracking apparatus. A continuous belt 4 feet long was revolving between two horizontal cylinders at a constant speed of 1 foot per 10 seconds. Along a 2.5 inch wide and 40-inch long track, 100 holes ($\frac{1}{16}$ inch) were punched at irregular intervals through the cellulose acetate belt. The track was concealed from view, except for 5 inches visible through a window of which the last $\frac{3}{4}$ inch was cut out to give a rectangular aperture. As the belt moved along, and one or more holes appeared under the aperture side by side, the subject's task was to hit with a stylus as many of these as he could. He was sitting by the instrument, the belt moving just above knee level, resting his dominant hand at the side of the aperture, and sliding the tip of the stylus along the smooth surface of the belt. Contact of the stylus with a copper plate under the belt closed an electric circuit, automatically tallying the score on a counter, and also allowing for a buzzer signal after each success. Three pilot runs preceded the twelve trials, on which 20 Korsakoff patients achieved a mean score of 17.8 (SD 3.1) per trial, a very significantly ($t=7.59$) lower total than 25.6 (SD 2.8) of 18 control (A) subjects. In neither group was there clear evidence of a consistent trend from first to last trial.

## Writing and Drawing

Speed of writing was tested in a group of 16 Korsakoff patients and 16 control (A) subjects. A 12-word sentence printed in 1-inch type was first presented for copying; another sentence of the same length and the cowboy story of 97 words (see p. 235-236) were dictated for writing. The words were read at the rate of 1 to 2 seconds so that the subject should not fall behind; for the story, a limit of 3 minutes was set. Copying the print took the Korsakoff patients 45.6 seconds, the control group 33.9 seconds ($t=2.34$, $p<.05$). In writing to dictation the difference between the group means was not significant with the single sentence (37.7 as compared with 30.2 seconds), but in 3 minutes the control group wrote down significantly more words than the Korsakoff patients: 71.1 versus 53.1 ($t=2.69$, $p<.02$). It seems probable that the latter had lost none of their speed in carrying out the motor operations of writing, but were somewhat handicapped both in copying and in writing to dictation by their limited storage capacity for strings of words.

Incidentally, most of the Korsakoff patients' handwriting was remarkably neat and mature looking, and their spelling too would have done credit to many a college student. Their few spelling errors were contextually inappropriate homonyms and there were omissions in punctuation. Some members of both groups tended to capitalize nouns, and one control subject did that even with the definite article.

In contrast with their writing, the Korsakoff patients' drawings, whether copied from models or done from memory, were slovenly and inaccurate. In the copying task of Benton's Visual Retention test 20 Korsakoff patients averaged 7.40 correct reproductions, a mean not significantly below the control group's (16 A) 8.93. Since any one copy can include several mistakes, the error score of the Korsakoff group exceeded their total of incorrect copies: 61 as against 52. Following Benton's classification of errors the bulk, 39, came from misplacements; distortions accounted for 13, omissions and additions for 7, rotations for 2. There were no size errors, nor any due to perseverations.

## Reversal of Motor Set

Perseveration is an ambiguous concept. In its narrower sense it means the continuation of certain responses beyond the point at which they cease to be appropriate to the situation. In a looser sense the term is also used to denote a preference for or reversion to some much rehearsed behavior pattern from one that is less familiar. The circumstances that make for one type of perseveration are not the same as those that favor the other. While Korsakoff patients do not tend to perseverate in the narrower sense of the term, they do show difficulties in carrying out responses that conflict with ingrained habits or skills. This was most apparent in a mirror drawing test of tracing a pattern with a pencil, while the subject watched it and his own hand through a mirror, i.e., saw his movements in reverse. More than half of the 18 Korsakoff patients tested could not perform even a relatively simple mirror drawing task; the older ones shared this incapacity with their contemporaries who had no clinically diagnosed brain damage.

Another test of reversal required the subject to write the letter S on a ruled page as many times as he could, first in the standard direction for 30 seconds, then in reverse for 60 seconds, and finally again forward for 30 seconds. Following trials in both directions, 20 Korsakoff patients averaged 78.0, 15 control (A) subjects 78.2 letters forward in 60 seconds, 35.3 and 65.8 letters in reverse. The two groups wrote standard S-s at the same rate, but differed significantly ($t=4.83$) in their differential scores (forward-reverse) with means of 42.7 (SD 18.3) and 12.4 (SD 17.1). The decrement in performance between the first and the final 30-second periods was slightly but not significantly larger with the Korsakoff patients (2.4 as against 1.6), in accordance with their general tendency to reach the optimum level quickly and show little or no improvement with practice.

## Summary

Although brought together under one chapter heading, the experiments surveyed tested several functions that can be impaired independently. In the general population, the manual skills investigated by these experiments represent three or possibly more motor capacities that are only partially interdependent. On the evidence of factor analysis (Seashore *et al.*, 1940; King, 1954), the initiation of response as tested in finger reaction, the repetitive performance of a movement, and finer tasks in manual dexterity are skills not highly correlated. Rank order correlations were calculated between pairs of the following scores: simple RT (Experiment I); mean bimanual tallying; moving metal beads; tracking; and writing S-s in reverse. The coefficients ranged from—0.02 to + 0.38 in the Korsakoff,—0.04 to + 0.37 in the control group. Korsakoff's disease clearly does not exert a uniform effect on the patient's motor abilities.

The several experiments confirmed the clinical impression that amnesic patients are relatively unaffected in the performance of long established skills, such as verbal facility or writing. Their comprehension of words and accuracy in spelling seem to be unimpaired; they can produce and follow speech at an undiminished rate. Their skills in reading and drawing, however, appear to have deteriorated, and both deficiencies are attributable to perceptual rather than to motor disturbances.

By the evidence of the word fluency and association tests, closely defined directives help to speed up Korsakoff patients with no detriment to accuracy, and also increase their output in continuous production. If, however, the directive goes counter to well established sets or habits, it impedes their activity more severely than that of the control subjects. The results of the cancellation task can be explained most satisfactorily by regarding it as a test of perceptual flexibility. In its simplest version cancellation calls for continuous and rapid scanning. This slowed down the progress of the Korsakoff group sufficiently so that, in proportion to the print covered, neither their correct responses, nor their errors differed significantly from the control group's. In its more complex version, the cancellation test demanded a continuous alteration of set from one type of cue to another, that might occur jointly with the first but also might not. Under these instructions, the Korsakoff patients performed much less efficiently than the control group.

As long as the perceptual component of the task was within their capacity, the Korsakoff patients did not show any marked deficit in motor performance. It appears that, at least in comparison with the control group of this research, the peripheral mechanisms involved in quick response and in continuous action are undamaged in the chronic phase of the Korsakoff syndrome; neither did performance fluctuate more, nor fatigue set in sooner. Even the comparatively fine skill required for picking up small beads appeared to be unimpaired. Evidence of undiminished motor skill in these patients is of interest in view of the severe peripheral neuritis that afflicted them in the initial phase of their disease.

Motor performance showed defects in the Korsakoff patients when the task demanded that they divide their attention between two dissimilar operations or that they process information presented to them successively and for a limited time. An example of the former deficit was observed when they had to tally with a counter while moving beads, and the addition of a third assignment—sorting out blue beads—resulted in a further decrement. One test in which the patients' limited perceptual capacity restricted their motor output was the tracking task; cancellation provided another instance of the same impairment.

As was expected, disjunctive RT demanding a divided perceptual set, placed the Korsakoff patients at a greater disadvantage than simple tests of manual response. This effect became accentuated when more than one sensory channel was involved in the transmission of signals, and also increased with the amount of information per signal. The paradoxical effect of alerting signals, prolonging rather than shortening latencies, is not unique to Korsakoff patients; we have observed it also in healthy older persons (Talland and Cairnie, 1961). Possibly this happens because each response is preceded by some active inhibitory phase, and the proper immediate reaction to a preparatory cue is continued inhibition until the response signal arrives. Korsakoff patients may be slower in releasing the inhibitory reaction, or they may have greater difficulties in coding information received in multiple signals. Either explanation concurs with observations of their low flexibility in switching sets.

*Chapter 6*

# PERCEPTION

Psychological terms common in general usage or, for that matter, in the technical literature do not correspond to stable functional units of the organism. Divisions within the domain of cognitive processes are, to some extent, dictated by considerations of convenience. Since memory implies the storage of information and its appropriate application, its reference could be stretched to include both genetically transmitted patterns of behavior and skills acquired in the course of individual development. Whatever the arguments in favor of or against such an inflation of the term, it is clear from the foregoing chapters that amnesic patients are not characteristically barred from access to those types of information.

At the other extreme, memory could denote a function involved in those very brief storage processes that subserve even the seemingly instantaneous accomplishments of perception. A signal or pattern can be distinguished only by setting it against others that surround it, and that is an operation extended in time. Conceivably, an organism unable to store information for a second could not make such distinctions. In fact, even severely amnesic Korsakoff patients are able to retain information within this microscopic range. Their perceptual functions are not grossly disturbed, and deficiencies that may show in finer perceptual performance could be attributed to their memory impairment.

There is a region over which the boundaries between perception and memory are not sharply discernible, but criteria of differentiating the two can be established without recourse to arbitrary rules. If a person is asked to report what he is about to see or hear, his perception is tested, even though the information may be transmitted to him item by item over a short span of time. If, however, he is told to remember that which he is about to see or hear, or is in the process of perceiving, then his memory is probed and an immediate trial tests his registration. In this study, registration is distinguished from perception primarily in terms of intention, and intention is inferred from the experimental instruction. When a subject is asked to remember what he sees or hears, this means to remember for a while, not just for a moment and then forget it.

The distinction advocated conforms to general usage by which perception is not limited to operations that depend entirely on signals actually impinging on the receptors. The reproduction of an involved sentence may be credited as a feat of memory, but not the utterance of a word that flashed on and off before the viewer could emit a sound. Although often unimportant, this distinction must not be neglected in a study of the amnesic syndrome, since in that context it does matter whether a perceptual anomaly can be attributed to defective memory function or should be treated as a primary symptom. In accordance with the rule proposed above, this chapter includes several experiments in which the subject had to keep count for brief periods or was required to report information that accumulated over a span of a few seconds, though not that he retain this information beyond its first report.

## Span of Perception

Information from the environment is apprehended either concurrently or in succession. The amount that appears to be received simultaneously is closely limited; it depends on grouping, spacing, and other formal properties of the material, as well as on the total number of items. Beyond that limit simultaneous displays are registered sequentially, and in the process some information could be lost. The limit of the simultaneous perceptual span must therefore be determined by short exposure, i.e., by preventing the accumulation of information in successive steps. It is questionable whether even so the perceptual act is instantaneous rather than progressive, but in any case the simultaneous span measures speed of perception. In contrast, the successive span of apprehension is entirely contingent on the type of information so presented and on the schedule of presentation.

*Visual Span: (a) Figures.* Pen drawings of ten familiar objects were shown on a single card in brief exposure. In this, as in other experiments, a Gerbrands tachistoscope was used, which illuminates a 7¾ square inch field 2 feet from the viewer's eye, shielded to peer into a dark chamber. Six of the test figures (tea kettle, airplane, violin, watch, hat, scissors) were in black, apple and hammer in red, fish in blue, and chair in green ink. The figures were roughly matched in size, and spaced evenly over the card. The subject's task was to name immediately after exposure as many of the objects as he had seen. Each subject's threshold was first determined by showing him two larger black pen drawings, with exposure times ascending from .01 second by steps of .01 second. The test card with ten figures was first shown at the threshold level and, unless this was above the following, successively with exposures of .1, .25, .5, and 1.0 second.

**Table 6**

NUMBER OF FIGURES RECOGNIZED AND INCREMENT WITH LONGER EXPOSURE

| | *Korsakoff* | | | *Control (15A, 6H)a* | | | |
|---|---|---|---|---|---|---|---|
| | *N* | *Mean* | *SD* | *N* | *Mean* | *SD* | *t-Ratio* |
| Subject's own threshold | 22 | .68 | .32 | 21 | 1.67 | .73 | 4.88 |
| .10 second | 19 | 1.10 | .70 | 20 | 1.90 | .64 | 3.64 |
| .25 second | 21 | 1.21 | .62 | 21 | 2.52 | .74 | 5.96 |
| .50 second | 22 | 1.59 | .59 | 21 | 3.48 | .68 | 9.50 |
| 1.0 second | 22 | 2.27 | .89 | 21 | 4.57 | .96 | 7.90 |
| .10 – .25 sec. | 19 | .11 | .63 | 20 | .75 | .46 | 3.98 |
| .25 – .50 sec. | 21 | .38 | .64 | 21 | .95 | .49 | 3.20 |
| .50 –1.0 sec. | 22 | .68 | .48 | 21 | 1.09 | .53 | 2.50 |
| Threshold – 1.0 sec. | 22 | 1.59 | .65 | 21 | 2.90 | .69 | 6.12 |

*a* For identification of code letters A, H, X, P used in conjunction with control groups see "Prefatory Note" at the beginning of this Part.

Table 6 lists scores at each exposure, and mean increment with increasing exposure, and shows that all between-group differences were statistically significant. Two incidental findings are of interest. First, while every member of the control group noticed the colors in which some of the figures were drawn, 6 Korsakoff patients did not. Although none of them was color blind, when questioned, they reported that all the figures were in black and white. Several other members of their group and most control subjects spontaneously remarked on the colors. The other observation concerns a tendency to generalize a class from a single instance. On first encounter with the test card 10 Korsakoff patients reported that they had seen fishes, or pots and pans, or musical instruments, and altogether 16 members of their group responded with an inaccurate generalization at some stage of the experiment. The same kind of error occurred in the first response of 2 control subjects and once more subsequently in that group.

*(b) Words.* Employing the same instrument and procedure as in the previous experiment, single words were shown, each centered and printed in heavy black, 1-inch square type. Of the nine words in the series (prop, wrist, enamel, indulge, despatch, inspector, fertilizer, slag, spurt), the first seven were matched for frequency in usage and ranged in length from four to ten letters.

After determining the threshold, the test cards were presented at that level in standard order. Words that could not be read correctly were shown again after intervals with exposure increased by steps of .05 second. Scores, representing the total exposure time needed for correct recognition of all nine words, averaged 14.4 (SD 9.0) seconds in the Korsakoff, 7.1 seconds in the control group. The two control samples deviated in opposite directions from the Korsakoff group; the 16 alcoholic patients with a mean of 2.6 seconds (SD 1.5) differed significantly ($z = 4.3$), while the mean, 19.4 (SD 13.7) of the 6 neurological patients was not significantly higher. Since the latter were chosen to control for the effects of prolonged hospitalization, it is possible that lack of practice, or reading without pressure of time, may account for this result.

The pictorial test confirms the finding that, at relatively short exposures, the perception span of the two hospitalized groups did not differ significantly. As soon as the special difficulties raised by very brief exposure were eliminated, however, both sections of the control group increased their span and gained with progressively longer exposures significantly more than the Korsakoff patients. One explanation is that Korsakoff patients show a deficit not so much in their initial or immediate grasp of the material presented to them as in their capacity to shift attention from one discrete item to another. It seems quite safe to rule out the alternative argument that they cannot recall all the figures perceived, since the immediate reproduction of a list of four or five items was well within the capacity of our patients.

*Digit Span.* Strings of numbers or letters provide a suitable test of the successive span of unrelated items. Previous studies have shown that this is not abnormally short in Korsakoff patients, and our study has confirmed their conclusion. The task was administered as part of Wechsler's (1944) intelligence test to 22 of our patients, whose mean digit span came well within the population norm, and 16 of them retested 2 years later further improved their forward and reverse digit span.

If the digit retention test measures the span of focused attention, the running digit span tests capacity to shift the focus of perception. In this test the instruction was not to reproduce the whole series from the beginning, but only the last five items in the original order. Four lists of single digits and four lists of letters, 10, 18, 8, and 12 items long, were read aloud at the rate of one item every 2 seconds, so that the subject had no foreknowledge of the length of each string. Single trials were scored for the number of items reproduced in the right order. Mean group scores derived from the four strings of letters and separately from the four strings of numbers were 10.9 (SD 2.9) and 8.4 (SD 3.3) for 24 Korsakoff patients, 15.1 (SD 4.0) and 13.9 (SD 3.0) for the control group (20A, 8H). In contrast with the stable digit span, in this test the Korsakoff patients performed at a level significantly below that of the control group. ($t$=4.10 and 6.17).

*Sentence Span.* Six sentences ranging in length from three to twelve words (5-18 syllables) were presented one day from a tape, another time in the tachistoscope, alternating in order. Immediate verbal reproduction after auditory presentation proved quite an easy task for 21 Korsakoff patients. Repeated brief visual presentation, on the other hand, presented difficulties.

Printed in black 1-inch type, each sentence was shown repeatedly for periods of 1 second until the subject completed reading it. Except for the shortest two sentences most patients accomplished this only by installments. After reading the last installment, the subject had to repeat the entire sentence and, if unsuccessful on first trial, he was shown the card again for as many periods of 1 second as he needed to reproduce the sentence in full, but not more than 20 times.

The control group (15A, 6H) needed a mean of 11.4 (SD 2.4) trials to complete piecemeal reading of the six sentences, 20 Korsakoff patients needed 13.9 (SD 2.5). The difference ($t=3.27$) was statistically significant, but it should be noted that the in-patient component of the control group, with a mean of 13.5, barely differed from the Korsakoff patients. All but two control subjects reported the entire sentence on first trial after reading the last instalment. None of the Korsakoff patients did, and several of them needed more repeated exposures to achieve this than for first piecemeal reading of the sentence. Furthermore, the more repeated presentations a subject required to complete a sentence by installments, the more additional exposures was he likely to need for reproducing it in full, as indicated by a correlation of $r=.53$ ($p. <.01$).

Previous experiments showed that Korsakoff patients are troubled with the integrative processes of reading rather than with the immediate apprehension of printed words. The present observations point to the same difficulty in progressively building up the information received. This disability may account alike for the discrepancy between the patients' stable and running digit spans and their reproduction of aurally and visually presented sentences. Both tests that handicapped the Korsakoff patients demand the retention in short-term storage of new information while additional information is being processed. For the running digit span new items must be added stepwise to those already accumulated, and some of the latter must also be discarded. A similar operation is also involved in reading a sentence without an opportunity to check back, and while the information is transposed from the visual to the vocal processing mechanism.

No inference should be drawn from these findings in regard to the relative efficiency of the visual and auditory systems in Korsakoff's syndrome; they reflect the effects on a central mechanism. Visual processing of sentences longer than five words always proceeded by discrete stages, and no doubt so did subvocal transposition as well. While the spoken sentences may indeed also have been taken in by segments, that process was continuous. The storage mechanism involved in the progressive accumulation of information plays no crucial part in reproducing a short spoken sentence, any more than in the stable digit span. It certainly does in the running digit span, and very likely also in the reproduction of printed sentences. A disturbance in this hypothetical mechanism would also account for the Korsakoff patients' defective registration of memories.

## Perceptual Identification and Discrimination

An elementary process in perception is the identification of an object or pattern, its distinction from other patterns. Discrimination may be in terms of a single attribute or several; the criteria can be explicitly stated or demand the discovery of cues. Further, in accordance with the foregoing definition of perception, attributes can extend over a very short span in the temporal dimension.

*Visual Judgment of Length.* Following a simple matching task, three tests of relational comparisons were set, all in a single dimension. The material consisted of 12 rectangular flat bars, 1 inch wide and ¼ inch thick, and two each 3, 5, and 9 inches long, one each 4, 6, 12, 15, 18, and 24 inches long. The bars were spread out on a flat surface, at various angles in a standard randomized display. The subject indicated his choice by pointing and was not allowed to lift up a bar or push it alongside another.

In the matching test, with three sizes that could and three that could not be matched, the Korsakoff patients proved themselves quite capable of handling the problem. Relational judgment was tested first by presenting the four longest bars, 12 times in randomized order, and asking the subject to point to the pieces that measured $\frac{1}{2}$, $\frac{1}{4}$, $\frac{1}{6}$, $\frac{1}{8}$ of the longest, $\frac{1}{2}$, $\frac{1}{3}$, and $\frac{1}{2}$ of the second, $\frac{1}{3}$ and $\frac{1}{5}$ of the third, $\frac{1}{2}$, $\frac{1}{3}$, and $\frac{1}{4}$ of the fourth in length. The second task was the reverse; all but the three longest pieces were presented in random order with the instruction to single out those that were twice, three times, etc., as long as the object of comparison. Last, the subject was shown pairs of appropriately matched pieces, and he had to estimate how many times the shorter went into the longer. The combinations were identical with those of the first and second series, and therefore the correct answer was always an integer. As shown in Table 7, the Korsakoff patients' mean error was significantly higher in all three tasks than the control (A) group's. Both groups tended to overestimate the longer of two bars, and in the first two series few errors were wider of the mark than one size.

Table 7

VISUAL JUDGMENT OF LENGTH: MEAN ERROR SCORE

| | *Korsakoff* *N=20* | | *Control* *N=20* | | |
|---|---|---|---|---|---|
| | *Mean* | *SD* | *Mean* | *SD* | *t-Ratio* |
| Series I | 7.20 | 2.31 | 2.95 | 3.39 | 4.52 |
| Series II | 7.20 | 2.28 | 3.10 | 3.19 | 4.78 |
| Series III | 6.50 | 2.98 | 3.30 | 3.28 | 3.15 |

*Tactual-kinesthetic judgment of width* was tested incidentally in an experiment designed to explore the extent of "figural after-effect" which, following Klein and Krech (1952), should be more pronounced in Korsakoff patients than in control subjects (18A, 6H) who had no clinically diagnosed brain injury, but in fact differed in the opposite direction. The apparatus, modelled on that used by the authors quoted, consisted of a 1.5 inch wide wooden bar and a comparison gauge tapering from 4 inches to $\frac{3}{4}$ inch, both mounted on 4-inch stands. Riders sliding above the top allowed only the tips of thumb and forefinger to touch the sides of the bar or gauge. The blindfolded subject began by marking the position on the comparison gauge where it matched the width of the bar. He had two trials with his dominant hand, first starting from the wide end, next from the narrow end. Twenty of the 22 Korsakoff patients and 15 of the 24 (18A and 6H) control subjects repeated the experiment under identical conditions after 2 or more weeks. Thus three measures of tactile judgment were obtained: (a) accuracy of judgment, i.e., deviation from the correct position of 1.5 inches on the comparison gauge; (b) consistency of judgment, i.e., difference between

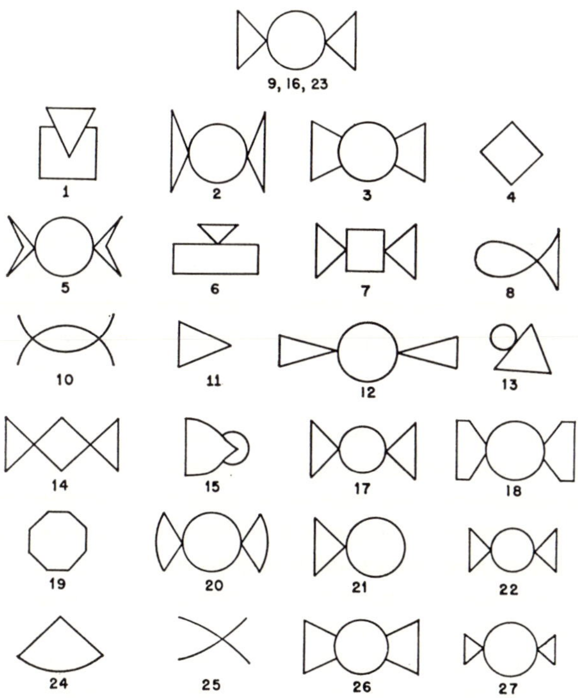


Fig. 1. Figures for visual discrimination.

position marked in descending and ascending approach; (c) discrepancy between judgment on first and second test. Scores for (a) and (c) were based on arithmetic means of the two judgments. With mean scores of .42 (SD .48) and .46 (SD .50) inch for (a), .24 (SD .20) and .22 (SD .22) inch for (b), .33 (SD .33), and .28 (SD .21) inch for (c) no significant difference was found between the two groups.

*Visual pattern discrimination* was tested on the series of designs in Fig. 1. The task was to identify the top figure which was shown in serial positions 9, 16, and 23. Each of the other figures was presented once in the order illustrated; except that 3 was identical with 26. It is apparent that the figures varied widely between those that had little in common with the standard and others that were of the same general pattern but drawn on a smaller or larger scale, or differed only in the proportion of a detail to the whole.

The figures were presented singly in a tachistoscope, though the exposure time of .5 second was not intended to create ambiguity and could be extended to suit the subject's convenience. In case of doubt, a figure was presented a second time. Initially the subject was given a model of the standard on a card, and was asked to remember it, because he would see a number of figures, one by one for a short time, "some exactly like the one he was looking at, others similar but not identical in every respect, and still others that are entirely different." He was told that he was to say "yes" each time he saw exactly the same figure, "no" when it was not exactly the same in shape or size. He could examine the model for as long as he needed to be certain of recognition, and subsequently saw it once more in the tachistoscope. On completion of the 27 presentations and responses, the same task was performed a second time in reverse order, but now the subject was instructed to check the model before each exposure.

With very few exceptions, all responses were prompt and definite. Frequencies of positive responses, both correct and mistaken, are listed in Table 8. A shorter time gap between inspecting the model and matching the figure evidently did not help correct identification. Incorrect calls were somewhat

**Table 8**

IDENTIFICATION OF VISUAL PATTERN ("WINGED" FIGURE): FREQUENCIES

| | *Figure* | *Korsakoff* $(N=22)$ | | *Control* $(N=24, 16A, 8H)$ | |
|---|---|---|---|---|---|
| | | *Forward* | *Reverse* | *Forward* | *Reverse* |
| Correct | | | | | |
| | 9 | 19 | 18 | 22 | 23 |
| | 16 | 19 | 18 | 23 | 22 |
| | 23 | 20 | 18 | 20 | 22 |
| Incorrect | | | | | |
| | 2 | 14 | 5 | 8 | 1 |
| | 17 | 20 | 18 | 15 | 11 |
| | 22 | 16 | 15 | 11 | 11 |
| | 27 | 11 | 16 | 9 | 4 |
| | All others | 41 | 35 | 5 | 1 |

fewer in the reverse series, but in neither group was the difference statistically significant. Errors of both kinds averaged 5.0 (SD 2.0) forward and 4.4 (SD 2.6) in reverse for the Korsakoff patients, 2.0 (SD 1.6) and 1.7 (SD 1.9) for the control group. With $t=5.35$ and 3.90, both between-group differences with significant.

*Auditory discrimination* was tested by the identification method of the previous experiment, using nonsense words (e.g., *taran*) in place of complex patterns, natural words instead of simple figures. All but 1 of the 24 control subjects (16A, 8H) and 12 of the 21 Korsakoff patients correctly indicated the standard on all three occasions. In errors the groups again differed significantly ($t=3.26$), with means of 2.6 (SD 1.6) and 1.9 (SD 0.9). Since the Korsakoff patients' success in judging width (see pp. 138-139) suggested that the elimination of signals irrelevant to the task, i.e., reducing distraction, might also improve their accuracy in auditory discrimination, the same experiment was repeated with blindfolded subjects. The results, however, failed to support the hypothesis.

Another experiment in auditory discrimination formed part of Halstead's (1947) battery. On prerecorded tape 60 nonsense syllables were presented for recognition by marking 1 of 4 printed syllables for each. The mean error of 19 Korsakoff patients was 19.4 (SD 7.8), only one scoring below 7, Halstead's upper limit for normal performance.

*Recognition and Reproduction of Rhythms.* Halstead also demonstrated the diagnostic significance of recognizing rhythmic patterns and included Seashore's (1919) procedure among his tests of brain damage. This presents 30 pairs of recorded acoustic patterns, setting the subject the task of deciding whether each pair consists of the same pattern sounded twice or of two different rhythms. Halstead's scoring method assigned a mean rank score of 8.9 (SD 2.4) to 19 Korsakoff patients, of whom 2 performed within the normal range.

Reproducing rhythms is not only a more difficult task than recognizing their identity, it also reaches deeper into the borderline territory between perception and memory. A test suggested by Ploog was given to 18 Korsakoff patients and 18 control (X) subjects. Using Morse notation, the following rhythmic patterns were sounded on a buzzer, always twice in succession, and the subject was also required to repeat each two or more times: (a) ... ... (b) _._ _._ (c) .._ .._ (d) .__. .__. (e) __.. __.. (f) __.._. __.._. (g) ._._..._._.. The number of subjects who passed the criterion of two successful reproductions by sounding a buzzer with a telegraph key are listed in Table 9.

**Table 9**

Reproduction of Rhythmic Patterns

| | *Pattern* | | | | | | |
|---|---|---|---|---|---|---|---|
| | *a* | *b* | *c* | *d* | *e* | *f* | *g* |
| Korsakoff ($N = 18$) | 16 | 6 | 10 | 2 | 9 | 1 | 1 |
| Control ($N = 18X$) | 18 | 11 | 18 | 6 | 15 | 7 | 5 |

At first glance it looks as if the Korsakoff patients had been inferior on all trials except the first. By the evidence of a statistical test (Latscha, 1953), however, differences between the two groups proved to be significant in three trials only: in *c* ($p < .01$), *e*, and *f* ($p < .05$). Qualitative analysis indicates that alternation of double and single alternation is wellnigh beyond the capacity of the Korsakoff group, as is double alternation when the pattern begins midway (*d*); but neither did most control subjects master these rhythms. Since younger people of average ability tend to perform this task successfully, the high incidence of failure in both our groups could be attributed to an aging effect. It should be stressed that the criterion of mastery, i.e., two consecutive reproductions of the rhythm, did not especially penalize the Korsakoff patients by requiring retention as well as acquisition of a pattern. There were only four instances in that group, two on trial *c* and two on *f*, in which a subject correctly tapped the rhythm once but not a second time; in the control group the same partial failure occurred seven times.

*Time Judgment.* Estimates of short durations and intervals were tested by immediate reproduction, experimenter and subject controlling the same buzzer at two ends of the laboratory. Four series of trials tested: matching (a) duration, i.e.,

**Table 10**

TIME JUDGMENT: MEAN ERROR SCORE
(RATIO OF DISCREPANCY TO STANDARD)

| | *Standard: Seconds* | | | | | | |
|---|---|---|---|---|---|---|---|
| | *2* | *5* | *7* | *10* | *15* | *30* | *All* |
| *Task: Match* | | | | | | | |
| | *Duration* | | | | | | |
| Korsakoff ($N = 20$) | 288 | 375 | 258 | 212 | 343 | 386 | 1856 |
| Control (16A, 6H) | 136 | 177 | 117 | 93 | 149 | 137 | 814 |
| | *Interval* | | | | | | |
| Korsakoff ($N = 20$) | 276 | 274 | 186 | 208 | 200 | 310 | 1450 |
| Control (16A, 6H) | 182 | 187 | 124 | 125 | 148 | 138 | 899 |
| *Task:* | *Multiply by* | | | *Divide by* | | | |
| | *3* | *2* | *2* | *2* | *3* | *2* | |
| | *Duration* | | | | | | |
| Korsakoff ($N = 20$) | 258 | 135 | 210 | 176 | 264 | 150 | 1260 |
| Control (16A, 6H) | 143 | 84 | 124 | 48 | 136 | 130 | 666 |
| | *Interval* | | | | | | |
| Korsakoff ($N = 20$) | 487 | 413 | 320 | 321 | 416 | 228 | 2182 |
| Control (16A, 6H) | 171 | 93 | 68 | 123 | 169 | 89 | 702 |

uninterrupted buzzer signals over periods of 5, 15, 30, 2, 7, and 10 seconds; (b) time intervals of the same lengths, marked at start and termination, reproducing a multiple or a fraction of the same (c) durations, and (d) intervals; a third of 15 seconds, treble 2 seconds, half of 10 and 30 seconds, double 5 and 7 seconds. Duration and intervals were measured by an electric clock in $\frac{1}{100}$ second, and the scores listed in Table 10 were calculated by dividing the error in estimate—irrespective of direction—by the standard, and multiplying by 1000.

Nonparametric tests applied to all four arrays of total scores gave $z$ scores significant at the .01 level. The Korsakoff patients made consistently larger errors than the control subjects, but in neither group was the error in estimate a direct function of the length of the time to be judged. Testing mean differences between a subject's score on one and either of the other two types of task (duration versus interval; matching versus multiplying and dividing) no significant differences were found between the two groups. The requirement to form proportionate time estimates did not further impair the Korsakoff patients' performance. All four sets of time judgment were repeated with the Korsakoff patients blindfolded. Mean group scores were about the same, and neither did individual subjects show greater accuracy when guarded against possible visual distraction.

Two other tests of time judgment were given, one requiring the subject to keep count of time, the other to estimate it retrospectively. In the former the instruction was to rest and signal when (A) 30 seconds and (B) 3 minutes had elapsed; (C) stop drawing geometric figures after 30 seconds and (D) stop cancelling capital letters after 3 minutes. In the other task subjects were required (E) to rest and (F) to write to dictation; after 3 minutes they were asked how much time had elapsed while they were resting or writing. Each trial took place on a different day. Error scores calculated in the same manner as above are given in Table 11 for 16 Korsakoff patients and a control (X) group of the same size.

Neither group made significantly more or fewer errors in estimating time spans occupied by writing or resting. When

**Table 11**

TIME ESTIMATION: MEAN ERROR SCORE
(RATIO OF DISCREPANCY TO STANDARD) IN SECONDS

| *Task* | *Korsakoff* | | *Control* | | |
|---|---|---|---|---|---|
| | *Mean* | *SD* | *Mean* | *SD* | *Wilcoxon T* |
| A. Signal after 30 seconds rest | 530 | 340 | 303 | 36 | 228[a] |
| B. Signal after 3 minutes rest | 484 | 283 | 271 | 101 | 227[a] |
| C. Stop drawing after 30 seconds | 380 | 336 | 227 | 82 | 245 |
| D. Stop cancellation after 3 minutes | 428 | 246 | 200 | 71 | 206[b] |
| E. Estimated time spent resting (3 minutes) | 1116 | 64 | 427 | 26 | 340 |
| F. Estimated time spent writing (3 minutes) | 646 | 38 | 411 | 26 | 253 |

[a] $p < .02$; [b] $p < .01$.

the task was to stop after a given period, both groups erred by underestimation, and the Korsakoff patients tended to make larger errors, particularly when the intervals were as long as 3 minutes. In retrospective judgment, the control group tended to overestimate the period that had elapsed, while the Korsakoff patients were evenly divided between the two types of error. They also erred more widely in judgment but this difference was not reliable. These experiments would show that memorizing or keeping in evidence some information is a task more difficult for amnesic patients than recollecting or reconstructing the same type of information. Other experiments, however, do not allow for wide generalization of this conclusion. The findings are of interest chiefly in view of the many speculative observations about the effect of Korsakoff's disease on the patient's temporal sense.

## Completion of Fragmentary Patterns

Normal perception involves considerable reconstruction of total patterns from partial cues, especially when the information is presented under less than optimal conditions, e.g., amidst noise, or with short exposure. A defective operation of this process has been recognized in various neurological patients, and could indeed form part of the amnesic syndrome, since the process of perceptual completion entails the matching of the momentary information against stored models. Bürger-Prinz and Kaila advanced still another reason for the amnesic patients' failure in this perceptual function, i.e., that they tend to adopt a perceptual attitude toward parts and cannot shift to an orientation toward the whole pattern.

*Mutilated Words.* A series of words, printed in large, clearly readable type, was presented in the tachistoscope, with successively longer exposure, as required. Some of the words had their first, last, or one or two middle letters deleted, but in each sufficient cues were left for the reconstruction of one, and only one, meaningful word, e.g., SW ET. The test material also included several complete words, some printed in the usual upright horizontal position, others sloping up or down, or upside down.

In the Korsakoff group ($N = 18$) the percentage of correct responses or speed of recognition of the mutilated words was not lower than of the control words in the familiar or disoriented position. There were three exceptions to this rule: two words in which the entire upper or lower half was missing, and SAMPLE from which the letter P had been omitted. This last word furnishes the only instance of the Korsakoff patients performing less efficiently than the control (A) group ($N = 16$), and that happened because most of them appeared to be quite satisfied with the recognition of SAM LE as the name of a Chinaman. The evidence of this experiment argues against the Korsakoff patients' relative inability to elaborate cues or to integrate fragments into wholes.

*Picture Completion.* Twelve figures from Street's (1931) test, shown in Fig. 2, were presented singly for recognition, in the order shown (cat, dog, etc.). Each figure, printed on a $6 \times 6$-inch card, was handed in the upright position to the subject, who could turn it around if he wished to, while inspecting it for at most 4 minutes. As soon as he gave the right answer, he received the next card; if his response was incorrect, he was told so and asked to try again.

Table 12 lists frequencies of correct recognition of each card, but the two groups were compared on mean individual

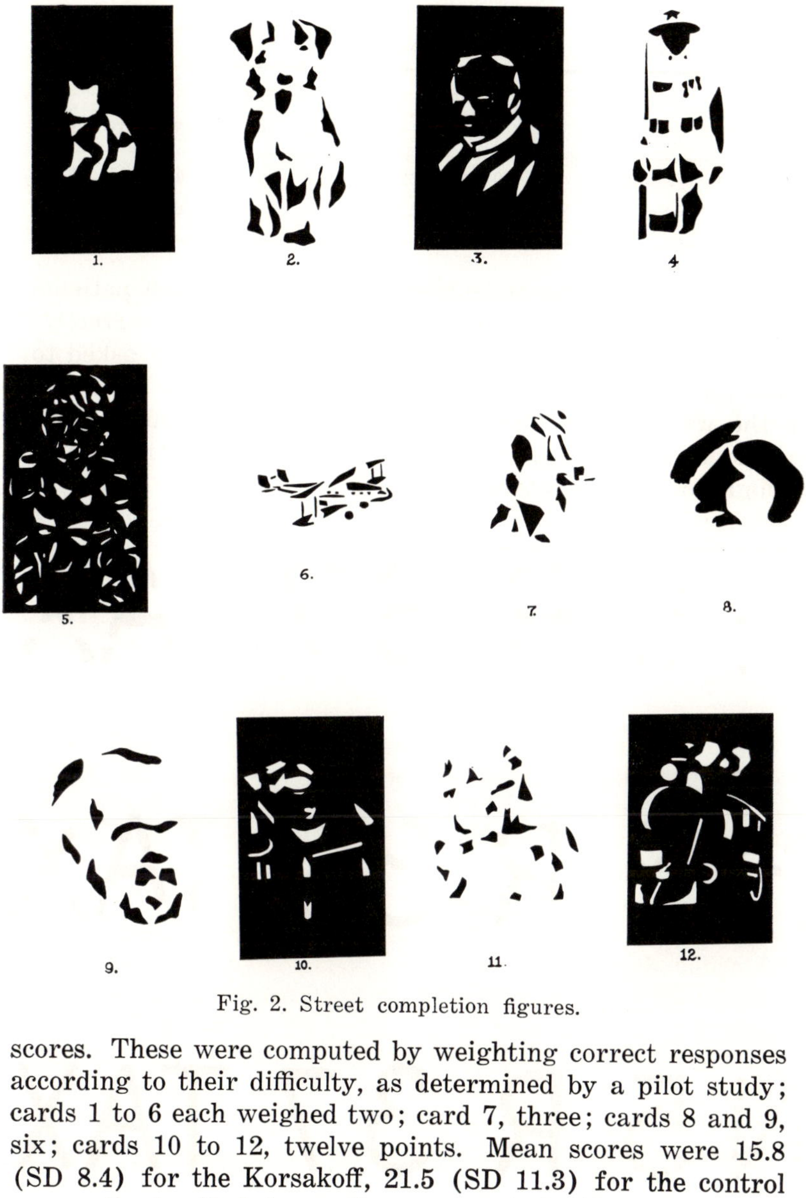


Fig. 2. Street completion figures.

scores. These were computed by weighting correct responses according to their difficulty, as determined by a pilot study; cards 1 to 6 each weighed two; card 7, three; cards 8 and 9, six; cards 10 to 12, twelve points. Mean scores were 15.8 (SD 8.4) for the Korsakoff, 21.5 (SD 11.3) for the control group; the $t$-ratio between these was not significant at the .05

Table 12

STREET COMPLETION CARDS: NUMBER OF CORRECT RECOGNITION

| | *Cards* | | | | | | | | | | | |
|---|---|---|---|---|---|---|---|---|---|---|---|---|
| | *1* | *2* | *3* | *4* | *5* | *6* | *7* | *8* | *9* | *10* | *11* | *12* |
| Korsakoff (*N*=22) | 20 | 22 | 22 | 20 | 19 | 18 | 10 | 4 | 4 | 3 | 1 | 0 |
| Control (*N*=24; 16A, 8H) | 21 | 22 | 22 | 22 | 20 | 18 | 14 | 8 | 6 | 4 | 2 | 2 |

level. Faced with the difficult pictures, the Korsakoff patients tended to respond more readily, although often incorrectly; they were also more apt to pick out a detail and, if asked to make another effort, to add yet another detail rather than take in the whole figure. Since they made more mistakes, their revisions were also more frequent than in the control group, though not as often correct.

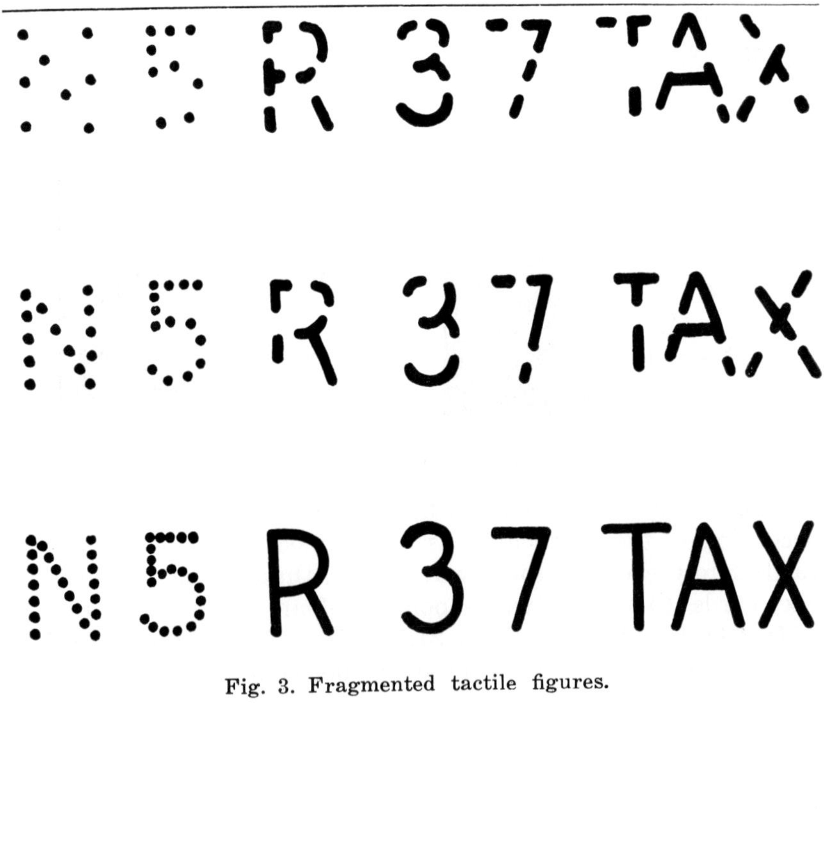


Fig. 3. Fragmented tactile figures.

*Tactual Completion.* Perceptual integration was tested in another sense modality, on blindfolded subjects palpating a 3.5-inch square surface on which a letter, a number, or a short word was outlined with pinheads, or in an elevated ridge of baked clay. Each figure was presented in three graded stages of fragmentation, as shown in Fig. 3, beginning with the least complete model. Subjects could use any finger on either hand to palpate the test object, each for as long as 90 seconds. After recognition the fuller variants of that figure were omitted from the test.

**Table 13**

TACTUAL RECOGNITION: NUMBER OF CORRECT RESPONSE WITH DIMINISHING FRAGMENTATION

| | *Figure* | | | | | | | | | | | | | | |
|---|---|---|---|---|---|---|---|---|---|---|---|---|---|---|---|
| | *N* | | | *5* | | | *R* | | | *37* | | | *TAX* | | |
| | | | | | | | *Model* | | | | | | | | |
| | 1 | 2 | 3 | 1 | 2 | 3 | 1 | 2 | 3 | 1 | 2 | 3 | 1 | 2 | 3 |
| Korsakoff ($N = 21$) | 3 | 8 | 7 | 2 | 9 | 8 | 9 | 2 | 9 | 6 | 2 | 11 | 2 | 0 | 6 |
| Control ($N = 20$; 16A, 4H) | 8 | 7 | 5 | 6 | 7 | 5 | 9 | 7 | 4 | 8 | 4 | 7 | 1 | 3 | 10 |

Converting the frequencies shown in Table 13 into individual scores, by assigning values of three, two, and one to models in descending order of difficulty, the Korsakoff patients with a mean of 7.4 (SD 2.3) did not differ significantly from the control (16A, 4H) group's 8.0 (SD 2.7). Scoring for correct recognition of single letters or digits, instead of complete models, did not make for significant differences; neither did *chi square* tests on frequencies of success for any of the five figures.

## Differentiation

The preceding experiments show that Korsakoff patients are not deficient in completing perceptual patterns from fragmentary cues. The reverse of this synthetic process is involved in the sorting out of patterns, in disentangling figures from a background that is not clearly demarcated. Several experiments tested this analytic component of perception for accuracy, speed, or both.

*Hidden Words.* In each of twelve lines of a page one, and only one, meaningful word of three to five letters was embedded among twenty capital letters. On page A each word named a color and appeared in the center of the line; those on page B all represented some item of clothing but were randomly positioned along the lines; on page C they occupied the same positions as on B, but differed in one or two letters, e.g., *ham* instead of *hat, coal* instead of *coat,* and they were not drawn from one conceptual class. All the words on pages D and E were derived from different categories, the former occupying the middle four positions of each line, the latter randomly placed. The subjects were given detailed instructions, shown an example, and asked to proceed as fast as they could, by underlining the words they found, but no time limit was set.

**Table 14**

MEAN SOLUTION AND TIME TAKEN IN FINDING HIDDEN WORDS

| | *Korsakoff* | | | | | | | *Control* | | | | | | |
|---|---|---|---|---|---|---|---|---|---|---|---|---|---|---|
| | | *Success* | | *Seconds* | | *Seconds ÷ Success* | | | *Success* | | *Seconds* | | *Seconds ÷ Success* | |
| *Task* | *N* | *Mean* | *SD* | *Mean* | *SD* | *Mean* | *SD* | *N* | *Mean* | *SD* | *Mean* | *SD* | *Mean* | *SD* |
| A | 13 | 8.5 | 3.5 | 250.5 | 169.5 | — | — | 16 | 11.6 | .6 | 95.6 | 50.6 | — | — |
| B | 13 | 8.8 | 2.5 | 271.7 | 137.7 | — | — | 16 | 11.3 | .8 | 114.5 | 43.6 | — | — |
| C | 13 | 8.9 | 3.8 | 250.1 | 141.5 | — | — | 16 | 11.1 | 1.4 | 103.2 | 35.7 | — | — |
| D | 12 | 9.8 | 2.3 | 199.4 | 107.5 | — | — | 16 | 11.9 | .5 | 68.4 | 37.1 | — | — |
| E | 11 | 9.2 | 3.4 | 192.2 | 115.0 | — | — | 16 | 11.3 | 1.3 | 96.7 | 33.2 | — | — |
| ABCDE | — | — | — | — | — | 33.3 | 30.9 | — | — | — | — | — | 8.3 | 2.4 |

Of 16 Korsakoff patients 3 could not perform this task, including 2 who had difficulty in reading regular sized print; 1 patient completed three, another four pages, 11 got through all five. Although the mean success score of those who attempted the task was consistently below that of the control (X) group, the difference reached statistical significance only for the first two pages. On every trial a number of Korsakoff patients managed to find all twelve hidden words, but it took them much longer than the control subjects. As shown in Table 14, both the raw time score and mean time taken over successful trials were of an entirely different order in the two

groups; in fact there was barely any overlap between the two arrays. Neither group seemed to benefit from finding all the hidden words in the center of the rows, or in the same conceptual class.

*Line Tracing.* Tangled lines were presented in four patterns of graded difficulty, with the instruction to follow each line from left to right, starting with number 1, and to write the number printed at its point of origin in the box against which it terminates. Figure 4 reproduces the trial task. The four

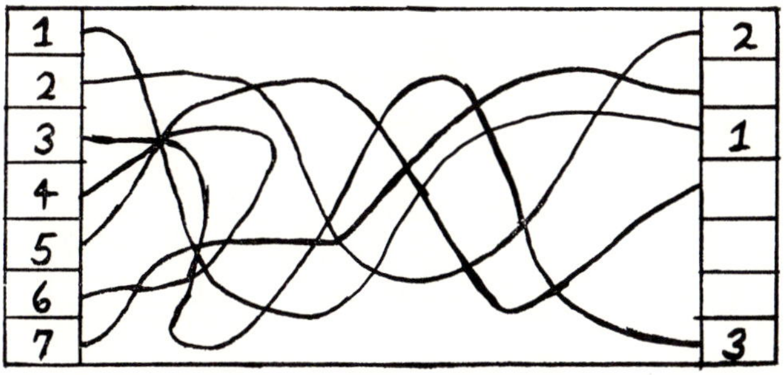


Fig. 4. Tangled lines.

test patterns differed either in the number of lines originating on the left or the number terminating on the right or in both, these being: A: 6/5; B: 10/7; C: 12/10; D: 16/10. Subjects were asked to work as fast as they could, but no time limit was set.

Table 15 shows that the two easiest tasks were well within

**Table 15**

Mean Success and Time in Tracing Lines

| | *Korsakoff (N = 16)* | | | | *Control (= 16)* | | | |
|---|---|---|---|---|---|---|---|---|
| | *Success* | | *Seconds ÷ Success* | | *Success* | | *Seconds ÷ Success* | |
| *Task* | *Mean* | *SD* | *Mean* | *SD* | *Mean* | *SD* | *Mean* | *SD* |
| A | 4.4 | 1.1 | 18.4 | 21.2 | 5.0 | 0 | 3.4 | 2.1 |
| B | 6.7 | .8 | 17.6 | 11.2 | 7.0 | 0 | 6.3 | 4.8 |
| C | 8.1 | 2.3 | 28.9 | 39.6 | 9.6 | 0.9 | 9.6 | 4.7 |
| D | 4.7 | 2.0 | 62.6 | 40.2 | 8.5 | 1.1 | 22.9 | 6.8 |

the capacity of both groups; in the two more difficult tests, however, the control group (X) traced significantly more lines correctly. The Korsakoff patients were also significantly slower. Members of both groups tried to follow all the lines on the first three tasks; on D control subjects averaged nine, the Korsakoff patients seven.

*Embedded Figures.* Gottschaldt (1929) designed a series of patterns to demonstrate that these, far from being just aggregates of their component parts, absorb those parts to

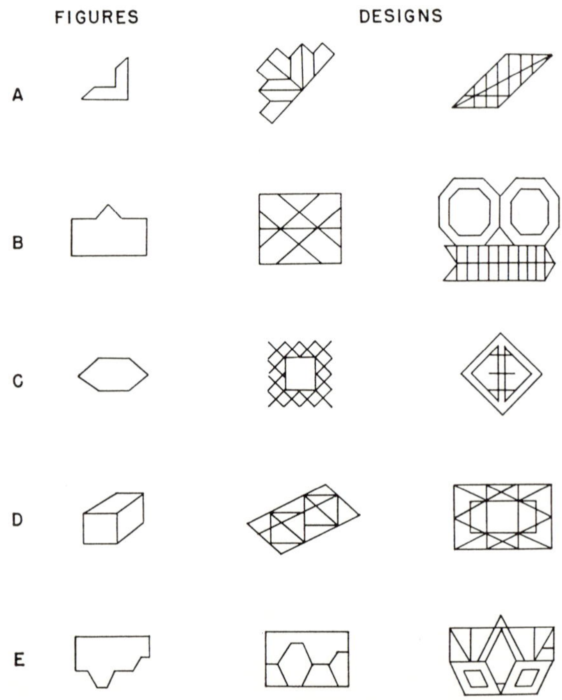


Fig. 5. Embedded figures.

such an extent that they are difficult to recognize or identify. Proficiency in locating the simple figures within the associated complex designs in Fig. 5 is thought (Pemberton, 1952; Keehn, 1956) to indicate an ability to hold in mind simultaneously several aspects of the same situation. The test material used followed Thurstone's (1944) model, dividing the thirty-four designs into five sections. Section I included seven designs embedding Fig. A, while those in the other three sections embedded one or another of two figures.

Subjects were first instructed to find examples of Figure A in Section I, and shade it in with a pencil. The experimenter demonstrated the procedure with one instance. In the subsequent sections the figures to be identified were indicated only if the subject could not make any headway otherwise. All Korsakoff patients, but not every control subject, needed this help. Speedy progress was not encouraged, as 50 minutes were allowed for the series of 33 test designs.

Of the 21 Korsakoff patients, 4 scored no success at all and only 5 solved a problem beyond Section I. Even that subgroup of 5 averaged a mere 2.5 solutions, compared with 15.4 in a control group of 15 (10A, 5H). Unlike the other tests of perceptual differentiation, this task proved to be outside the capacity of the Korsakoff patients. The reason is probably that the Gottschaldt designs form tighter whole patterns than rows of disconnected words or tangles of lines. Even when the subject manages to change his set from the whole to a part, unless this part happens to be the hidden figure, he has to revert to the total pattern before dissecting it again. This involves repeated shifts of set from part to whole and back. Reading the letters he need not retrace the distance covered; following a line his success depends on his ability to focus on it and on not straying over the whole field.

*Visual Constancies and Illusions.* A special case of separating the perceptual object from its setting occurs in tests of perceptual constancy. Constancy, as a technical term, denotes the propensity to perceive objects as total figures within their context, and not as specific stimulus combinations, e.g., to recognize that the pencil in one's hand is smaller than a telegraph pole in the distance, regardless of their retinal projections. Since spatial relations between persons or between observer and object tend to change most of the time, there would be little continuity in the world but for our capacity to abstract the percept from its momentary geometric properties. If the amnesic patient were indeed composed of cross sections without a longitudinal dimension, as some students (Sollier, 1900; Bürger-Prinz and Kaila, 1930) thought, then he should be unable to recognize the identity of persons or objects even as they changed their position within his view. Teuber (1961) noted that in patients with extremely severe visual field defects perceptual anomalies of this type can occur, so that a passing motorcycle is seen "as a string of motorcycles standing still." Similar derangements have not been reported of amnesic patients even with the most ephemeral retention span, and certainly have not been observed in ours.

Experiments in perceptual constancy test not so much the recognition of identity but rather the degree to which objects retain their "real" properties under conditions of restricted cues. Their devices aim at a perceptual compromise between the physical attributes and the retinal projection or, as Vernon (1957) proposed, a compromise between two perceptual attitudes: sensory judgment and object judgment.

In the present study, a test of size constancy showed no difference between the Korsakoff patients and the control group. They judged the size of two triangles at some distance by manipulating a matching device, and the general tendency was towards overestimation. Judgments in tests of shape constancy demand more complex inferences from cues. Two experiments asked the subjects for "sensory judgment," i.e., to select the model that matched the apparent shape of tilted figures shown with minimal cues of their setting. In both these experiments the Korsakoff patients differed significantly in their judgments from the control group (Talland, 1957). They were less able to disregard the known or inferred geometric properties of the models, and also showed a wider range of equivalence, i.e., coarser discrimination.

Visual illusions, according to Teuber (1960), exemplify the operation of the constancy effect in inappropriate contexts, and have been used to test certain hypotheses about normal and deranged brain function. Though there was no reason to expect that Korsakoff patients would report atypical experiences, they were shown both Ames's (1951) trapezoid window and the Necker cube. Every one of the 18 Korsakoff patients observed the Ames illusions, i.e., oscillation and the independent rotation of the cube. They also noted the reversals at the same points as the control subjects. Following the experiment, on close observation, they recognized that the apparatus was in continuous circular motion, and that they had been exposed to a visual illusion. As in the constancy experiments, Korsakoff patients perceived the trapezoid window in accordance with object-related expectancies, but in this instance differed in no respect from the control group.

Fig. 6. Trapezoid window.

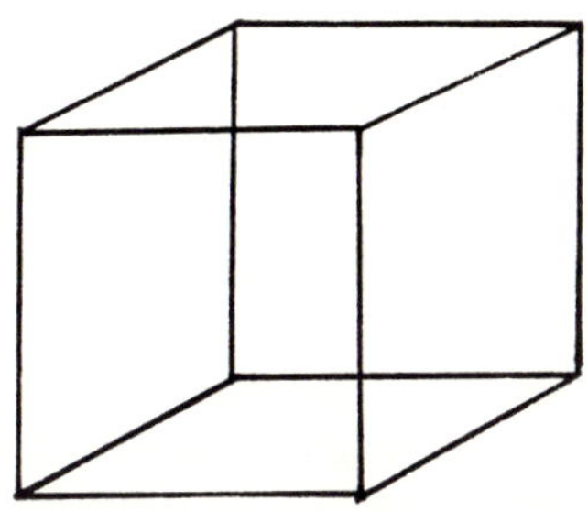

Fig. 7. Necker cube.

While all control subjects observed the illusion with Necker's cube, half of the Korsakoff group could see no reversal at all during the preparatory period or the test proper. The remaining 11 Korsakoff patients did not differ reliably from the control group in the number of reversals of perspective during two 60-second periods with no instruction to control the rate of reversal, or when asked to stem it. When they were encouraged to speed up the frequency of reversals, only 4 Korsakoff patients succeeded in this, compared with 19 control subjects; consequently the mean scores of the two groups differed significantly. To this extent, the experiment supports the hypothesis that Korsakoff patients are hindered in tasks that require flexible perceptual sets.

## Expectancy Effects

The foregoing experiments support the view that Korsakoff patients tend to adhere to their first response to a situation, no matter how incorrect that be, and are hampered in changing their set. Percepts are a joint product of the sensory input and such selective dispositions as expectancy, familiarity, and interest. Failure or deficiency in perceptual performance can be caused by derangements in these dispositions as well as by the impairment of the sensory apparatus. With an appropriate expectancy, sensory input of a lower intensity will be sufficient for accurate perception than is necessary in the absence of such an expectancy. Inappropriate sets must be changed, and if the switching mechanism is sluggish more intensive stimuli may be needed to activate it.

An experiment of auditory perception was designed to test the Korsakoff patients' capacity to utilize prescribed expectancies, to formulate their own sets, and to discard those that cease to be appropriate to the information given. Two experiments were conducted with 21 and 20 Korsakoff patients, and a control group of 18 (12A and 6H) participated in the first. Several lists of words were presented on a tape at or near each subject's threshold of intelligibility. This was determined by setting the volume control so as to allow for the correct reproduction of half the words in a pilot list. Some test lists that followed consisted of words drawn from a single conceptual class, e.g., animal names; others combined two classes; still others mixed classified with randomly assorted words.

Expectancy for words of a certain class would lower their threshold of intelligibility, so that more than half of them should be correctly reported. A set was established explicitly by advising the subject that he would be hearing names of animals, or implicitly by presenting him with several words of one category, so that he would expect more words of the same class. In addition, the experiment also included countersets, by first confirming an explicit set with several instances, then following these with words drawn from a different conceptual class. The original set would thus become inappropriate and tend to hinder the development of an appropriate new set. Single sets were tested when expectancy had been established or induced for one class of words only, double sets when two classes were equally likely to provide the instances. Sets were followed by "complete confirmation" if the lists consisted entirely of words congruent with expectancy, or by "partial confirmation" if such words were mixed with others from the assorted stock. Each set was confirmed by twelve words, and the same number of assorted words was mixed in for partial confirmation. The test lists therefore varied in length from twelve to thirty-six items. Implicit set was induced by a pre-list of six words. Except in tests of explicit set

**Table 16**

MEAN CORRECT REPORT FROM LISTS OF TWELVE WORDS

| *Set* | *Explicit single* | | | | *Explicit double* | | | |
|---|---|---|---|---|---|---|---|---|
| *Confirmation* | *Complete* | | *Partial* | | *Complete* | | *Partial* | |
| Experiment and position | I-6 | II-4 | I-4 | II-2 | I-3 | I-3 | I-5 | I-5 |
| List | $P_2$ | $A_1/A_2$ | $F_2$ | $F_1$ | $A_1$ | $P_1$ | B | C |
| Words reported | | | | | | | | |
| Korsakoff | | | | | | | | |
| Mean | 8.95 | 8.10 | 5.57 | 7.95 | 5.19 | 6.95 | 5.81 | 5.90 |
| SD | 2.66 | 1.81 | 2.91 | 2.28 | 2.84 | 3.14 | 3.47 | 2.07 |
| Control | | | | | | | | |
| Mean | 9.94 | — | 7.72 | — | 7.95 | 8.83 | 9.72 | 8.56 |
| SD | 2.16 | — | 2.34 | — | 2.00 | 2.25 | 3.74 | 1.53 |
| t-Ratio | 1.23 | | 2.50 | | | 3.80 | | 4.78 |

| *Set* | *Implicit single* | | | | *Counter single* | | *Mixed Words* | | | | |
|---|---|---|---|---|---|---|---|---|---|---|---|
| *Confirmation* | *Complete* | | *Partial* | | *Complete* | | | | | | |
| Experiment and position | 1-2 | II-3 | I-1 | II-1 | I-7 | II-5 | I-1 | I-4 | I-5 | II-2 | II-1 |
| List | G | $A_1/A_2$ | $F_1$ | $F_2$ | $A_2$ | $P_2$ | $X_1$ | $X_2$ | $X_3$ | $X_1$ | $X_2$ |
| Words reported | | | | | | | | | | | |
| Korsakoff | | | | | | | | | | | |
| Mean | 6.57 | 6.25 | 7.71 | 5.35 | 6.19 | 6.00 | 2.71 | 1.67 | 2.52 | 1.65 | 2.40 |
| SD | 1.89 | 1.32 | 2.55 | 2.82 | 2.85 | 3.14 | 1.63 | 1.65 | 2.03 | 1.78 | 1.91 |
| Control | | | | | | | | | | | |
| Mean | 8.50 | — | 8.50 | — | 6.83 | — | 4.06 | 1.94 | 2.39 | — | — |
| SD | 1.68 | — | 2.22 | — | 2.57 | — | 1.73 | 1.53 | 1.94 | — | — |
| | | | | | | | | .52 | | | |
| *t*-Ratio | 3.26 | | 1.02 | | .72 | | 2.46 | | .20 | — | — |

with complete confirmation, not more than two names drawn from the same category or two mixed words followed in a run.

Expectancy effects were tested on the following classes of words: animals (A), food (F), parts of the body (P), birds (B), colors (C), garments (G). Alternate lists of twelve compiled from one category or of mixed words are distinguished by suffixes. Experiment I consisted of the seven tests listed in Table 16; Experiment II reversed the sets for the F lists, and presented each A list to half the group with explicit set, the alternate list with implicit set, the former providing a counter-set for P. Instruction giving an explicit set included two examples from the class, those for an implicit set merely stated that a list of words would be presented. Subjects were repeatedly asked to report every word just as it had sounded to them; the silent interval after each word was five times the length necessary for reproducing it.

Group means of correct response for each list of twelve words are set out in Table 16 for both experiments. Expectancy effects are in evidence in both groups, since these means are much lower for mixed than for categorized words, although they did not inherently differ in intelligibility. Between-group differences were statistically significant for explicit set with partial confirmation and implicit set with complete confirmation, and for double sets. Given the latter, the Korsakoff patients behaved as if they had a single set, e.g., for birds or colors, but not both. While correct recognition was evenly divided between the two associated classes of words in both groups, the difference between the two for any one subject was much wider in the Korsakoff than in the control group. Tabulating correct responses in accordance with the more effective or major set, irrespective of its category, and for the less operative or minor set, the means shown in Table 17 were obtained. Clearly, the two groups differed more markedly in their scores with the minor than with the major set, and their difference between mean differential scores (major-minor) was statistically significant in both tests with double set. More illustrative still is a comparison between group scores for the minor set and for the associated mixed words in test I–5, as it shows that for the Korsakoff patients the minor set was barely more effective than no set at all.

Experiment II resolved a paradox, by pointing out that the two F lists differed in intelligibility, and thus an implicit set

**Table 17**

CORRECT REPORT WITH DOUBLE SET FOR MAJOR SET, MINOR SET AND MIXED WORDS

| | *Double set: Complete confirmation* | | | | *Double set: Partial confirmation* | | | | | | | | |
|---|---|---|---|---|---|---|---|---|---|---|---|---|---|
| | | | | | | | | *Difference between* | | | | | |
| | *Major set* | *Minor set* | *Difference* | | *Major* | *Minor* | *Mixed* | *Major-minor* | | *Major-mixed* | | *Minor-mixed* | |
| | *Mean* | *Mean* | *Mean* | *SD* | *set* | *set* | *words* | *Mean* | *SD* | *Mean* | *SD* | *Mean* | *SD* |
| Korsakoff | 8.38 | 3.76 | 4.62 | 1.71 | 7.50 | 4.21 | 2.52 | 3.29 | 2.28 | 4.98 | 2.35 | 1.69 | 1.92 |
| Control | 9.33 | 7.45 | 1.88 | 1.08 | 9.83 | 8.44 | 2.39 | 1.39 | 1.79 | 7.44 | 2.21 | 6.05 | 2.31 |
| $t$-Ratio | — | — | — | — | — | — | — | 2.77 | | 3.31 | | 6.61 | |
| $z$ | — | — | 3.51 | — | — | — | — | — | | — | | — | |

does not favor perception more than explicit set with partial confirmation. In fact, on the evidence of the two A lists, the difference is in the opposite direction ($t = 4.20$). Counter set facilitated correct recognition less than an explicit set ($P_2$) but did not differ from an implicit set ($A_2$). From this one would conclude that Korsakoff patients do not perseverate with abnormal rigidity, although exceptions did occur; e.g., a patient either kept silent or distorted into parts of the body the animal names presented under a counter set.

The experiment also demonstrated that amnesic patients do not select randomly from the environmental information. They are quite capable of following a single set provided for them and of holding it as long as events tend to confirm it. Failing this, they discard it readily enough but are virtually unable to keep it in reserve in case it might be appropriate again. They are able to formulate an appropriate expectancy for themselves, though possibly not quite as readily as the control subjects. Perhaps they are only more cautious. This they certainly proved to be by often refusing to respond altogether rather than risk an incorrect answer. Although clearly instructed and, if necessary, repeatedly reminded to reproduce each word as it sounded to him, a subject could always keep silent. This made failure a certainty, yet more mistakes were made by omission than by commission, and especially in the Korsakoff group. For them the ratio of errors through failure to respond to those made by incorrect words was 1.41, compared with 1.13 in the control group. Considering the subjects individually, only 5 Korsakoff patients made the larger part of their mistakes by incorrect response, while half of the control group did. The difference could be attributed to motivation as much as to cautiousness, but is in either case inconsistent with the view that amnesic patients, supposedly so easily given to confabulation, will offer any plausible reply to please the interviewer, or discharge their assignment without much care for its truthfulness.

## Apparent Motion

Faced with those gross defects in immediate memory, several observers have proposed that amnesic patients are unable properly to link the present impression with their previous experiences. If indeed they suffer from such an incapacity, the question arises whether they are able to integrate two temporally or spatially discrete stimuli into a unitary pattern, although they have no difficulty with the perception of real motion. Real motion is continuous, but in other situations, e.g., in watching movies, the illusion of motion is created by the rapid sequential yet disjointed exposures of images. The range of conditions suitable for creating this illusion can be wider or narrower, allowing for more or less spatial or temporal displacement, utilizing or neglecting structural or thematic properties that favor the perception of movement.

Two experiments (Talland, 1958b) explored the range of linear and rotary displacement and of the time gap between successive exposures, that allow Korsakoff patients to perceive the illusion. The test material included both abstract figures (lines, blots, geometric designs), and the scene in

Fig. 8 which by its very theme suggests motion. Table 18 lists the steps of spatial and temporal intervals tested.

Of 22 Korsakoff patients 10 failed to perceive motion under any of the experimental conditions, 7 others saw it with the car but not with the line, and only 5 with both figures. Only 1

Fig. 8. Car "moving" along the road.

member of the control group (14A and 7H) was unable to see the illusion at all; 18 perceived it with both types of figure. Not only did fewer Korsakoff patients perceive apparent motion, but those who did succeeded over a narrower range of intervals, with each upper threshold below the control group's. Frequencies of reports of motion perceived in the 27 trials are listed in Table 18.

**Table 18**

NUMBER OF SUBJECTS PERCEIVING MOTION

| | *Karsakoff (N=22)* | | | *Control (N=21)* | | |
|---|---|---|---|---|---|---|
| Line sideways | 1″ | 2″ | 3″ | 1″ | 2″ | 3″ |
| 20 msec | 4 | 5 | 4 | 15 | 15 | 12 |
| 100 msec | 3 | 3 | 3 | 13 | 15 | 15 |
| 200 msec | 0 | 1 | 2 | 12 | 13 | 13 |
| Line rotating | 45° | 67.5° | 90° | 45° | 67.5° | 90° |
| 20 msec | 4 | 4 | 4 | 15 | 15 | 12 |
| 100 msec | 2 | 2 | 2 | 14 | 13 | 12 |
| 200 msec | 0 | 0 | 0 | 13 | 13 | 12 |
| Car | 1.5″ | 3.5″ | 5.5″ | 1.5″ | 3.5″ | 5.5″ |
| 20 msec | 12 | 12 | 6 | 15 | 16 | 16 |
| 100 msec | 8 | 8 | 7 | 13 | 14 | 15 |
| 200 msec | 7 | 7 | 6 | 12 | 13 | 11 |

A second experiment was conducted 10 months later with 20 Korsakoff patients, in which the sequence of the two types of figure—line and car—was reversed, and several other figures were also presented under the same experimental conditions in order to test the hypotheses that: (a) displacement in line with its longest dimension; (b) the blot-like shape; (c) the surroundedness of the car may have favored perception of its motion as compared with the vertical line. The results furnished no evidence in support of the alternative hypotheses, and the subjects' performance proved to be remarkably consistent on the two occasions. The automobile was seen in motion more readily because this is a familiar, expected, meaningful occurrence, to use Jones and Bruner's (1954) threefold definition of the attitudinal factor which influences the perception of apparent motion. There is considerable experimental evidence to show that the perception of apparent motion depends on an appropriate set, and evidently it is harder to induce in Korsakoff patients, who tend to perceive two consecutive impressions as discrete events rather than interpret them as two phases in a single process.

This tendency can be attributed to several circumstances. Defects in the visual apparatus are unlikely to account for it, since performance on this task was not found to be related to acuity of eyesight or severity of nystagmus, and neither did our Korsakoff patients differ from control subjects in critical flicker fusion frequency. A misinterpretation of the purpose of the experiment cannot be entirely ruled out. Unlike the control subjects, the Korsakoff patients may have thought that the experiment tested their sanity and, by implication, their immunity to illusions. Half their number, however, also failed to see the autokinetic phenomenon, even though normal expectancy was in favor of positive response. The most likely explanation remains their abnormally high threshold for the sequential integration of information.

## Microgenesis of Perception

Although perception appears to be instantaneous, in fact it is a developmental process over a microscopic scale of time

(Sander, 1928; Flavell and Draguns, 1957). Normally the process is too rapid to yield either to introspective or to objective analysis, although there are situations as e.g., walking in heavy fog, when shapes and outlines literally emerge by stages in front of our eyes. The process can also be subjected to observation under suitable experimental conditions, e.g., by showing a figure in successive brief exposures, any one of which may be insufficient for forming an accurate image. In order to arrive at a complete and veridical percept the information obtained in each successive exposure must be integrated with those that preceded it. If Korsakoff patients are indeed deficient in progressive perceptual integration, their impairment should be manifested in the microgenetic process. They would arrive more slowly at the structured percept than control subjects, and no more rapidly under conditions of continuously successive exposures of the figure than with its presentation repeated after intervals.

*Composite Figures.* Three experiments were conducted, the first two with 16 Korsakoff patients and two separate control groups (P) of 15 and 10 respectively; 14 Korsakoff patients took part in the third. The five figures[2] shown in Fig. 9 were used as the test material: (a) the winged bull of ancient Assyria and the Evangelist St. Luke; (b) the hippogriff, a composite of horse, eagle, and lion; (c) merman and mermaid; (d) the Etruscan hippocamp, half horse, half dolphin; (e) a caricature of the Chevalier d'Eon, French diplomat and famed duelist whose transvestite habits gained him considerable notoriety in London society of the 1770s (White, 1952). These inherently ambiguous figures were chosen for their relative incongruity and unfamiliarity, attributes that demand repeated checking and reconciliation of details, and thus extend the process of recognition. Photographs of these figures, 6 × 4 inches, were shown in the tachistoscope.

In all three experiments the subject was told to be alert and to report on the picture he has seen flashing in the instrument.

[2] The mythical beasts were copied from Lum (1951); the picture of the Chevalier d'Eon originally appeared in the September 1777 issue of the *London Magazine*.

He was warned that the exposure would be brief, and was asked to give as much information as he had gathered. If he reported nothing or gave a very meagre response, the experimenter prompted him further with such nondirective questions as "Is that all?", "Anything else"? or by repeating his words with an inflection of incompleteness.

Fig. 9. Composite figures.

In Experiment I the figures were shown under the conditions of *repeated presentation,* in standard sequence from A to E, first with an exposure of .1 second, then again in the same order with exposures of .25, .5, and 1.0 second. Experiment II was conducted under the conditions of *successive presentation,* in which each figure was shown four times with exposures of .1, .25, .5, and 1.0 second before presenting the next one. Since the two experiments were conducted 6 months apart it was unlikely that any memory effect would carry over from the first to the second occasion in the amnesic patients;[3] the two control groups were different.

Experiment III was administered to 14 Korsakoff patients 4 weeks later. The method of *successive presentation* was used with a variable schedule. Each figure was shown three times with the shortest exposure before proceeding stepwise to single presentations with longer exposures. Balancing the order of the five figures across the subjects, one each was first shown for .01, .1, .25, .5, and 1.0 second. The last of these was presented three times altogether, the first seven times. Finally the subjects were asked to describe each figure, after unlimited inspection outside the tachistoscope, a procedure applied to the control group at the end of Experiment II.

Responses were recorded verbatim and those given to the second or subsequent presentations of a figure were tabulated under the headings of: (a) elaboration; (b) change; or (c) replication of a previous description. Elaboration was further divided into correct and incorrect, and included any modification of a previous response in the direction of a structured percept, a new detail, or the correction of a detail, as well as a specific definition instead of a generic one (e.g., horse for animal). Change meant the replacement of a specific response by another, correct or incorrect. Replication could either be a verbatim repetition of a previous response, or words amounting to much the same. Only a small fraction of the responses failed to fit under these headings, e.g., those that were quite vague, meaningless, poorer in content than the previous description, or when the subject could not report anything at all.

Since the experiment was concerned with trends toward perceptual structuring, only the second and subsequent exposures were scored, by compounding a subject's reports on all five figures and converting the tally into a percentage of the highest possible total, i.e., 15 in Experiments I and II. Mean scores of the two groups are set out in Table 19, and offer a comparison of their tendencies to elaborate, change, and replicate under the two experimental conditions. The tabulation

[3]Learning effects would have favored recognition under *successive presentation.*

takes care of the few instances in which a subject could see nothing distinct at all with the shortest exposure.

**Table 19**

MEAN ELABORATION, CORRECT ELABORATION, CHANGE, AND REPLICATION SCORES OF THE KORSAKOFF AND CONTROL GROUPS IN EXPERIMENTS I AND II AFTER SECOND, THIRD, AND FOURTH PRESENTATIONS OF THE COMBINED FIVE COMPOSITE FIGURES[a]

| | *Elaboration* | | | | | *Correct Elaboration* | | | | |
|---|---|---|---|---|---|---|---|---|---|---|
| | *Korsakoff* | | *Control* | | *t-Ratio* | *Korsakoff* | | *Control* | | *t-Ratio* |
| | *Mean* | *SD* | *Mean* | *SD* | (*z*) | *Mean* | *SD* | *Mean* | *SD* | (*z*) |
| Repeated presentation | 41 | 16.6 | 62 | 22.7 | 2.83[b] | 23 | 10.8 | 41 | 17.3 | 3.37[b] |
| Successive presentation | 24 | 9.6 | 59 | 23.4 | $z$=3.48[b] | 17 | 8.0 | 42 | 19.8 | $z$=2.56[b] |
| $t$-Ratio | 4.85[b,d] | | .26 | | — | 2.35[c,d] | | .34 | | — |

| | *Change* | | | | | *Replication* | | | | |
|---|---|---|---|---|---|---|---|---|---|---|
| | *Korsakoff* | | *Control* | | *t-Ratio* | *Korsakoff* | | *Control* | | *t-Ratio* |
| | *Mean* | *SD* | *Mean* | *SD* | (*z*) | *Mean* | *SD* | *Mean* | *SD* | (*z*) |
| Repeated presentation | 23 | 13.7 | 11 | 10.0 | 2.68[c] | 24 | 13.5 | 18 | 15.5 | 1.10 |
| Successive presentation | 6 | 5.2 | 13 | 9.0 | $z$=1.60[c] | 65 | 13.6 | 20 | 16.0 | $z$=3.62[b] |
| $t$-Ratio | 4.11[b,d] | | .35 | | — | 11.50[b,d] | | .28 | | — |

[a]Scores express the actual response as a percentage of the possible total.

[b]$p < .01$. [c]$p < .05$.

[d] Calculated on mean difference of 14 patients.

In both experiments the rate of total and correct elaboration was lower in the Korsakoff than in the control group. The two groups also differed significantly in their rate of change, but the direction of the difference was the reverse in the two experiments. Replications were more common in the amnesic group, but significantly so only under *successive presentation.* The two control groups did not differ on these indices, even though one was tested under *repeated* and the other under *successive presentation.* In the Korsakoff group replication was significantly higher and the other three scores were significantly lower with *successive* than with *repeated presentation.*

**Table 20**

MEAN ELABORATION, CORRECT ELABORATION, CHANGE, AND REPLICATION SCORES OF THE KORSAKOFF GROUP IN EXPERIMENT III, FOLLOWING THE SECOND AND SUBSEQUENT PRESENTATIONS OF FIVE COMPOSITE FIGURES[a]

| | *Number of successive exposures* | | | | | |
|---|---|---|---|---|---|---|
| | *3* | *4* | *5* | *6* | *7* | *All* |
| Elaboration | 18 | 31 | 21 | 33 | 31 | 28 |
| Correct elaboration | 11 | 21 | 14 | 26 | 23 | 20 |
| Change | 7 | 7 | 5 | 9 | 4 | 6 |
| Replication | 68 | 55 | 64 | 53 | 56 | 58 |

[a] Scores express the actual response as a percentage of the possible total.

As set out in Table 20, the results of Experiment III show that neither elaboration nor replication was a direct function of the number of successive presentations. Neither of these trends in the microgenesis of perception varied with the mean length of presentation so as to suggest that—at any rate within the range of 1 second—briefness of exposure time accounted for the low rate at which the Korsakoff patients evolved their percepts. Elaboration occurred as often after a short as after a long exposure, and many of the replications came at the end of a series, i.e., following a longer exposure. Another finding in support of this conclusion is the absence of significant differences between any of the corresponding mean scores in Experiments II and III. Inspection outside the tachistoscope elicited from the Korsakoff patients hardly more descriptive material than tachistoscopic presentation; nevertheless 80 percent of it involved some elaboration and 70 percent was veridical. In the control group 78 percent of the responses to prolonged inspection constituted some elaboration of previous descriptions, all correct.

The major results of the microgenetic study present an apparent paradox: Korsakoff patients evolve and change their percepts more consistently when interrupted in this process than with no interruption. Their deficient perceptual function cannot be attributed to their memory impairment, for this would show its effect over the longer intervals between *repeated presentations* of a figure rather than over the brief pauses in *successive presentation.* The findings make more sense if viewed in relation to the patients' inability to reorient themselves to a situation, to modify their initial percept. Because of their rigid adherence to the first percept, *successive presentations,* even well above the threshold of clear discrimination, contribute little to its better structuring or its closer approximation to the veridical image. *Repeated presentation,* in contrast, interrupts the original set adopted toward the ambiguous figure and thus allows for a steadier advance in structuring and correction.

The interruption of an inappropriate set, however, can only indirectly advance the process of perception. Repeated attempts would be more or less successful according to chance unless there were some systematic influence to cause their improvement. Such an influence may have been the progressive lengthening of the exposure time in our experiment, although the results of Experiment III argue against this explanation. Alternately, the patients carried over some information from each exposure to the next. This hypothesis is by no means inconsistent with observations about the Korsokoff patients' amnesic derangement. It concurs with other experimental evidence that the perceptual anomalies of these patients are not secondary to their memory disorder, and that a tendency to isolate limited or fragmentary impressions from the flow of experience and the fixity of their originally adopted sets are basic disabilities in this syndrome.

*Fragmented Figures.* That amnesic patients can retain newly presented information for some length of time, and that this helps their perception was shown by another procedure of serial presentation. Drawings of seven objects were presented in six degrees of fragmentation: bridge, church, hammer, house, table, dog, elephant. In a pre-test with normal subjects it was found that the first three were the easiest to identify, the two animals the most difficult, and that longer exposure time or a lower degree of fragmentation alike helped correct recognition.

Fourteen Korsakoff patients, alternately began with .01-second tachistoscopic exposures of the church or the hammer, stepwise reducing the fragmentation of the figure until it was correctly identified. Next they were shown the house or the table, and the dog or elephant in the same manner, except that exposure time was .05 second for the former, .10 second for the latter. Last the bridge was presented in the three most fragmented versions, each for .20 second. This constituted

**Table 21**

FREQUENCY OF RECOGNITION OF FRAGMENTED FIGURES

*A. Three Familiar Figures*

| | Degree of fragmentation | | | | | | |
|---|---|---|---|---|---|---|---|
| *Exposure time (seconds)* | *1* | *2* | *3* | *4* | *5* | *6* | *Fail* |
| .01 | 4 | 9 | 9 | — | — | — | 20 |
| .05 | 14 | 4 | 5 | 3 | — | — | 12 |
| .10 | 8 | 5 | 2 | 4 | 1 | — | 4 |
| .20 | 7 | 1 | 3 | 0 | 4 | 0 | 1 |

*B. Three Unfamiliar Figures*

| | Degree of fragmentation | | | | | | |
|---|---|---|---|---|---|---|---|
| *Exposure time (seconds)* | *1* | *2* | *3* | *4* | *5* | *6* | *Fail* |
| .01 | 2 | 2 | 2 | — | — | — | 36 |
| .05 | 2 | 2 | 6 | 4 | — | — | 26 |
| .10 | 3 | 7 | 6 | 4 | 4 | — | 14 |
| .20 | 10 | 6 | 1 | 3 | 7 | 2 | 6 |

*C. Bridge*

| | Degree of fragmentation | | | | | | |
|---|---|---|---|---|---|---|---|
| *Exposure time (seconds)* | *1* | *2* | *3* | *4* | *5* | *6* | *Fail* |
| .01 | 0 | 0 | 3 | — | — | — | 11 |
| .05 | 1 | 1 | 4 | 1 | — | — | 7 |
| .10 | 1 | 3 | 2 | 2 | 1 | — | 4 |
| .20 | 2 | 4 | 2 | 2 | 1 | 0 | 1 |

a preparatory procedure in which at some stage all subjects identified each figure, except the bridge. In the test proper the seven figures were shown in a standard order, beginning with exposures of .01 second each in versions 1 to 3, then for .05 second in versions 1 to 4, next for .10 second in versions 1 to 5, and last for .20 second in versions 1 to 6, i.e., including the complete drawing. A figure correctly recognized was subsequently shown only in a more fragmented version.

Responses to the fragmented figures are given in Table 21 according to exposure time and degree of fragmentation. "Unfamiliar" denotes figures that were not included in the preparatory procedure. Comparing these with the matched figures, it is apparent that familiarity helped to reduce both the time and the amount of information in the outline that is necessary for correct recognition. Amnesic patients are evidently able to form and retain for a while memory images, in the sense that other persons do. Subliminal perception did not facilitate recognition of the bridge. Other subjects tested by this method progressed more rapidly, and for that reason benefited less from the previous presentation of a figure.

## Summary

The experiments presented support the view that Korsakoff patients are not subject to severe perceptual anomalies. Their immediate memory span is not so limited as to interfere with normal perception. They recognize objects for what they are and can follow them in movement; they understand causal connections in commonplace occurrences; things and events appear to them in their normal connectedness. Since our laboratory was not equipped for exact determination of sensory function, most of the experiments presented signals above threshold level. Several Korsakoff patients had difficulty in reading fine print, typically because they had no spectacles. The incidence of hearing or visual defects did not appear to be higher among them than in the general population, but 9 patients seemed to have no capacity for olfactory discrimination.[4]

In tests involving comparisons, Korsakoff patients performed quite well if both models to be matched were within their perceptual range, i.e., with visual and tactual rather than with auditory material. They were also able to use familiar models, and match the fragmentary data given them against such stored patterns. The experiments that showed no significant impairment in Korsakoff patients are significant for eliminating two hypotheses about their perceptual deficit where it does show up. Its source is neither a dulling of sensory acuity, nor is it a direct effect of their disturbed memory function, even though perception depends on the availability of memory images to supplement, check, and structure the momentary sensory input. This dependence, however, varies with the situation or task, and is particularly influential when fragmented letters or figures are to be completed, tasks our Korsakoff patients accomplished quite efficiently.

Other experimental findings also confirm this conclusion. In identifying the winged figure, checking the model immediately prior to judgment did not improve accuracy. In determining the identity or difference of two short musical patterns presented in quick succession, or in reproducing the briefest temporal interval, the Korsakoff patients performed as poorly as in judging longer phases or sequences. Yet they could repeat long sentences presented aurally without error, even though the load of information was heavier but also more familiar and more sharply defined than that of a musical pattern or of a sound of indeterminate length. There is also the paradoxical observation that the more repeated exposures the Korsakoff patients needed for reading sentences in installments, the more additional presentations they required still before they could reproduce them in full. Paradoxical it is if considered under the laws of learning, but not incompatible with an impairment in the sequential integration of

---

[4]This anomaly emerged in the course of an experiment designed to test suggestibility (see p. 56) with extracts representing various agreeable odors. Döblin's (1905) patient, proved insensitive to, and misidentified some potent offensive as well as pleasant odors.

input, a defect suggested by the experiments with apparent movement and in microgenesis.

A second hypothetical function that accounted for several observations about defective perception in the Korsakoff patients was that of reorientation, of changing sets. In completing fragmented images or letters, the patients either succeeded right away or were unlikely to correct the misperceived figure on repeated trials. Although at a slow rate, they were able to disentangle paths or words embedded in an amorphous background, but not the Gottschaldt figures that can be spotted only by shifting the focus from part to whole and back again while testing possible solutions. Studies of expectancy effects show that Korsakoff patients have a very restricted capacity to maintain two or more sets concurrently and alternate them. This inferred deficiency also offered an explanation of their performance in experiments with shape constancy and reversible perspective. Can it account though for their results in several tests of identification and discrimination and for their narrower perceptual span?

In order to combine the fragments of a human portrait into a whole, very likely an orientation toward the composite image is most helpful, and it matters little what route the eyes follow. A different situation arises when the visual field comprises several self-contained figures, for the perceptual process reaches closure with the recognition of each, and at that point the perceiver must redirect his attention to another figure. Beyond a certain limit, the width of the simultaneous perceptual span depends on the speed of reorientation. Amnesic patients, so prone to remain locked in their initial set, scan the field at a slow rate. If in the process they also have to keep in reserve the information received, and sift it in order to discard some and combine the rest with the subsequent input, these patients are at a serious disadvantage. Their short running digit span, like the several examples of their difficulties with the integration of sequential input, can be attributed to this impairment.

Both defects under consideration—in set flexibility and in sequential integration—could be held responsible for the Korsakoff patients' relative bluntness of perceptual discrimination. Their looser categorization may be simply a matter of missing cues because of a more or less fixed orientation to some grosser aspects of a figure, or may arise from a loss of information about these cues in the process of switching from one object of comparison to the other. Quite possibly the two defects exert their effects jointly, and indeed may be interdependent. In order to accomplish progressive integration in perception, it is necessary to hold the set adopted toward and confirmed by the last event, as well as the information received, until the next event occurs; yet the set must also be flexible enough to yield to disconfirming messages. Amnesic patients are quite capable of maintaining whatever set they have adopted, they can also hold some new information for a limited period, but hardly seem to alter the former and thus to modify and develop the latter.

*Chapter 7*

# INTELLIGENCE; REASONING

The effect of the Korsakoff syndrome on reasoning and other higher mental processes has been a controversial topic. Quite obviously, a distinction must be made between abilities to solve problems that require the utilization of new information, and others that depend on the application of long established intellectual skills. Only in the latter type of problem can one determine any mental impairment other than the memory defect characteristic of the amnesic syndrome.

## Intelligence Tests

*Wechsler-Bellevue Intelligence Scale.* In the first year of the research, the mean IQ of 22 Korsakoff patients, adjusted for age, was 103 (SD 9.3), i.e., well within the range of the population norm. Verbal IQ of 104 was above performance IQ of 99. Two years later, 16 members of this group were retested, with an IQ of 101, higher than their own previous mean of 98; there was no difference between verbal and performance test levels. Normal intelligence, as tested by the WBIS, is a reliable finding in the Korsakoff syndrome. In fact, it is recovered fairly soon during the early phase of the Wernicke-Korsakoff syndrome, with the remission of the confusional state (cf., Victor, Talland, and Adams, 1959).

Although we could find no statistically reliable WBIS profile associated with the Korsakoff syndrome, it is apparent from Fig. 10 that tests of factual knowledge and sound common sense tend to be least taxing, and Digit Symbol Substitution is most resistant to mastery. The latter task requires both new learning and rapid switching of set. Block Design is another test that depends on repeated shifts from model to the object of construction, checking one against the other. It also involves planning and literally combining and ordering elements into wholes. Arithmetic, the third subtest which

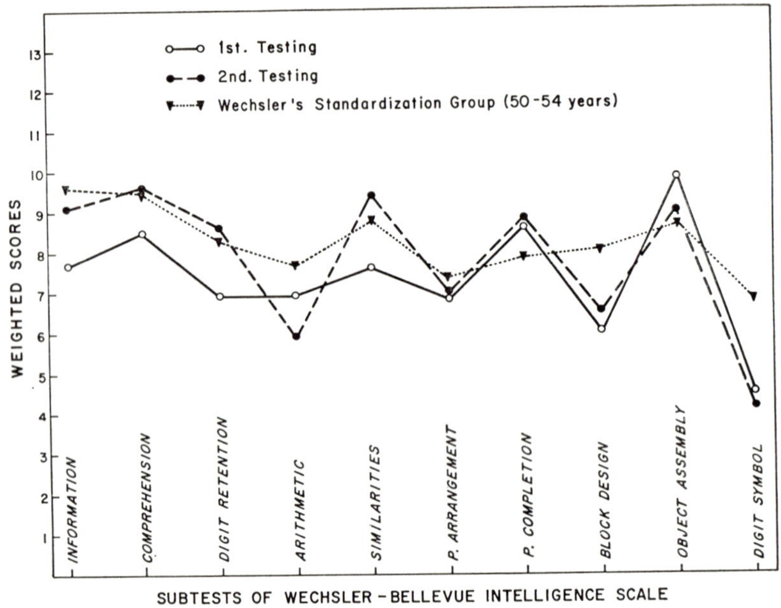


Fig. 10

showed a marked deficit on second testing, probably does not represent a typical dip in the Korsakoff patient's WBIS profile. The 10 patients whose scores pulled down the group mean were all women, who may never have mastered the multiplication table or who became easily confused by this test.

*Arithmetic.* Although simple addition and subtraction rarely caused difficulty, in serial addition less than half of the 14 patients tested accurately counted by 3's from 1 to 40. The extent to which the limitations in immediate storage of incoming information restrict the arithmetic operations of amnesic patients was pointedly shown by an experiment that required adding up simultaneously two or more columns of items. The first task was the following: "Take four cups and six plates; add two cups and seven plates. How many cups and plates do you have now?" Only 7 out of 17 Korsakoff patients solved this or the matched parallel problem. Two failed at the next step that required the addition of three items in one, two in the other column, and another at adding up three items in both columns. When allowed the use of paper and pencil, only three patients were unable to pass the same problems and to proceed successfully to the more difficult tasks.

*Progressive Matrices.* Raven's (1956) test was administered in the colored version, individually to 17 Korsakoff patients. Mean score on series A, Ab, and B was 20.4 (SD=7.8), mean performance time 588 seconds (SD 246). Six patients solved over half the problems in series B, thus qualifying for the sets with black figures, but only 2 patients did better than chance on C, one on D, and none on E. Using Raven's population norms for the oldest age group, and extrapolating from his published data, it appears that 5 Korsakoff patients scored above the top quartile, 5 just below the median, and 7 below the lower quartile. Their scores scattered more widely than on the WBIS, and the correlation between the two intelligence tests, although positive, was not high with *rho*=33; between matrices and block design it was still only *rho*=.35.

The progressive matrices provide a very questionable index of the general intellectual function and reasoning capacity of the type of patient studied. They set him problems that are both unfamiliar and meaningless and, furthermore, require the discovery of certain more or less concealed cues for categorization, thus facing him with disproportionate obstacles on three scores.

*Stencil design.* Arthur's (1943) test, originally constructed for measuring intelligence in children, consists of 20 symmetrical colored designs, in a series of graded difficulty (cf. Fig. 11). The task is to reproduce each pattern by superimposing one or several stencils on a solid colored base. Help can be given with the first five designs, the time limit is 4 minutes for each, and three consecutive failures or failure with any one of the last three designs terminate the test.

A control group (X)[1] of 21 performed significantly better

[1]For identification of code letters A, H, X, and P used in conjunction with control groups see "Prefatory Note" at the beginning of Part Four.

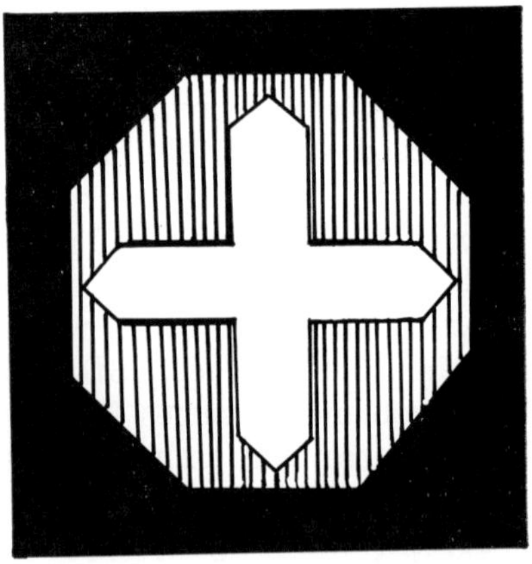

Fig. 11. Stencil number 3.

than the same number of Korsakoff patients, as shown in Table 22. At the lowest level of complexity, represented by the first three cards, there was no difference in proficiency or speed of performance. Extending Arthur's age norms beyond 15, by adding a year for each successful solution, the patients' mean mental age appeared to be 7.9, significantly lower than the control group's 12.1.

**Table 22**

STENCIL DESIGN TEST: MEAN GROUP SCORES AND SIGNIFICANCE OF DIFFERENCES

| | *Korsakoff (N = 21)* | | *Control (N = 21)* | | | |
|---|---|---|---|---|---|---|
| | *Mean* | *SD* | *Mean* | *SD* | *t-Ratio* | *z* |
| Correct solution | 6.3 | 3.3 | 11.7 | 3.3 | 5.29 | — |
| Level reached | 8.0 | 3.9 | 13.5 | 2.9 | 5.04 | — |
| Mean time of successful trials (in seconds) | 65.1 | 38.4 | 54.8 | 72.3 | — | 3.50[a] |
| Total time of first three trials (in seconds) | 83.6 | 70.2 | 77.4 | 61.0 | .30 | — |

[a] $p < .001$

Arthur proposed the stencils as an alternative to the block designs, and the two tests indeed share some important features. Both types of design are built up stepwise, but this is done most efficiently when the whole pattern is conceived in advance. There are also differences, most notably in that the block designs do not and the stencils do demand that the subject reverse his immediate line of attack. All the stencils have the same perimeter, but perforations of varying sizes and patterns. Designs are built up by laying a foundation with the solid card that corresponds to the color of the central area. Since, however, this area is relatively small, subjects are inclined to begin with the color of the surrounding field. Most Korsakoff patients consistently tried to place the solid card of that color on top, and thus covered up the stencils selected. They could not learn this cardinal principle of the test, even after its explication and demonstration.

Four years later 14 patients were retested by this method, but with relaxed rules that imposed no time limit and allowed for five consecutive errors. Their performance level rose to 9.5, and this improvement was not entirely attributable to the changed instructions. There was evident a greater willingness to experiment by crass trial and error tactics, and this accounted for quite a few successful solutions.

## Resumption of Unsolved Problem

Faced with problems testing intelligence, as with experimental tasks, the Korsakoff patients visibly tried to perform to the limits of their abilities. The incentive operating while they were engaged in a performance, however, did not outlast its conclusion. Ovsiankina (1928) has demonstrated the strong tendency of unsuccessful problem solvers to resume their incomplete tasks. An experiment investigating this tendency was conducted with 20 Korsakoff patients and a control (A) group of 18.

The task was the assembly of a jigsaw puzzle, a letter T, from four pieces of plywood. First the subject was shown the model assembled and asked to identify it. This they all managed to do. Then he was told that the pattern would be broken up, and he was allowed 4 minutes to piece it together again. If he arrived at an incorrect solution the experimenter told him so and encouraged him to try again. All subjects but one control failed to reach the correct solution in the time available, as indeed they were meant to with this difficult though not unsolvable puzzle.

This was the point at which the experiment proper began. The four pieces of the T were set aside but left on the table in front of the subject, who was given three successive brief experimental tasks, none that involved problem solving. Each task lasted 2 to 3 minutes and was separated from the last by a gap of 2 minutes. At the end of every task the experimenter said that he had to examine his records, and while he was busy the subject could rest or do as he wished. The experimenter then ostensibly immersed himself in his papers but could in fact watch any activity on the subject's table and record attempts to resume the interrupted puzzle. None of the subjects who failed in the first trial period solved the problem subsequently, but every member of the control group made at least one attempt, 11 reverting to it on all three available occasions. Only a single Korsakoff patient resumed the problem in one of the breaks, the others did not try even once. The experiment sorted Korsakoff patients and control subjects into two clearly distinct groups. In these impassive patients the urge to achieve a goal—at least of the type set in this experiment—fades even more rapidly and completely than do memories.

## Judgment

*Assessment of Tracking Skill.* In contrast to the poor judgment patients in the early stage of the Wernicke-Korsakoff syndrome express about their current capacities and past achievements, our chronic amnesic patients usually assessed quite accurately their limitations and powers. Their retrospective evaluation of test achievement, however, tended to be less reliable. The tracking task, described on page 125, afforded an opportunity to measure accuracy in assessing actual and potential achievement in a test of skill. The task was to hit with a stylus as many holes in a revolving belt as possible. Three pilot trials preceded the 12 test trials, and after each the subject was asked to estimate his previous score, i.e., the number of holes hit. Before starting on the next trial he had to predict his forthcoming score. By counting, he could keep an accurate record of his performance, and in the last six trials the experimenter gave him that information following the subject's own estimate. From the two estimates and actual performance three differential scores were obtained: (a) attainment discrepancy: the difference between the predicted and actual score; (b) judgment discrepancy: the difference between the estimated and actual value of a trial score; (c) goal discrepancy: the difference between the predicted score on the next trial and subjective judgment of the last score. For the last six trials a fourth differential score was also calculated; (d) objective goal discrepancy: the difference between the predicted score and the last score as reported by the experimenter. It was assumed that after a rise in performance the conventional move would be to predict a further rise or the same score, and the reverse after a drop in performance. Ignoring fluctuations with plus and minus one, an index of conventional moves was calculated for each subject. Means of these measures and of the discrepancies, without regard to direction, are given in Table 23 for 20 Korsakoff patients and a control group (A) of 14.

**Table 23**

MEAN ERRORS IN JUDGMENT AND PREDICTION OF TRACKING PERFORMANCE

| | *Korsakoff (N = 20)* | | | | *Control (N = 14)* | | | |
|---|---|---|---|---|---|---|---|---|
| | *Trials* | | | | *Trials* | | | |
| | *1–6* | *7–12* | *1–12* | | *1–6* | *7–12* | *1–12* | |
| | *Mean* | *Mean* | *Mean* | *SD* | *Mean* | *Mean* | *Mean* | *SD* |
| Attainment discrepancy | 58.5 | 34.4 | 92.9 | 108.4 | 39.0 | 27.9 | 67.0 | 24.6 |
| Judgment discrepancy | 51.6 | 16.6 | 68.2 | 94.2 | 22.9 | 10.4 | 33.4 | 30.1 |
| Subjective goal discrepancy | 21.2 | 19.1 | 40.3 | 15.6 | 17.3 | 20.3 | 37.6 | 9.8 |
| Objective goal discrepancy | — | 19.9 | — | 10.0 | — | 28.4 | — | 7.7 |
| Conventional prediction | 3.1 | 3.5 | 6.6 | 3.2 | 4.2 | 3.6 | 7.8 | 2.6 |

The numerous statistical tests calculated on these results will be only briefly summarized, since they showed no significant difference between the two groups, whether the scores were treated arithmetically or algebraically. Inter-subject variability was larger on all discrepancies in both groups than within-subject variability, i.e., individual subjects tended to make either large or small errors with some degree of consistency. Group means did not significantly differ on any of the three discrepancy scores based on 12 trials, but the Korsakoff patients' objective goal discrepancy was significantly ($t=2.58$; $p<.02$) lower than that of the control group. Attainment and judgment discrepancies decreased significantly ($p<.05$) in both groups from the first six to the second six test trials; there was no consistent trend in goal discrepancies. The two groups did not show significantly different changes on any of the three discrepancies between the two halves of the experiment. Members of both groups predicted their next score closer to what they thought to have reached than to the value reported by the experimenter. In both groups about half the predictions were conventional throughout the experiment; approximately two-thirds of the Korsakoff patients' and three-quarters of the control subjects' unconventional predictions aimed higher than the preceding score warranted.

Judging from the evidence of this experiment the Korsakoff patients showed no sign of detriment in assessing their own performance or capacities. Several of them began with very large discrepancies on all three counts, and substantially reduced the margin half way through the experiment. Since neither the pilot runs, nor the first six test trials had an effect on errors in estimate, it is reasonable to attribute this change to the information they received after each of the last trials. These patients evidently performed the task without paying much attention to their scores and improved their predictions without any marked change in motor skill. Some others gained nothing from learning their true score; these subjects—about a quarter of either group—seemed to keep a fairly accurate record of their hits while tracking, for they misjudged their tally at most by one or two through all twelve trials. Although, in order to accomplish this, they had to perform two operations more or less concurrently—to track and to count—this did not seem to hamper their manual dexterity, for they were about evenly divided among high, middle, and low scores. There is, of course, no way of telling whether their tracking performance might have been more efficient if they had not been set to achieve and note a numerical score.

*Risk-Taking Strategy.* This was investigated with two games based on the model of pinball machines; one did, the other did not allow for the application of manual dexterity.

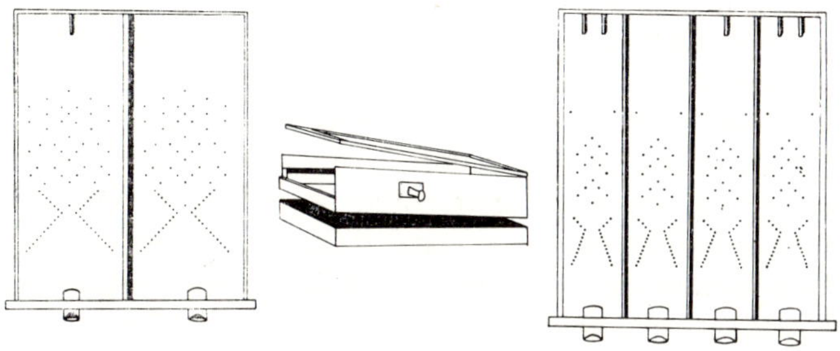

A. B.

Fig. 12. Pinball Game.

The apparatus (Fig. 12 C) consisted of a box 16 x 20 inches and 5 inches deep, supported on a tray by four compression springs, covered by a window, and with two handles mounted in the middle of the longer walls. Balanced by these, the box could be tilted at any angle up to a point at which its edge hit the tray; alternately it could be secured with hooks in a forward slant. Different bases were used for the two games, with appropriate gullies opening through the front panel, into which the subject fed half-inch steel balls. The base in game A was divided lengthwise into two equal halves, each studded with 76 pins in a symmetrical pattern so as to deflect the ball in its course. The goal strip of the right field was painted red, that of the left was divided by a ridge into equal halves of blue and green. The base of game B consisted of four channels 3.5 inches wide, each with its own gully and the same pattern of 42 pins. The goals of the two outer channels were divided into three equal strips, one in the middle was divided into two halves, the other was undivided. Number 3 was painted in the central goal strip of one, and in the inner goal strip of the other outer channel, number 2 in one side of the halved goal strip, number 1 in the undivided goal; all the other goal strips were marked with zero.

Game A was played with the box at a fixed slant, and consisted of 36 trials in which the subject's task was to accumulate the highest possible score. Each trial added to his score no less than one and no more than five points, and for each the subject was given a steel ball and a card. The cards showed three numbers, between 1 and 5, and no two the same—blue on the left, green in the middle, red on the right. The numbers indicated the score that could be made on that trial by hitting the blue, green, or red goal strip. If the red number was either the highest or the lowest of the three—each occurred on 8 cards—the rational choice was to prefer or alternately to avoid the right gully; chance would decide between the blue and green numbers when the ball was fed into the left gully. On 8 cards, the mean value of the two left numbers was the same as the red number; over many trials, therefore, the payoff would be the same for either gully. The left side was clearly preferable on the six trials which offered a red number midway between the other two but lower than their arithmetic mean. The remaining 6 cards also showed a red number in the middle position but its value was higher than the mean of the other two; conservative tactics would therefore favor its choice but the gambler might be attracted by the chance prospect of hitting the highest target. The cards were presented in a standard sequence within which the various payoff ratios were randomly distributed. Mean choices of the left field (blue/green) by 15 Korsakoff patients and 14 control (7 A, 7 P) subjects under the different payoff conditions are shown in Table 24.

**Table 24**

MEAN CHOICE BETWEEN BLUE/GREEN AND RED CHANNELS IN RISK-TAKING GAME A

| | *Korsakoff (N = 15)* | | *Control (N = 14)* | |
|---|---|---|---|---|
| | *Mean* | *SD* | *Mean* | *SD* |
| Irrational choice | 2.33 | 3.02 | 1.07 | 2.27 |
| Blue/green when mean value = red | 6.80 | 1.47 | 6.57 | 2.04 |
| Blue/green when mean value > red | 5.33 | .73 | 5.57 | .94 |
| Blue/green when mean value < red | 4.87 | 1.55 | 4.71 | 2.12 |

Although the Korsakoff patients made more irrational choices, these were not significantly higher than in the control group, and occurred on but 6.5 percent of the possible occasions. Eight patients made no irrational choice, but 3 patients made as many as 7 or 8, and 1 clearly followed a preference for red or right. Neither did the two groups differ significantly in their decisions when the odds were even on both sides of the game, or when the mean value of blue and green was below or above the red number. The choices were re-analyzed separately with a view to the effect of previous success in a "gamble," and again showed no significant differences between the decisions reached by the two groups. With so many agreements in their behavior, the mean scores of the two groups were also much the same: within the narrow scope allowed her, Fortune smiled or frowned alike on both.

Game B set the subject the same task of accumulating the highest score but allowed some application of manual skill, in that he could balance the box by the two handles. Each of the sixty trials presented him with the same decision: whether to play for a safe score of 1, to take the even chance of 2, or risk a one-in-three possibility of 3 and, if the latter, which channel to try. Neither group showed any strong tendency to play safe; the Korsakoff patients chose the single goal in 62, the control group in 61 instances, the bulk of the latter being contributed by a single subject. They did differ in their total choices between double and triple goals, with

203 to 635 in the Korsakoff against 338 to 501 in the control group. This difference could be attributed to the preferences shown by a few subjects, since it did not prove to be significant after calculating a risk-taking score for each individual, by adding up 3's for each choice of a triple goal, 2's for double goals, and 1's for the single channel. Mean scores thus obtained as well as other relevant group means are set out in Table 25. The division between the two triple goal channels was very even in both groups, with 1 or 2 subjects preferring either, and most of them trying both the same number of times. Alteration marks the number of occasions in which a subject changed the target in two consecutive trials; alteration after failure indicates the proportion of such instances following a zero hit.

**Table 25**

MEAN CHOICES AND SCORES IN RISK-TAKING GAME B

| | *Korsakoff (N = 15)* | | *Control (N = 15)* | |
|---|---|---|---|---|
| | *Mean* | *SD* | *Mean* | *SD* |
| Choice of single goal channel | 4.1 | 4.5 | 4.1 | 5.7 |
| Choice of double goal channel | 13.6 | 17.0 | 23.2 | 20.6 |
| Choice of triple goal channel | 42.3 | 14.5 | 32.7 | 17.4 |
| Risk score | 158.1 | 13.6 | 148.6 | 16.1 |
| Percent success: on double goal channel | 37.7 | 18.8 | 44.8 | 20.3 |
| Percent success on triple goal channels | 33.1 | 10.1 | 32.2 | 14.4 |
| Alteration of channel | 30.1 | 16.3 | 18.5 | 17.6 |
| Alteration after failure (ratio score) | 60.7 | 19.8 | 58.6 | 24.1 |

On none of the scores examined did the two groups differ significantly. Readiness to take risks and to switch from one target to another was somewhat higher in the Korsakoff patients, but not sufficiently so to indicate a more reckless gambling spirit or less task involvement. Taken as a test of skill, the game proved the two groups to possess about equal manual dexterity.

## Concept Formation

Most problems in concept formation involve the effective use of stored information, i.e., memory function, and would therefore be expected to show deficit in Korsakoff patients. Some problems in categorization, however, depend very little on memory, or the retention component can be controlled.

*Categorization.* It would follow from our observations of the Korsakoff patients' propensity to wide perceptual generalization that their conceptual classes also tend to be more than normally comprehensive, in disregard of finer distinctive cues. The hypothesis that this is so, and the extent to which this effect stems from a perceptual impairment, were tested by means of the designs of Figure 13. The figure on top served as standard of comparison, and was first shown as an instance of PAM—a meaningless word that, for the purpose of the experiment, denoted the properties of the design. The remaining designs were then displayed singly, on white cards, with the instruction that the subject say the word each time he saw a PAM.

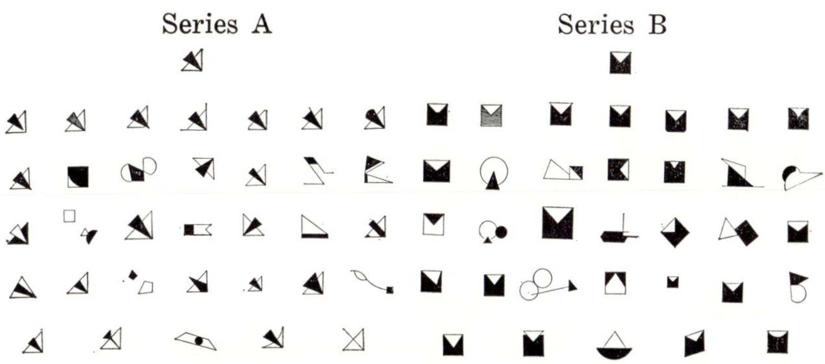


Fig. 13. Figures used for categorization.

The instruction was given in words suitable and in sufficient detail to be comprehended by the subject. If he then asked for a closer definition of PAM, i.e., whether size, color, or certain details of the design mattered, he was advised that this was for him to decide. After thorough inspection of the standard, he was shown the test series, in the order of the illustration, except that the standard appeared in positions 2, 6, 7, 11, 13, 22, and 30. Alternate subjects were shown series A or B, and their responses had to be "PAM" or "not PAM"; intermediate or qualifying definitions were not allowed. Although exposure time was unlimited, almost all responses were given instantaneously and rarely required as much as 1 minute. All through this test the standard was displayed in front of the subject.

Second, the same procedure was followed with the alternate series of cards, except that a different nonsense syllable, BIX, was attached to the standard, and that this card was concealed from the subject after initial inspection. A third and fourth test repeated these procedures with the difference that the instruction was to identify those figures that were exactly the same as the standard. Absolute identity was rigorously

**Table 26**

MEAN RECOGNITION AND GENERALIZATION OF STANDARD FIGURE

| | *Recognition* | | | | | | | |
|---|---|---|---|---|---|---|---|---|
| *Instruction:* | *BIX/PAM* | | | | *Same* | | | |
| | *Standard shown* | | *Standard hidden* | | *Standard shown* | | *Standard hidden* | |
| | *Mean* | *SD* | *Mean* | *SD* | *Mean* | *SD* | *Mean* | *SD* |
| Korsakoff ($N$=20) | 7.00 | 0 | 6.20 | 1.25 | 6.70 | .66 | 5.65 | 1.38 |
| Control (16A, 8H) | 6.83 | .90 | 6.83 | .87 | 6.67 | .70 | 6.54 | 1.01 |
| $t$-Ratio | .81 | | 1.90 | | .17 | | 2.40 | |
| $z$ | — | | — | | — | | — | |

| | *Generalization* | | | | | | | |
|---|---|---|---|---|---|---|---|---|
| *Instruction:* | *BIX/PAM* | | | | *Same* | | | |
| | *Standard shown* | | *Standard hidden* | | *Standard shown* | | *Standard hidden* | |
| | *Mean* | *SD* | *Mean* | *SD* | *Mean* | *SD* | *Mean* | *SD* |
| Korsakoff ($N$=20) | 15.40 | 6.75 | 16.00 | 8.55 | 2.10 | 2.00 | 2.65 | 2.65 |
| Control (16A, 8H) | 2.37 | 3.05 | 2.29 | 3.14 | 1.72 | 2.24 | 2.25 | 2.25 |
| $t$-Ratio | — | | — | | .59 | | .54 | |
| $z$ | 5.29[a] | | 5.15[a] | | — | | — | |

[a] $p < .01$

defined, with specific mention of size, shape, shading, position, and any other detail.

Performance was scored for: (a) correct identification, and (b) for width of categorization, i.e., instances of identifying with the standard a figure that is not the same in every respect. Differences between the two series of cards were statistically not significant. Mean scores under the two instructions (defining the class of BIX/PAM and testing perception of identity) are set out in Table 26. Korsakoff and control groups did not differ significantly in correct recognition of the standard, whether this was in view or not, whether the task was categorization or perception of identity. They did differ significantly in width of categorization, alike with the standard in view and hidden, but identified the standard in that process with equal accuracy.

These findings suggest that bluntness of perceptual discrimination made a negligible contribution to width of categorization by Korsakoff patients, defective memory made none whatever in this experiment. Nevertheless, their categories were wider and more loosely defined, and were so because the patients ignored certain defining attributes in categorization, even though capable of observing them under conditions of perceptual discrimination. Apparently, an attitude of reasonable accuracy in perceptual discrimination can be elicited from Korsakoff patients but, in the absence of appropriate instructions, they tend toward greater laxity which is also manifested in concept formation.

This tendency is even more pronounced when the material submitted for categorization does not offer simple and obvious cues for classification, as in a sorting task with 36 diverse objects that could be divided on several criteria into a smaller or larger number of classes. The instruction was to sort these objects into piles, no matter how many, so that all those that "belonged together" would be in one pile, those that were different in other piles. Qualitative as well as quantified assessment showed the inferiority of the 20 Korsakoff patients' performance to the control group's (16A, 8H), for 11 of the former proceeded without any explicit or recognizable principle of classification. When, on completion of first sorting, the subjects were asked to rearrange the objects in a different way, but still so that those belonging together would be in the same pile, only 6 Korsakoff patients could think of a new principle of sorting, in contrast with all but 2 of the control group. The same observation was confirmed by Weigl's color-form block test (Talland, 1959b).

*Halstead's Category Test.* This test of abstraction and generalization showed no marked deficit in Korsakoff patients at the level of difficulty represented by the first two series. Their task was to abstract a differentiating attribute from each successive display of four figures. At the level of complexity represented by series 3 to 7, the 20 Korsakoff patients failed in half to three-quarters of the trials, i.e., did little or no better than by random guessing. Over the entire test all scored far above 50 errors, Halstead's norm for brain damage; the group mean was 105 (SD 18.3).

*Negative Instances.* For a verbal task 12 rows of printed words were used, each containing four that represented the same class and one that differed. This principle was explained to the subject, with the instruction to underline the odd word, and was demonstrated in two practice trials. A row consisted of all nouns, all verbs, or all adjectives. In the first ten lines meaning provided the criterion of inclusion (e.g., cow hide horse pig goat); in the last two it was a formal attribute of the words, i.e., their rhyming (e.g., fly/sigh/try/sing/lie).

The Korsakoff and control (X) groups of 16 differed significantly in mean success (7.2, SD 1.97 versus 9.4, SD 1.41; $t=3.49$), in total time spent on the task (204 seconds, SD 55 versus 113 seconds, SD 37; $t=5.35$), or time per successful solution (31.3 versus 12.5 seconds; $T=161$, $p<.01$). Omission accounted for a single error in the Korsakoff, for three errors in the control group. The difference between the two groups, though narrower, remains significant after eliminating from analysis the three most difficult items. The "Einstellung effect," tested by switching the categorizing criterion in the last two items, appeared to be somewhat stronger in the Korsakoff group. This test did not require the acquisition or discovery of new concepts but the rediscovery and application of familiar ones; it did not hinge on a capacity to retain new information, but demanded that the subject hold a generic principle while he surveys specific instances and checks these against it.

*Discovery of Formal Concepts.* The problem in concept formation is first the identification of the one distinctive attribute which, in experiments, is often concealed; next it is to formulate and test alternate principles of categorization. When all instances, positive and negative, are simultaneously available for inspection, the burden placed on memory function is negligible. If, however, the instances appear singly in succession, reliance on information storage becomes considerable, varying in extent with the strategy adopted (Bruner, Goodnow, and Austin, 1956). The following experiments in concept formation employ this latter method of display, and could therefore properly be considered as tests of learning or short-term retention.

*(a) Blocks.* Concept formation by the discovery of a simple and unitary attribute in successive instances was tested with a set of 60 colored blocks, no two of which were identical in all four of their differentiating attributes (Talland, 1957). Half of their number were 1 inch high, the other 2 inches high, and they also differed in any one or more of the following characteristics: color (black, blue, green, red, white); shape (circle, square, triangle in cross section); size of base (three values each for the square and triangular, four for the circular blocks). The subject was told that he would be shown a number of blocks, one at a time, some of which were VEC, a name given to one group of blocks that had a certain feature in common and that distinguished them from the others. His task was to discover what was a VEC, what characteristic made a VEC, by naming each block a VEC or not-VEC, and the experimenter would tell him whether he was right or wrong.

The blocks were presented in a prearranged order in front of a screen, so that not more than one was visible to the subject at a time. He could select any of the four differentiating attributes as defining a VEC and, if his guess proved wrong, switch to another. According to the design, height was the defining attribute; all 2-inch tall blocks being VEC. The order of presentation provided for adequate opportunities to test the various hypotheses by forestalling runs of chance success; it allowed for at most four consecutive correct responses on the basis of any but the true criterion. After each response, the subject also had to state why he answered the way he had. The experiment concluded with a run of eight consecutive correct responses or with the 60th block, and the subject's definition of the concept.

None of the 21 Korsakoff patients succeeded in discovering the attribute that defined a VEC; 19 out of 20 control subjects did after a mean inspection of 8.9 blocks prior to the test series of 8. Not one of them hit on the correct criterion immediately; their modal shift of hypothesis preceding solution was two. Thirteen Korsakoff patients discovered the concept when four otherwise different blocks representing each of the two classes, i.e., 1- and 2-inch tall pieces, were shown them simultaneously, the one group as characteristic of VEC, the other of those that were not VEC. After this demonstration these subjects succeeded in responding correctly to other blocks shown them singly; another 4 subjects could do so only after the defining attribute was explained to them, and 4 failed after receiving this information.

All but 1 of the Korsakoff patients attempted solution by shape, and 7 also tried one or more other reasonable hypotheses, simple or composite, such as bulk or shape combined with color. Four thought of height but none stuck to this criterion, even though it was evidently confirmed; only 1 patient chose color, and none selected size. One subject experimented with 4 hypotheses, 4 patients with 3, and 1 patient proceeded without any recognizable criterion. Many of the hypotheses by shape were defined in somewhat roundabout terms, such as "uniform top and bottom"; "same on all sides." There was also a remarkable tendency to drag in entirely irrelevant utilitarian considerations, e.g., "this could be a doorstep; it is not a VEC"; "it does not look like a VEC, rather like a hat."

The task itself elicited some resentment on account of its pointlessness, or the meaninglessness of the term VEC. Nonetheless, the subjects seemed to grasp the instructions sufficiently well to proceed with the experiment, though some of their explanations were far from enlightening about their strategy of concept formation, e.g., "does not look like that which was a VEC"; "different from last one"; "odd looking."

*(b) Figures.* Four years later a similar task was given to 16 members of the Korsakoff group, with two differences in the test material. Instead of three-dimensional blocks, flat colored figures were used, each drawn and painted on a white card. Further, the experiment consisted of several phases, each differing in difficulty. Table 27 lists the seven decks of cards used in this experiment. The first trials were with $C_1$ and B; if the subject failed both he continued with $A_1$ and, after a further failure, with $A_2$. Success on $A_1$ led to $C_2$. A subject who solved either or both $C_1$ and B was then given D and E and, if successful on either, he finished with F. If he failed both D and E he was given $C_2$; success at that point concluded the experiment, failure was followed by the two A decks. The experimental design is diagrammatically shown in Fig. 14.

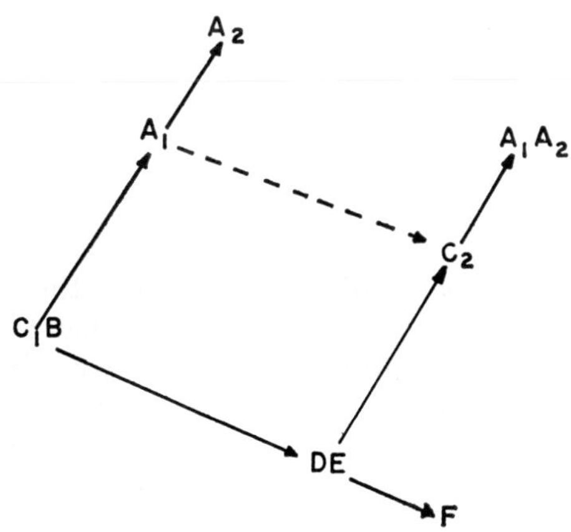


Fig. 14. Concept formation: experimental design.

**Table 27**

DECKS IN TEST OF CONCEPT ATTAINMENT
(CRITERION IN ITALICS)

| *Deck* | *Level of Complexity* | *Variable attributes* |
|---|---|---|
| $A_1$ | 2 x 2 | POSITION: *center*/side HATCHING: cross/parallel |
| $A_2$ | 2 x 2 | SHAPE: *circle*/square SURFACE: hatched/plain |
| B | 3 x 2 | BORDER: *present*/absent SIZE: large/small FIGURE WITHIN: parallel/crossed lines |
| $C_1$ | 2 x 3 | SHAPE: *triangle*/circle/square COLOR: green/red/yellow |
| $C_2$ | 2 x 3 | COLOR: *blue*/orange/purple SHAPE: circle/square/triangle |
| D | 4 x 2 | SIZE: *small*/large COLOR: blue/yellow SHAPE: circle/square FIGURE WITHIN: upright cross/diagonal cross |
| E | 3 x 3 | COLOR: *red*/blue/green SHAPE: circle/square/triangle POSITION: top/center/bottom |
| F | 4 x 3 | HATCHING: *cross*/diagonal/parallel COLOR OF BORDER: blue/green/red COLOR OF FIGURE: blue/green/red SHAPE: circle/square/triangle |

**Table 28**

LEVEL OF SUCCESSFUL CONCEPT ATTAINMENT

| | *Level of complexity* | | | | | | | | |
|---|---|---|---|---|---|---|---|---|---|
| | *F* | *DE* | *CE* | $C_1C_2$ | $C_1/C_2$ | $A_1A_2$ | $A_1/A_2$ | *Failed at all levels* | *Total* |
| Number of patients successful | 8 | 1 | 1 | 2 | 2 | 0 | 1 | 1 | 16 |

Table 28 shows that 8 Korsakoff patients passed all levels of difficulty, and only 1 failed to solve even the simplest problem. No adequate control data are available for comparison but the results are significant in their contrast with those of the earlier experiment. In sheer load of information processing and storage, deck F hardly differed from the set of blocks, yet 8 Korsakoff patients who had failed with those discovered the concept embedded in the two-dimensional designs. Three different explanations come to mind to account for this discrepancy. Over the years and having served as subjects in so many psychological experiments, our patients had acquired some problem solving skill, in fact had learned a new skill. They also learned in the course of the single experiment. The blocks presented a relatively complex problem in concept formation without prior practice with easier tasks; the cards, by progressively increasing the level of difficulty, allowed the subject to acquaint himself with the operative cues and also to gain confidence in his ability to cope with the problem, so that the more complex test did not overwhelm him. Although attractive, this explanation is weakened by the results of Halstead's category test. Finally, the task set may have been more effective in this instance, in that the two-dimensional patterns suggested no such irrelevant considerations as the colored blocks.

*Sequential concept formation* tests memory function both in the process of discovery, and subsequently in retention. Maze learning is the most familiar experimental method to probe this capacity, but the pattern need not be in spatial dimensions. One device employed in this research built a sequential pattern into a deck of playing cards. Two decks, without the aces, were stacked to give 16 runs of B-B-R-B-R-R, B meaning black for spades and clubs, R red for hearts and diamonds. All our subjects were familiar with playing cards, and understood their task, i.e., to discover the order in which black and red cards were piled. They were assured that a fairly simple and regular pattern of ordering could be found in the deck, and their instruction was to discover this by predicting whether the next card the experimenter would turn face up was black or red. The subject proceeded at his own chosen pace over 16 sequences of the pattern, unless he predicted at least three consecutive sequences, i.e., 18 cards, correctly. Failing this, the experimenter told him what the pattern was, demonstrated it with four sequences, made the subject repeat it several times, and then resumed the procedure. If the subject now could predict three sequences without error, he was interrupted half-way through a sequence with some such comment as "you see, you can do this all right," and then the task was resumed; further successful performance was interrupted once more. In case of failure the subject was tested on the 16 sequences, and then shown the sequential pattern again. On third trial a model of the pattern (a single sequence if sufficient, or else one showing three sequences) was left in front of the subject; otherwise the procedure was the same as on second trial. Finally, the subject was asked to reconstruct the pattern from randomly assorted cards.

Of the 20 Korsakoff patients 2 solved the problem, 1 patient after two, the other after five sequences. Both were men; another 2 men were successful when shown the pattern, but only one maintained his performance after interruption. On the third trial every patient could follow the pattern displayed in front of him, 4 managed to resume it after interruption, and only one—the same man who did not quite make the second trial—continued to perform accurately after removal of the model. Some of the others continued successfully after losing sight of the model through as many as six sequences, but then the concept escaped them and they could not recover it. In several instances a model of a single sequence proved of little help, but one of three sequences did enable the subject to make a good start, though not in resuming after interruption. Successful resumption was almost always delayed by a few errors. In reconstructing the pattern only those 3 subjects proved successful who had either discovered it for themselves or had applied it after interruption in the second trial. Of 20 control (14A, 6H) subjects 10 discovered and correctly applied the pattern in the first, 9 applied it correctly in the second trial after interruption; one had to be given a third trial, in which he performed well after interruption.

All but 1 of the Korsakoff patients began by formulating hypotheses in an attempt to discover the pattern, but as they went along several of them turned it into a game of chance. They either volunteered or were asked to assess their performance after the first trial and tended grossly to misjudge it, whether their guesses were mostly incorrect or right. Their principal difficulty was in conceptualizing a combination of single and double alternation; many errors arose from a continuous double alternation (B-B-R-R-B-B-R-R) or two-one sequence (B-B-R-B-B-R). Correct verbal recall of the model was itself no more effective in assuring successful performance than its display; several Korsakoff patients remembered it well into the second trial, yet were unable to make the requisite number of correct predictions on single cards. Some of them gratuitously remarked in the first trial that there were never more than two of a color in a run, but would still call "black" immediately following two black cards. It is interesting that, in addition to their impairment in forming sequential concepts, amnesic patients appear to encounter still further difficulties in applying such concepts, even though they had previously grasped and memorized them.

When the experiment was repeated 4 years later with 14 of the old and 2 new patients, the same 2 men again discovered the concept in the first trial series. Following its demonstration, 8 more Korsakoff patients attained the concept, after a mean of 4.5 runs. For the remaining 6 subjects a different procedure was then introduced. The sequence of six was divided into its component halves, and an attempt was made to teach them these sequences of three, first separately, and subsequently in combination. This experiment failed in every instance, and again 1 patient mistook the test for a game of chance.

An easier test in sequential concept formation also demonstrated the ineptness of amnesic patients with that type of problem. White cards with one of five geometric figures drawn in black ink were used: small (1-inch) circle, two small circles, triangle, square, large (2-inch) circle. Procedure and task were the same as in the other experiment, this time to predict the large circle. Three consecutive correct predictions, without intervening false positive responses, constituted success. The decks were sorted on the following principles: (A) varying number of cards with small circle, double circle, one small circle, large circle; (B) varying number of blank cards, small circle, two blank cards, large circle; (C) varying number of blank cards, among which one square and one triangle was placed each time in a different position—the large circle immediately followed the second of these figures. Of the 21 Korsakoff patients tested, 18 solved and managed to apply concept A, 10 succeeded with B, 7 with C. Ability to predict accurately, when apprised of the pattern, also diminished from A to C. Several patients guessed the principle correctly, verbalized it, but failed to follow it. A control (X) group of 21 registered not a single failure in discovering and applying concepts A and B; 4 had to be told the principle of C, and then proceeded without error.

A very easy test of sequential concept formulation used playing cards sorted into sequences of diamond-spade-club-heart. Before each card was turned face up, the subject had to name its suit. All but 3 of the 20 Korsakoff patients discovered the pattern, after a mean of 8.41 sequences (SD 2.00), but 6 wavered in its continued application. All 20 control subjects (16A, 4H) arrived at the principle, with a mean of 3.0 sequences, and proceeded with faultless predictions.

## Summary

Intelligence tests measure in varying degrees different special abilities, the compound of innate endowment and its development or decline. In most Korsakoff patients the development had taken its normal course over a wide spectrum of aptitudes, but degradation occurred at different rates in the various special areas. Information acquired early in life, the ability to draw inferences and to apply even some recent information in forming judgments and making predictions are generally well retained in the amnesic syndrome. There is no evidence of a derangement in formal reasoning. In certain special areas, however, intellectual performance is severely impaired by an inability to assimilate and apply unfamiliar data, or to perform operations that involve the formation and simultaneous testing of alternative plans. This latter defect implies a difficulty in perceptual reorientation and accounts for the Korsakoff patients' poor performance in tests of spatial designs.

Their assessment of objective probabilities in simple situations was realistic, their evaluation of possibilities dependent on their own skill could be sound or wildly misjudged. The latter happened chiefly because the patients neglected to gather the available information. This explanation is pertinent to other anomalies in reasoning that occur with amnesic patients. Their capacity in problem solving is very closely related to the novelty and load of information—particularly in discrete items held concurrently—that is necessary for successful performance. In classifying objects, amnesic patients established wider categories than control subjects, with boundaries looser than could be attributed entirely to their perceptual defects. They also showed deficiencies in the discovery of distinctive attributes, and consequently of appropriate criteria for classification. This latter shortcoming may, in part at least, account for their looser rules of categorization. Their impaired memory function certainly hampered their concept attainment, particularly when the examples drawn from a class were presented serially, but reluctance to adopt alternative criteria also contributed to their ineffective performance. These patients were predisposed toward certain definite principles of classification, e.g., shape or utility, and if those proved inappropriate they were less inclined to test another criterion than the control subjects.

The greatest defect in the Korsakoff patients' concept attainment was directly related to their amnesic derangement, namely, their virtual inability to form concepts in the temporal dimension. The few successes recorded in the relatively more difficult sequential concept tests remain among the many paradoxical observations of the amnesic syndrome, and can best be explained by crediting them to the transfer of long-established skills, though the evidence to support this interpretation is lacking. The easier tests in sequential concept formation seemed to be within the range of several Korsakoff patients' immediate memory span, and the task itself was evidently not too difficult to master.

Certain defects our Korsakoff patients showed, alike in tests of perception and of higher mental functions, fit Goldstein's (1942) theory that brain damage, without regard to its site, forces the patient to function at a level of reduced complexity, in a concrete rather than abstract or symbolic fashion. Over and above the signs of passivity, Goldstein and Scheerer (1941) proposed a multiple criterion for determining an impairment of the abstract attitude. Among these a relative inability to change mental sets, to keep in mind various aspects of a task simultaneously, and voluntarily to evoke previous experiences, are defects highly characteristic of the amnesic syndrome. Some of our patients' responses to the colored blocks furnish quite direct evidence for a concrete attitude.

A global construct with a unidimensional scale from the abstract to the concrete pole, however, is not fully consistent with our findings. The Korsakoff patients' tendency to adopt a concrete attitude was but the most common example of their more general orientational inflexibility. Indeed, they regularly failed to switch from a concrete to the abstract aspects of an object or situation, but this impairment did not preclude their original adoption of an abstract principle. Both the Weigl-Goldstein-Scheerer test and Halstead's categorization task showed that these patients were quite capable of abstracting common attributes from concrete examples. In the former, several of them failed in shifting spontaneously from one abstraction to another, but not in arriving at the first abstraction; in the latter they were defeated only by the complexity of the criterion for abstraction. They could certainly list instances of a class concept, such as names of animals, and were able to recategorize objects—at least under instruction—in a manner contrary to their customary classification, e.g., when they sorted playing cards into red and black instead of the four suits.

Goldstein's concrete attitude and Bürger-Prinz and Kaila's proposition that Korsakoff patients cannot adopt a perceptual set to the whole figure, are alike instances of a more generic derangement. These patients have great difficulty in changing their set, whatever that be directed to, and since first it is more likely to be toward a detail, to a concrete attribute, they are unlikely so to reorient themselves as to take in other aspects of the object or situation, concrete or abstract.

Sequential concept formation pointed to still another source of the amnesic patients' defective functioning. In a number of instances, even though a patient might grasp such a concept (whether he had discovered it himself or been told what it was), he could not apply it consistently. This failure was clearly not due simply to forgetting after comprehension, because often he was still able to verbalize the concept long after he had ceased to apply it effectively, or could put it in words but never succeed in applying it. Application, of course, requires attention to the material presented as well as knowledge of the principle it illustrates, checking one against the other, the fragmentary sensory input against the image of the whole.

Some defects in concept formation are manifestly not derived from but are superimposed on the perceptual impairment of amnesic patients. There are also obvious parallels between the two areas of dysfunction that in turn suggest more basic constructs common to perceptual and conceptual processes. Loose conceptual categorization has a parallel in wider perceptual generalization, rigid adherence to preconceived criteria in dependence on the sensory input, inability to form sequential concepts in failure to integrate successive percepts. Set rigidity, an incapacity to alter one's approach in the face of evidence that shows it to be inappropriate, was a characteristic common to the Korsakoff patients' perceptual and conceptual functioning. In both perceptual and conceptual tasks their failure suggested an inability to check performance against images or models, a process that itself may involve rapid shifts in mental set. Some defects in perception and concept formation could not be attributed to the patients' memory impairment, but deficiencies in processes common to both might help to account for the latter, since experiences insufficiently ordered and integrated are not reliably available for recall.

*Chapter 8*

# LEARNING AND REMEMBERING

In the context of our clinical observations, various examples were listed both of the Korsakoff patients' capacities to learn and remember, and of their extensive areas of forgetting. They included instances of retrograde amnesia as well as of the recall of memories from the pre-morbid years, numerous illustrations of an apparent inability to acquire or retain new information, and a few exceptions to this rule. Some of the preceding experiments also touched on the patients' memory and learning capacities—on certain borders of perception, and more directly in several tests of intelligence and concept formation. The latter set the subjects relatively complex tasks; the experiments discussed in the present chapter and the next tested new learning at lower levels of difficulty. They formed part of a project designed in accordance with the express assumptions that the amnesic syndrome does not involve a complete loss of learning and retention, but rather that it exemplifies a severe disturbance of these functions, and that the investigator's task is to determine, not the presence or absence of a capacity, but the extent to which it is available and the conditions that are more or less conducive to its exercise.

## Recall of Instructions

Most experimental studies depend on the subject's ability to follow instructions. Our amnesic patients proved remarkably efficient in following instructions and in pursuing their tasks. Interruption of their activity, however, was liable to abolish their work-set; even after a short break they rarely managed to resume where they had left off, whether deflected from their pursuit by some other activity, or just by a question or comment. That a mere break interferes with the Korsakoff patients' memory much less than one which also changes their work-set, was demonstrated by a simple counting task.

*Counting.* Ability to follow a directive to terminate and resume a continuous performance was tested by asking the subject to count slowly from 1 to 22, to stop and later when told, to continue on to 37 from where he had left off. If he completed the first assignment, the instruction for the second part was repeated, and a break of 3 minutes followed. On one occasion this time was occupied by drawing a simple picture, on another by rest. On the first trial all but 1 of 16 Korsakoff patients counted accurately up to 22 and then stopped; on the second occasion 2 members of the same group passed that mark. Following the rest period, 10 of the 14 patients completed the task correctly, and 2 made errors of one place only. After the interpolated activity only 4 of the 15 followed the instruction; this represented a success ratio of little over one-quarter in contrast with two-thirds when the task-set remained unbroken. Furthermore, after the interpolated activity 3 patients could not remember at all what to do. All 16 control (A) subjects performed the first half of the test correctly on both occasions; 14 completed it accurately after a rest break, 11 after drawing, but the remaining 5 all remembered to resume counting and made only small errors at one or the other end of the number series.

*Vigilance.* The limits of the amnesic patients' capacity to follow instructions was probed by four vigilance tests, in which signals for appropriate responses were presented intermittently at relatively long intervals, either amidst other signals or in isolation. Sixteen Korsakoff patients were tested by all four procedures in balanced order. Seated in a soundproof chamber, they received signals by means of a bell, buzzer, or the speaker of a tape recorder, and responded either by pressing a telegraph key or by talking into a microphone. Their responses were recorded outside the chamber.

Each program lasted 30 minutes and included nine response signals placed in the same positions, at intervals varying between 45 seconds and 5 minutes. Test A used a nonsense word for signal to which the proper response was made with the telegraph key. Test B presented the subject with a recorded periodic auditory input: a list randomly compiled from the days of the week, one word every 15 seconds. The signal, "Sunday," occurred at the same nine intervals as the nonsense word on tape A, and response to it only was to say aloud "church." Test C followed the program of A, except that the bell served as signal and that cumulative responses were required; tapping on the key once after the first, twice after the second signal, and so forth up to nine. Test D required the same cumulative response to the bell, but the intervals were occupied by a buzzer sounding briefly every 15 seconds.

All but one of the 16 Korsakoff patients gave the correct response to every signal in test A, and all but 3 in B; in these two tests 99 and 86% of the group's responses were correct. In test B 2 patients twice answered with "church" to neutral signals; one responded to Sunday with the wrong word 5 times, another once. Only 3 members of the group passed test C, and one patient D without error; the percentages of correct responses, however, amounted to 71 and 53. Most of the errors occurred in the second half of the tests, when the subjects could no longer keep count of their previous responses. Failures to respond totaled 12 in test C, and 16 in D, one subject contributing 10 to the first, 7 to the other total.

The experiment illustrates a considerable resistance not only to forgetting the instruction but also to interference of two kinds. The interference effect of neutral signals was quite negligible, and even the taxing demand to keep count of repeated occurrences barely affected the ability of our Korsakoff patients to follow their instructions. This was evident from the fact that the majority of their errors were multiple taps on the telegraph key, i.e., attempts to respond in the prescribed manner. Of course, with an increasing load of information to store, most of these attempts were inaccurate, though not all. The relatively high proportion of complete and partial successes in these tests was unexpected and out of keeping with other observations made on Korsakoff patients. A likely explanation is that the experimental conditions, i.e., a soundproof room with nothing to distract attention from the apparatus employed for the test, helped to keep the patients oriented to their task which, in spite of its double assignment, depended on a unitary set.

*Recall of Previous Performance.* In contrast to their efficient retention of instructions, Korsakoff patients barely ever managed to recollect their previous experimental tasks. In one laboratory session of 12 short experiments, 16 Korsakoff patients were asked half-way through, and again at the end, to list as many as they could recall of the tasks they had been engaged on. Their mean listings were 2.4 and 2.9 as compared with 4.3 and 6.9 of 16 control (A)[1] subjects. At both stages the difference between the two groups was statistically significant ($t$=4.66; $T$=135,$p$<.01). The modal responses of the Korsakoff patients were 3 at first, 2 and 4 at the end; usually they included the last procedure and one or two others of which some visible reminder had remained in sight.

## Recognition

*Test Material.* Recognition of nonsense syllables was probed in two experiments (see p. 217) of learning and relearning after 5 minutes. On the second presentation of the list, the subjects were asked whether they had seen it before and, if their answer was affirmative, when they had seen it. Every member of a control group of 23 (15A, 8H) recognized the list on both occasions as identical with one seen a few minutes earlier. Only 2 of 20 Korsakoff patients identified it correctly on both occasions; 5 others did so without and 3 after an intervening task, the others thought they could recognize some of the words or that they had seen the same list a week or two earlier.

A remarkable example of instant forgetting occurred in the experiment with apparent movement. When faced with the picture of a car and road for the fourth time within some 3 minutes, one patient insisted that she had not seen it or its

---

[1]For identification of code letters A, H, X, and P used in conjunction with control groups see "Prefatory Note" at the beginning of Part Four.

like before; yet the only intervening events were the exposures of a straight line. Let it be noted, though, that on many other occasions she, as well as other patients, correctly recognized an instrument and described its use, even after intervals of several weeks.

*Objects.* A pencil sharpener and a stapler were shown to the subject, with the instruction to name and remember them. All 22 Korsakoff patients correctly named or described the two objects, and these were then mixed with eight other metal articles. After busying themselves with a different task for 5 minutes, all the patients correctly picked out the objects earlier shown them.

Another day, 16 Korsakoff patients were shown four objects placed wide apart in the room, and asked first to name them, and then to remember them in the same order. They all correctly named the four objects and recalled them after a minute, but 6 failed to list them in the original sequence. After an hour's interval, 6 patients could still list the four items, two in the correct order, one of them having memorized this by means of a formula invented for the purpose.

*Pictures:*

*(a) Identification.* The covering pages of two issues of the *New Yorker* magazine were used as test material. One represented a lady rider as she is being helped off with her boots by a maid, sitting in the middle of a period-furnished bedroom. The other scene was that of children leaving Sunday School and running to the cars in which their fathers are waiting. On two different occasions 15 Korsakoff patients were shown these pictures with the instruction to observe them carefully so that they could remember them later. One day, alternating both pictures and sequence, the subject described the scene immediately after inspection. On the other he was immediately engaged in a different task to prevent verbalizing his impressions.

The purpose of the experiment was threefold: (a) to serve as a simple test of recognition; (b) to investigate any distortion verbal reconstruction may cause, an effect demonstrated by Belbin (1950); (c) to replicate Zangwill's (1941) observation about a variety of paramnesia he found to be characteristic of alcoholic Korsakoff psychosis (see p. 82). Recognition was tested by a standard method, when, following a simple motor task lasting 3 minutes, the picture was presented a second time. Handing it to the subject, the experimenter first asked him whether he had seen that picture before. If the reply was affirmative, he next put the question: "is it exactly the same?", and in response to a further assent: "are you quite sure it is the same?" In spite of this very considerable counter-suggestion, there were only 6 instances in a total of 30 tests when a patient wavered from absolute certainty, and none did so in both tests. The wording typical of the 24 standard responses was "yes . . . the same . . . quite sure," while the exceptions were: "little different," "color lighter," "mostly same," "was it more finished?", "not so many children," and a single "no." These answers were equally split between the two pictures, first and second test, recall with and without description, and all but the last were given in response to the second question. Although asked in what way the picture was different, if thought to be so, the 6 subjects gave no details beyond the brief remarks quoted above.[2]

*(b) Selection.* The same type of material was used; the covers of 40 issues of the same magazine. Half of them were shown to the subject, one by one for 10 seconds, without any special instruction to remember them. An hour later he was presented with all 40 cards in a mixed pile, and was asked to sort out those he had seen earlier. A group of 14 control (A) subjects as well as 16 Korsakoff patients were tested.

Three Korsakoff patients and 4 control subjects recognized all 20 pictures, but only 3 of the latter accomplished this without misidentifying at least one other card. Means of correct

---

[2] I have since succeeded in reproducing the "Zangwill effect" in a patient with severe brain damage whose symptoms, however, were very different from those characteristic of the Korsakoff syndrome. His memory defect was primarily one of uncertainty, doubt about the identity of objects or persons recognized. This type of disturbance I have not observed in Korsakoff patients with an alcoholic history, or with an etiology of inclusion body encephalitis.

recognition were 17.6 (SD 2.1) in the control, 12.9 (SD 5.6) in the Korsakoff group, means of differential scores (correct minus incorrect identification) 15.4 (SD 3.9) and 10.3 (SD 5.1). The difference between the last two was significant at the .01 level ($t$=2.94), that between the former two at the .02 level ($z$=2.41). Only 2 Korsakoff patients failed to recognize at least one-third of the pictures shown, both of whom performed relatively well on other tests. The Korsakoff patients took significantly ($z$=3.85, $p$. <.0004) longer over the recognition test than the control group, 162.8 seconds (SD 74.0) as against 90.2 seconds (SD 9.0).

Over the hour, as would be expected, the Korsakoff patients forgot more of the information. Their total error score was higher than the control, but it should be noted that, in this as in other tests that allowed for both types of error, their omissions far exceeded false positives; only 26 per cent of their mistakes were by mis-recognition as compared with 43 per cent in the control group.

Evidently, these patients, even though free to do so, are not apt to resort to any available answer rather than admit ignorance. The same conclusion was borne out by another more informal experiment when, in the course of an interview I showed the patients a cartoon with a humorous caption. Only 1 of the 16 Korsakoff patients grasped the joke, though it was simple enough, but when about 25 minutes later they were asked to find it in one of the two magazines lying about none of them selected a substitute; 7 discovered the right page, and all remembered they had been shown a humorous picture. My failure to reproduce the paramnesic responses reported by Zangwill could be attributed to the radical change in the patients' confabulatory propensities as they settle in the chronic phase of the disease, and possibly also to their test sophistication.

*Successive Recognition.* Several figures previously used in a test of perceptual discrimination (see p. 139) were shown on another occasion to investigate progressive trends in pattern recognition. The set of 12 cards also included some new designs, as shown in Fig. 15. Testing was by repeated recogni-

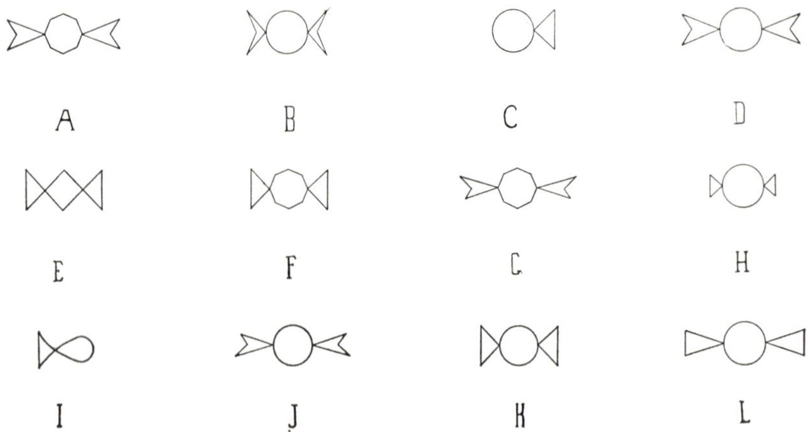


Fig. 15. Designs in recognition experiment.

tion. The figure marked here (but not in the experiment) with G was shown, with the instruction to remember its design for subsequent recognition. As soon as the subject felt confident that he could remember it, the 12 cards were spread out before him in a standard order of three rows. His task was to point out the figure and, whether his choice was right or wrong, the cards were immediately removed. This procedure was repeated after intervals of 15, 30, and 60 minutes during which the subject was kept occupied. Each time the cards were displayed in a different but standardized order of three rows, and on no occasion was the subject told whether his choice was correct. Table 29 lists the selections of Korsakoff and control (A) groups of 16.

**Table 29**

CHOICE OF WINGED FIGURE IN SUCCESSIVE RECOGNITION

| | *Korsakoff (N = 16)* | | | | *Control (N = 16)* | | | |
|---|---|---|---|---|---|---|---|---|
| *Figure chosen* Delay: | *0 Minutes* | *15 Minutes* | *30 Minutes* | *60 Minutes* | *0 Minutes* | *15 Minutes* | *30 Minutes* | *60 Minutes* |
| G | 9 | 5 | 5 | 3 | 15 | 15 | 15 | 15 |
| A | 6 | 8 | 6 | 8 | 1 | 1 | 1 | 1 |
| J | 0 | 2 | 2 | 0 | 0 | 0 | 0 | 0 |
| F | 1 | 1 | 0 | 2 | 0 | 0 | 0 | 0 |
| D | 0 | 0 | 3 | 3 | 0 | 0 | 0 | 0 |

This proved an easy task for the control group, since only one of its members made a mistake, and that remained constant through the experiment. None of the Korsakoff patients chose the correct card on all four trials. Two pointed to G a second time but after 30 minutes switched to other figures, one persisted with A throughout the session, all the others shifted once or more often in their selection. If A and J represent one, F and D two steps toward simpler design, the cumulative effect of errors in recognition was by normalizing, as the term is used in gestalt theory (Wulf, 1922; Koffka, 1935). The initial error, of course, could not but follow that trend on account of the experimental design. The progression toward simpler forms, however, was not consistent throughout the Korsakoff group, except in so far as they selected F only in the last two trials, following previous choices of G and A. With the model in view, all but 1 of the Korsakoff patients correctly matched it by selecting G from among the 12 cards.

## Reproduction of Patterns

*Benton's Test.* This test demonstrated the inaccuracy and clumsiness of the Korsakoff patients' line drawings in mere copying (p. 126). With a delay of 10 seconds between inspection and reproduction, their errors were increased in magnitude and frequency alike. All 20 patients fell below Benton's norm for correct reproduction (mean 2.4) and exceeded his norm of errors (mean 14.4). *Distortion* accounted for 21 per cent of all errors in copying, for 28 per cent in delayed reproduction, or 94 out of 303 instances; *omission* with a total of 77 rose from 10 to 25 per cent. The incidence of *misplacements* was barely higher, 41 as compared with 39, but there were as many examples of *perseveration* and *rotation* (43 and 41) which had not occurred in copying or only very rarely (0 and 2), and seven *size* errors against one with the model in view. Compared with our control records, the increment due to the delay in the Korsakoff patients' errors was abnormally high.

Benton's procedure was reversed in an experiment with 22 Korsakoff patients and a control group of 23 (15 A, 8 H). A red diamond on top of a blue square and an asymmetric design in black, shown in Fig. 16, were presented first for reproduction from memory, next for copying, and finally for recognition. No phase of the experiment was limited in time.

Because of the poor performance of the neurological control subjects, the reproductions showed a less reliable deficit in the Korsakoff patients, in spite of their crude distortions, omissions, and total failures, than did the copying task, in which none of the latter succeeded satisfactorily with both designs.

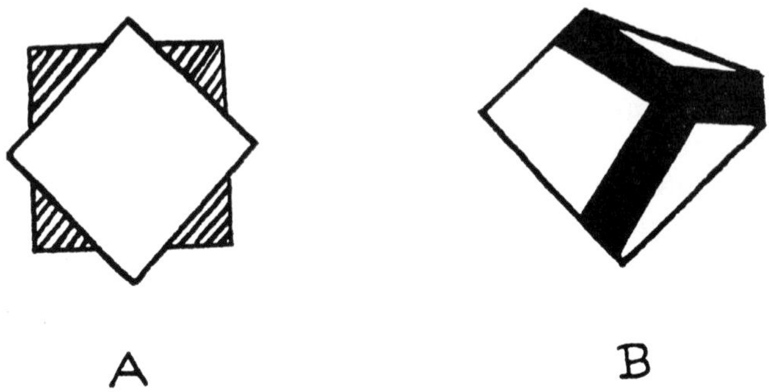


Fig. 16. Designs for reproduction.

An interesting feature of both hospitalized groups was their indifference to color. Although they had four pencils in front of them—black, blue, green, and red—they almost always chose only one for both patterns, usually the black. If they used color, it was as likely to be green as those in model A. Other errors common to these two groups were the reversal of figure and ground in A, and distortions of B towards symmetry.

Following reproduction, recognition was tested by shuffling the two figures into a deck with eight other drawings that resembled them, some more others less closely, 6 in two colors and 2 in black. Only 6 Korsakoff patients, but 20 control subjects, picked out both correctly.

## Associative Learning

*Conditioning.* Several experimenters, who tried to condition our Korsakoff patients, were inclined to concur with Gantt and Muncie's negative findings. In view of these unsuccessful attempts, my own venture is presented with some diffidence as a genuine example of conditioning.[3] It applied a modification of an apparatus described by Franks and Withers (1955) for conditioning eyelid closure. Air puff served as the unconditional (US), buzzer as the conditional stimulus (CS); the latter also triggered an electric clock, and lowering of the subject's eyelid stopped it by means of a photoelectric cell. Each signal, US and CS, lasted .5 second with an interval of .3 second between them.

Each subject was given a pre-test of 5 consecutive buzzer signals, in order to determine that he would not close his eye in response to the sound alone. If he did, the procedure continued until this effect ceased for 5 consecutive trials. The conditioning schedule followed a standard randomized design of 30 reinforced and 30 unreinforced buzzer signals, the former being more closely spaced in the first half, and neither running in sequences longer than 3. A series of unreinforced buzzer signals, the test, followed. Two criteria of conditioning were applied: (a) eyelid response within .3 second to 5 of the first 6 unreinforced test signals and (b) response within .2 second to over half of the unreinforced signals. The criterion of extinction was the absence of the conditioned response to 9 out of 10 test signals.

Of 16 Korsakoff patients 11 satisfied the first and the remaining 5 patients the second criterion of conditioning, but only 4 met both criteria. This suggests that those who conditioned more slowly retained the effect somewhat longer, though none of them for long. All 11 patients showed extremely rapid extinction, with a mean of 7.8 unreinforced signals. All 4 control (A) subjects available for this experiment satisfied criterion (a), and 3 criterion (b); their rate of extinction was considerably slower than that of the amnesic patients.

*Sign-Response Pairing.* Capacity to establish new associations between a visual sign and a motor response was tested

[3]Linskii (1954), however, reported that speed of conditioning was about the same in normal subjects and Korsakoff patients.

at several levels of difficulty. Simple geometrical figures provided the signs for response by tapping a telegraph key or stepping on a pedal. Although a tachistoscope was used in order to limit the field of vision, the exposure time of .6 second was well above the threshold of recognition and, on request, any figure was shown a second time. The experiment consisted of 5 series of trials, each following a standard schedule within which the order of the figures was randomized, except that each occurred the same number of times as any other alike in the first and second half of the schedule. Throughout the first half the subject was told after each response whether it was right or wrong, but in the second half no information was given.

Series A consisted of 10 triangles and 10 crosses; in B a circle was added to these, each appearing eight times. Series C combined triangle and circle with two new symbols, star and square, shown eight times. Series D presented the 5 previously introduced figures and a diamond, equally distributed in a sequence of 36. The response to cross, square, and star was always with the foot, to the others with the hand. Series E differed from the others in adding a third possibility to the alternative response by hand or foot, abstention from either. Its symbols, triangle, square, and shield, each occurred 8 times, the latter calling for no response. Latency was not timed, but unusually long delays were recorded; errors spontaneously corrected were scored as correct, changes in the reverse direction as errors.

**Table 30**

SIGN-RESPONSE PAIRING: MEAN ERRORS

| | *Series A* | *Series B* | *Series C* | *Series D* | *Series E* |
|---|---|---|---|---|---|
| | *Number of figures shown* | | | | |
| | *2* | *3* | *4* | *6* | *3* |
| Korsakoff ($N = 18$) | 1.7 | 1.5 | 7.2 | 11.0 | 4.0 |
| Control ($N = 18A$) | .3 | .2 | .6 | 1.6 | 0 |
| Wilcoxon's $T$ | 274 | 325 | 212[a] | 199½[a] | 180[a] |

[a] $p < .01$

Since the incidence of delayed reaction was too small in either group to warrant analysis, only the errors listed in Table 30 indicate the difference between their levels of performance. The leap from Series B to C marks the boundary beyond which the Korsakoff patients could not follow their instructions efficiently. In series A "information transmitted" was equal in both groups with a mean *T* of .81; beyond that it increased in the control group apace with the number of symbols, reaching its peak in C. In the Korsakoff group the trend was in the opposite direction, *T* hitting its lowest in Series C. Beyond that point the situation of those patients was one of utter confusion.

The results were also examined with a view to learning effects. Since the cross and the triangle appeared in every one of the first four series, and each was constantly associated with the same response, practice with these might have shown effects in the later series, as compared with the newly introduced symbols. In Series B and C the Korsakoff patients showed a slight learning effect, but in Series D they made errors in response to the relatively unfamiliar circle only half as frequently as either to the much practiced triangle or to the entirely novel diamond. In Series E, of their 56 errors, 25 followed the triangle and only 18 the shield which was both a new figure and called for a new type of response. Neither were the control group's errors any more consistent with a learning effect. None of the subjects in either group showed a marked preference for responding with foot or finger.

*Paired Words.* Wechsler (1917) used pairs of meaningful words to demonstrate that his Korsakoff patients were unable to form new associations, and subsequently included a test of that type in his memory scale (1945). It consists of ten word pairs, 6 easy or conventional (e.g., metal-iron, baby-cries, north-south) and 4 difficult or arbitrary (e.g., cabbage-pen) The list is read aloud, and the subject is warned that subsequently, when only the first half of each pair would be presented, he is to respond with the associated item. In each of the three trials the order of the pairs changes. Correct responses are scored separately for easy and for difficult pairs.

Unlike Wechsler's patients, every one of our 16 Korsakoff patients succeeded in learning some of the associations, with a mean of 13.9 (SD 2.4) from a possible 18 easy and 1.6 (SD 3.0) from a possible 12 difficult pairs in three trials. The corresponding means of a control (X) group of 16 were 15.9 (SD 2.0) and 4.6 (SD 2.3) of which only the latter was significantly higher ($t=3.11$). At times it became apparent that the difficulty of the unconventional pairs for some Korsakoff patients arose not so much from the novelty of the combination as from its meaninglessness. No trend from first to third trial could be traced in the records of the Korsakoff group.

On a different occasion the four difficult pairs were presented by means of a memory drum, i.e., visually, and repeatedly until a criterion of complete mastery was achieved. Of the 16 Korsakoff patients 2 refused to complete the experiment, another 2 failed in 12 trials, the remaining 12 learned the four pairs in 2 to 10 trials. Relearning after 1 hour was accomplished in fewer trials by 8 patients, but required more trials for 3 patients; one did it with the same number of presentations. Two patients completed the relearning test in a single trial. The selected group of 12 Korsakoff patients needed 6.5 presentations to learn the 4 word pairs in the first place; though almost twice as high, this mean was not significantly larger than the control mean of 3.4. The control group was not tested for relearning.

Word association with spatial cues was tested on a cardboard divided into 2, 3, or 4 equal areas, each imprinted with an adjective. In Series A the two adjectives were "old" and "clean," and the subject had to remember these and also which was on the right, which on the left. As soon as he would do this, the print was covered, and the experimenter proceeded to place, one by one, 5 cards over either area, in randomized order. Each card carried a noun, to which either of the two adjectives could be appropriate, e.g., "shirt." The subject's task was to attach the proper adjective to the noun, according to the placement of the card. In Series B and C, 6 and 9 cards were evenly divided among three areas, in D, 10 cards were placed over one or another of four adjectives.

A fair proportion of the 16 Korsakoff patients performed faultlessly in one or more tests, 3 making no error throughout the experiment. Their mean scores of correct response 9.0, 3.5, 7.7, and 8.2 were in no instance significantly lower than those of 14 control (A) subjects: 10.0, 5.8, 8.5, and 9.1; neither did they spend more time over it, except for the first series.

## Verbal Rote Learning

*Successive Recall.* In order to determine the rate at which amnesic patients forget newly acquired learning, they were asked to memorize lists of ten words. Two lists were used in different experimental sessions, the one consisting of nonsense syllables, therefore as unrelated to the subject's prior experience as any verbal material is likely to be, the other of meaningful words. Both kinds of words were made up of three letters: a consonant, a vowel, and a different consonant, e.g., PEZ or BAR. The 5 vowels occurred the same number of times, similarities in print or sound and associations by meaning or rhyme were avoided within each list. Nonsense syllables had an association value of 40% or less, according to Glaze (1928).

Printed in ¾-inch type, the words were arrayed vertically on a card that was handed to the subject with the instruction to memorize accurately as many of them as he could in 3 minutes. If he asked whether meaningless words should be pronounced or spelled, he was advised to pronounce them as words. Spelled answers were, nevertheless, accepted and, in case of doubtful pronunciation, called for. Since pilot experiments had shown that lists of 10 words exceeded the learning capacity of Korsakoff patients, no criterion of complete mastery was imposed. They also indicated that 3 minutes made about the optimal learning period, and that alternate modes of presentation tended to be less favorable.

Testing proceeded by unaided reproduction immediately after the learning period, and again 90, 180, 360, 540, and 720 seconds later. Words or syllables were accepted in any order listed. All incorrect as well as correct responses were recorded, except when they occurred repeatedly. If asked for confirmation, the experimenter always nodded affirmatively, whether the word reported was correct or not.

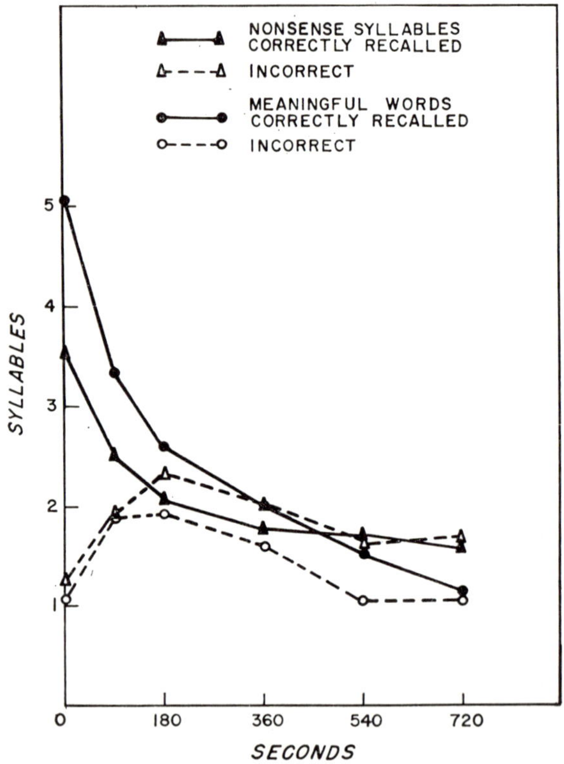


Fig. 17. Recall of syllables and words: Korsakoff group.

Between repeated tests the subjects were not engaged in any task or conversation that would prevent silent rehearsal which might reduce the rate of forgetting but also tend to augment errors by substitution. Although in successive recall, the rate of forgetting is considerably slower than in tests of single reproduction (Hanawalt, 1937), Figure 17 shows a steep initial decline in retention for 16 Korsakoff patients. Their incorrect responses increased during the same 3 minutes, but not beyond that period. As in so many other experiments these patients made no effort to compensate for their memory defect by arbitrary inventions. Their mean incorrect reproduction was not significantly more than that of the con-

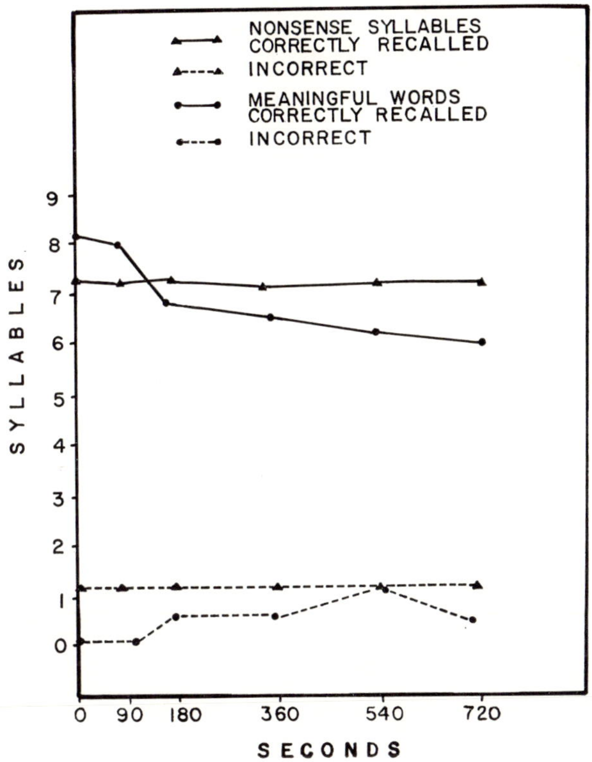


Fig. 18. Recall of syllables and words: control group.

trol group of 16, shown in Fig. 18. In respect to correct reproduction, the difference between the two groups was considerable and highly significant, both in immediate test of acquisition ($T=166\frac{1}{2}$ for meaningful, $t=6.09$ for nonsense) and at subsequent stages. Loss of retention in the first 90 seconds was also significantly different between the 2 groups ($T=166$ for meaningful; $z=2.45$ for nonsense; both $p<.01$).

*Relearning.* Both types of list were used on three other occasions to determine the effect of proactive and retroactive interference on the amnesic patients' retention of new learning. A modified version of the savings method was used, with the instruction to reproduce as many items as a subject could in any sequence. Control subjects memorized lists of 20 meaningful words or 15 nonsense syllables, to allow them scope for gain in relearning. Since each group served as its own control, this discrepancy in the test material did not contaminate the results.

Experiment I tested retroactive interference; the subject was allowed 3 minutes to memorize list A or B, reproduced the words he could recall, then proceeded to learn the other list, and finally relearned the original list. Experiment II tested retention without interference; the 5-minutes interval between learning and relearning the same list was spent resting. Experiment III tested proactive interference; list A or B was memorized and recalled in the standard manner, next the other list was learned and tested, and then relearned and tested. Schematically the design was A-B-A; B-o-B; B-A-A for the three experiments, alternate subjects beginning with A or B. Testing by reproduction began 30 seconds after the

**Table 31**

MEANS AND STANDARD DEVIATIONS OF RECALL SCORES

| | *Retroactive interference* | | | *No interference* | | *Proactive interference* | | |
|---|---|---|---|---|---|---|---|---|
| *Test* | *I* | *II* | *III* | *I* | *II* | *I* | *II* | *III* |
| Korsakoff Group: | (*N* = 20) | | | (*N* = 20) | | (*N* = 18) | | |
| Nonsense syllables | | | | | | | | |
| Mean score | 2.85 | 2.15 | 2.75 | 2.45 | 2.70 | 2.50 | 2.50 | 2.78 |
| SD | 2.18 | 1.71 | 1.21 | 1.38 | 1.56 | 1.20 | 1.62 | 1.83 |
| Meaningful words | | | | | | | | |
| Mean score | 4.60 | 4.90 | 5.45 | 5.25 | 5.10 | 4.61 | 5.17 | 5.17 |
| SD | 1.57 | 2.27 | 2.34 | 1.86 | 1.72 | 2.23 | 1.85 | 2.28 |
| Control Group: | (*N* = 23) | | | (*N* = 23) | | (*N* = 12) | | |
| Nonsense syllables | | | | | | | | |
| Mean score | 5.70 | 5.26 | 6.83 | 5.65 | 7.39 | 7.92 | 6.75 | 8.75 |
| SD | 2.82 | 2.32 | 2.74 | 2.74 | 3.04 | 3.03 | 3.22 | 3.47 |
| Meaningful words | | | | | | | | |
| Mean score | 8.96 | 8.83 | 9.52 | 10.26 | 12.26 | 10.67 | 10.83 | 12.50 |
| SD | 3.40 | 3.78 | 3.36 | 2.85 | 3.68 | 4.19 | 2.82 | 4.19 |

subject returned the list to the experimenter. Intervals between any two consecutive experiments ranged from 2 to 4 weeks.

The acquisition score with the first list in any experiment was about the same for the Korsakoff patients in the three parallel testing sessions, but the control group improved on the second occasion with natural words, on the third with nonsense syllables. Since in neither group and for neither type of material were there significant differences between the alternate lists, means in Table 31 combine A and B. Retention was measured by the difference between each subject's reproduction score in relearning and first learning of the same list; means and *t*-ratios calculated on these differences are given in Table 32.

**Table 32**

DIFFERENCES BETWEEN RECALL SCORES ON FIRST AND SECOND TEST OF LEARNING

| | *Nonsense Syllables* | | *Meaningful Words* | |
|---|---|---|---|---|
| | *Mean Difference* | *t-Ratio* | *Mean Difference* | *t-Ratio* |
| Korsakoff group | | | | |
| No interference | .25 | 1.32 | –.15 | 1.00 |
| Retroactive interference | –.10 | .90 | .85 | 2.24 |
| Proactive interference | .28 | .91 | 0 | 0 |
| Control group | | | | |
| No interference | 1.74 | 5.38 | 2.00 | 4.38 |
| Retroactive interference | 1.13 | 3.70 | .56 | 1.53 |
| Proactive interference | 2.00 | 3.78 | 1.67 | 2.29 |

The control group (15 A, 8H in Experiments I and II; 12 A in Experiment III) reported significantly more correct items in each of the 16 tests than the Korsakoff patients, and also increased its recall on relearning, significantly so when there was no interference, and with nonsense syllables even against retroactive or proactive interference. The Korsakoff patients were as likely to drop their score after relearning as to register some gain, and any gain was negligibly small. Retention scores in the absence of interference were significantly higher

( $t$=4.16 and 6.14) than with retroactive, though not with proactive, interference in the control group; no such difference was found for the Korsakoff patients.

An analysis of incorrect responses is of interest on two counts. In more than half the tests with meaningful words the Korsakoff patients did not give one incorrect response, and 12 members of their group averaged less than one such error over the 16 tests. Here again there is no evidence for their supposed propensity to fabricate answers when memory fails. Furthermore, the majority of their incorrect responses conformed to the model of a vowel flanked by two different consonants. At no time were the patients told that the material had been constructed on that pattern, so it seems that this much they had learned spontaneously. Apart from a second listing in the same test, few of the incorrect responses were likely to perseverate. In some instances, however, a patient reproduced the same erroneous nonsense syllable not only within one testing session but again several months later.

After an interval of 20 months, test of retention without interference and with retroactive interference was repeated with a Korsakoff group of 18, following the original design in every respect except that test was by recognition. The 10 words of the test list had to be selected from a display that included 20 more cards with items of the same type, none of which appeared in list A or B. No time limit was set, nor was

**Table 33**

Mean Ratios of Correct to Total Choices in Recognition Tests with and without Interference, and Mean Gain on Relearning

| | *Retroactive Interference* | | | | *No Interference* | | |
|---|---|---|---|---|---|---|---|
| | *Test I* | *Test II* | *Test III* | *Gain* | *Test I* | *Test II* | *Gain* |
| Nonsense syllables | | | | | | | |
| Mean | .72 | .72 | .59 | –.13 | .69 | .70 | .01 |
| SD | .18 | .23 | .19 | .28 | .18 | .18 | .18 |
| $t$-Ratio | — | — | — | 1.89 | — | — | 1.29 |
| Meaningful words | | | | | | | |
| Mean | .77 | .74 | .67 | –.10 | .75 | .70 | –.05 |
| SD | .14 | .12 | .15 | .23 | .18 | .13 | .16 |
| $t$-Ratio | — | — | — | 1.93 | — | — | 1.24 |

the number of choices restricted but, to avoid repeated selections of the same item, the subject placed the chosen cards to the side of the display.

Mean correct recognition exceeded recall on every trial, but so did incorrect responses, and to a much greater extent. Over all five tests, mean correct recognition was 5.4 for nonsense, 6.3 for natural words; mean incorrect choices were 3.5 and 4.6. Both types of choice were higher, though not significantly, after relearning. Measuring performance by the ratio of correct to total choice, the recognition scores are set out in Table 33, and they confirm the conclusion of the earlier study that no retention can be demonstrated in Korsakoff patients with this type of learning material, also that this negative finding cannot be attributed to retroactive interference.

Eight Korsakoff patients were able to learn a list of 6 natural words, in 5 successive presentations on a memory drum. The procedure was repeated after a rest of 15 minutes and again the next 2 days, always following a test of free recall, and another 3 consecutive days with six nonsense syllables. Each test concluded with complete success or the fifth trial. Every day some improvement showed between first to fifth trial, but the trend was not reliable, and no savings occurred from first to third day. By the evidence of savings there seemed to be no retention, by that of unaided recall there was a little or more after 15 minutes and even a whole day. Using the latter method in our previous experiments, we evidently missed no memory effects that would show up on the alternate procedure.

*Sentences.* The Korsakoff patients did better with word lists presented all at once than itemwise on a memory drum. These two methods of visual display, auditory presentation, and three types of interference were also compared by the learning of 6 matched 10-word sentences. Instruction was for verbatim reproduction immediately after presentation and again 5 minutes later. In each of 6 sessions, 16 Korsakoff patients and 16 control (X) subjects learned one sentence, following a design that balanced the order of the 6 experimental conditions and the assignment of the sentences to each.

In Experiments A, B, C, and D the sentence was read aloud to the subject at an even pace; in E he read it himself from a card; in F it unfolded in front of him stepwise on a memory drum, one word per second. In Experiments A, E, and F the 5 minutes were spent resting; in B they were occupied by a manual task that involved neither learning nor vocalization; in C by an interview focused on the subject's recollection of early life, i.e., verbal performance but no new learning; in D the interpolated activity was memorizing a short narrative passage. Sentence recall was scored on a 5-point scale, and group means calculated on that basis are listed in Table 34.

**Table 34**

IMMEDIATE AND DELAYED RECALL OF A TEN-WORD SENTENCE

| | | *Korsakoff (N = 16)* | | *Control (N = 16)* | |
|---|---|---|---|---|---|
| *Presentation* | *Interpolated activity* | *Immediate* | *After 5 Minutes* | *Immediate* | *After 5 Minutes* |
| A Read by experimenter | None | 4.75 | 3.94 | 4.75 | 4.75 |
| B Read by experimenter | Manual task | 4.88 | 3.31 | 4.75 | 4.19 |
| C Read by experimenter | Interview | 4.81 | .94 | 4.38 | 3.88 |
| D Read by experimenter | Learning | 4.69 | 2.31 | 4.31 | 3.75 |
| E Read by subject | None | 4.88 | 4.69 | 4.88 | 4.75 |
| F Memory drum | None | 4.94 | 4.13 | 4.88 | 4.94 |

Mode of presentation did not significantly influence recall either on immediate or on delayed testing. Immediate reproduction of a sentence of ten words clearly does not test the amnesic disturbance, since it showed no difference between the two groups. In the subsequent 5 minutes, however, the Korsakoff patients forgot more under all six experimental conditions, and most when that period was occupied by an interview. Their decrement in retention was significantly greater under treatment C than during either rest or performance of a manual task ($t$=5.70 and 4.61). This differential effect also characterized the control group but to a significantly smaller extent ($t$=6.96 and $T$=187 : $p$<.01, between groups). The interpolated learning task also interfered with retention, even though the Korsakoff patients remembered little of the story.

The conclusions to be drawn from these results seem to conflict with those of the preceding experiment. Interference effects in forgetting will be considered in Chapter 10, but it may be noted at this point that "relearning provides a complex measure of the persisting effects of original practice" (Luh, 1922; cf. also Postman and Rau, 1957; Florès, 1958). Quite possibly the contrasting results reflect the differential rate at which Korsakoff patients learn the two types of verbal material. There is also a difference between learning as a partial accomplishment and learning in the sense of mastery. The interference of interpolated activity may not become effective unless original learning has reached a certain measure of achievement.

## Learning Skills and Maps

In adulthood, the acquisition of skills very largely consists of applying the available repertory to new situations. To some extent a few of the Korsakoff patients accomplished this in doing a job at the mental hospital. This involved less of an adaptation for a waitress who worked in the cafeteria, or a woman who sewed clothes than for a laborer who became a storekeeper. No systematic provision was made to teach them new skills, none seemed to wish to learn any, and probably none would have been able to. The nearest attempt made in that direction in the present study was to determine the effects of practice on unfamiliar motor skills and on the solution of puzzles.

*Manual Skill.* Modified versions of our bead-picking task (pp. 123-125) tested the acquisition of new motor skills. In its more difficult variant, small beads had to be moved from one receptacle to another by means of crossed forceps, so that compression loosened the grip and release brought the points together. Another version used larger beads and an instrument that worked with a plunger action, picking up beads as the shaft was pushed down and dropping them when it was released. Korsakoff and control (X) groups of 12 were tested on the following schedule: 3 practice trials and 12 test trials of 60 seconds, with a break after the sixth, in the morning;

6 trials in the afternoon about 3 hours later; 6 more trials the following afternoon; 6 trials after a week. The patients had another six trials a month later. Tests with the two instruments took place in one session, balancing the order across the subjects. Performance was scored for the number of beads dropped into the receiving bowl in each 60-second period.

Neither group found the plunger action difficult, but 2 Korsakoff patients could not learn to use the crossed forceps. Disregarding variations among its members, both groups improved their rate with the plunger from each trial to the next. Statistical tests showed this improvement to be reliable on the first and second day, and for the Korsakoff patients also after a week, but not after a month. While differences in improvement were not significant, those between mean scores were significant between the groups on every occasion. Table 35 also shows that with the forceps neither group improved steadily in repeated tests, and that between group differences were not significant. Within a single session work rate tended to rise with successive trials but this trend not not reliable.

**Table 35**

PERFORMANCE RATE WITH PLUNGER AND CROSSED FORCEPS ON REPEATED TESTINGS

| | *Mean of beads moved with plunger* | | | | | *Mean of beads moved with forceps* | | | | |
|---|---|---|---|---|---|---|---|---|---|---|
| | *Test 1* | *Test 2* | *Test 3* | *Test 4* | *Test 5* | *Test 1* | *Test 2* | *Test 3* | *Test 4* | *Test 5* |
| Control ($N=12$) | | | | | | | | | | |
| Mean | 37.5 | 47.4 | 52.6 | 53.8 | — | 9.3 | 10.6 | 12.9 | 13.6 | — |
| SR | 14.0 | 16.3 | 17.1 | 19.9 | — | 4.5 | 4.9 | 7.0 | 6.6 | — |
| Korsakoff ($N=12$) | | | | | | | | | | |
| Mean | 21.6 | 24.6 | 31.3 | 35.6 | 38.5 | 7.1 | 6.6 | 8.7 | 8.9 | 8.3 |
| SD | 7.3 | 7.2 | 11.5 | 14.0 | 13.5 | 3.7 | 5.1 | 9.6 | 6.0 | 6.1 |
| $t$-Ratio | — | — | 3.49 | 2.47 | — | .50 | .76 | 1.17 | 1.74 | — |
| $T$ | 89 | 85 | — | — | — | — | — | — | — | — |

*Map Puzzle.* Acquisition and retention of a skill that does not depend on manual dexterity was tested on the puzzle outlined in Fig. 19. The task was to move a rider from point A to D, but this could not be done along the shortest track because the path was barred by concealed obstacles (marked in dotted lines). In order to clear the way, the rider had to slide first to B and next to C, and thus unlock the gates. On

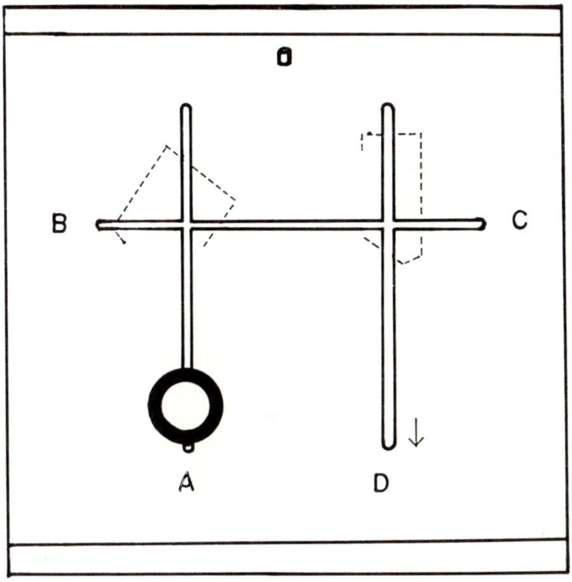


Fig. 19. Pattern of puzzle.

first trial all the patients got stuck, and none discovered the device to open the course. The experimenter then showed the trick by guiding the subject's hand, and after that encouraged him to try again without aid.

In three trials, of 16 Korsakoff patients 3 opened both, and another 5 patients one of the gates. They were given twelve more practice trials immediately, and a delayed test after an hour, when on first attempt only 1 patient remembered to unlock both gates. Two more thought of it before the second obstacle, and progressed smoothly all the way on the next trial; the others tackled the problem as if they had never before learned its secret. Retested after 12 to 15 days, even the 3 more or less successful learners had forgotten the simple trick. To 16 control (X) subjects this puzzle posed no serious difficulty; 13 discovered the clue to unlock the gates by trial and error, the others with the experimenter's help, and all remembered it after an hour, and a week or two later.

*Maze.* The maze in Fig. 20 represents a spatial version of the sequential pattern (B-B-R-B-R-R) tested in concept

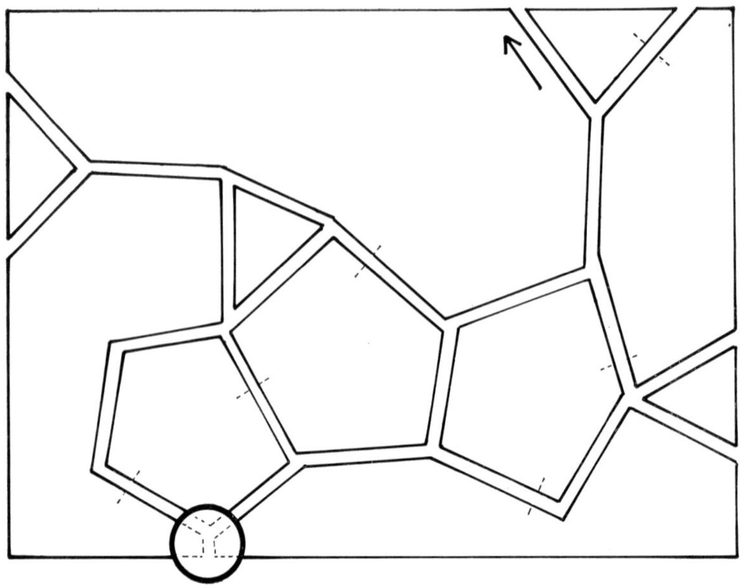

Fig. 20. Maze pattern: R-R-L-R-L-L.

formation (pp. 195-198). Most of the grooves in the 8-inch square wooden box led into blind alleys, except for a path followed by two turns right, one left, one right, and two left (R-R-L-R-L-L). Along this path the blindfolded subject had to slide a rider from the starting point to the terminal; passage through the blind alleys was barred in the positions marked.

After one demonstration by the experimenter, the subject was blindfolded and allowed 20 trials. If he met the criterion of three consecutive successes, he was given 5 more tests, all with the same criteria and limits. The third and fifth were identical with the first, the second differed from it by turning the entire maze around 180°, the fourth by requiring performance with the nondominant hand in the original orientation, and the sixth with the dominant hand starting from the terminal point. The entire procedure was repeated an hour later.

Only 5 of 15 Korsakoff patients met the criterion in the

first test, with a mean of 7.2 trials, and again in the second test after 16.6 trials. Four of these mastered the task in the last four tests, with mean trials of 7.0, 8.2, 9.2, and 7.0. There was clearly no practice or learning effect. An hour later 4 patients passed the first test with a mean of 7.0 trials, and 3 the other tests, with little or no savings. Turning the sequential formula into a motor test evidently did not greatly benefit these patients, and those who discovered the pattern of turns formed but a precarious visual-kinesthetic map. All 15 control (X) subjects solved and remembered the maze pattern in its original orientation, though several failed to apply it in reverse.

*Pegboards.* To probe incidental as well as deliberate map learning, the Rey-Davis test (Zangwill, 1946) was used in a modified form. The subject faced a row of four square boards, each with nine pegs spaced equidistantly in three rows, eight glued to the base, the ninth lifting out of its socket. The position of the loose peg varied from board to board. One set of boards and pegs was plain wood. The other set was painted; the base was white, three pegs were in one color, two pairs in two different colors, varying from board to board, one each black and in the fourth color. The last was the loose peg—red, yellow, green, and blue in order from left to right. Presented with the colored boards first, the subject was told that on each, eight of the pegs were firm, and his task was to discover the loose pegs by trial and error, and then remember them.

Up to ten trials were allowed for learning, and then the boards were turned to different angles, 270°, 360°, 180°, and 90°. As he was doing this, the experimenter fully explained his action. After no more than ten trials, the boards were turned back to their original position to repeat the first test. Next the unpainted boards were laid out in the basic position, and the subject was informed that each was identical with the painted board it replaced, so that the loose pegs would be in the same places as in the last test. The procedure differed only in the middle phase, when all the boards were rotated uniformly, first by 90° and then by 180°, before reversing them to the original position.

Each test terminated with success or the tenth trial. The criterion of learning was correct first choice on all four boards from left to right in two successive trials; the criterion of successful transposition was correct first choice on all four boards in the first two trials. Table 36 lists frequencies of successes and estimates of the significance of between-group differences by Fisher's (1934) Exact Test.

Of the 16 Korsakoff patients 8 were able to learn the color sequence, and several of them retained this after rotation, but only 1 remembered the position sequence; 3 more could learn but not transpose it. The gap between the two parts of the experiment proved narrower for the 16 control (A) subjects, several of whom transposed successfully after rotation, although only a few learned the position sequence as long as the color code provided sufficient information. While most of the Korsakoff patients could learn the position of the first two loose pegs, they often confused the third and fourth, or chose randomly on the last two boards.

**Table 36**

PEGBOARDS: SUCCESSFUL LEARNING (L) AND TRANSPOSITION (T)

| | *Colored pegboards* | | | *Plain pegboards* | | | |
|---|---|---|---|---|---|---|---|
| | *Basic (L)* | *Rotated (T)* | *Basic (T)* | *Basic (T+L)* | *90° (T)* | *180° (T)* | *Basic (T)* |
| Korsakoff ($N = 16$) | 8 | 5 | 5 | 1 + 3 | 0 | 0 | 0 |
| Control ($N = 16$) | 15 | 10 | 11 | 5 +11 | 9 | 8 | 5 |
| p | 0.01 | 0.08 | 0.02 | 0.09 —0.01 | 0.0004 | 0.001 | 0.02 |

## Incidental Learning

In all preceding experiments we studied the Korsakoff patients' aptitude for intentional learning. A few examples of their incidental learning emerged in clinical observations and one instance in the laboratory, when they followed the formal properties of test words that they could not memorize. The pegboards also furnished an occasion for incidental learning to subjects who noted the positions of the loose pegs while remembering them by their colors.

To provide a direct test of incidental learning, a news report, rich in details, was converted into a jigsaw puzzle. Spread over six and a half lines, its 66 words were printed in 3/8-inch letters on a cardboard, into which six identical rectangular windows were carved, so that each cut across two adjacent words in two or three lines. Board and rectangles were handed to the subject who was told to fit each into its proper window and that this could be easily done by checking that the words reassembled made sense. No further instruction was given. When the subject had fitted all six windows, he was asked whether he had finished, and if he had the board was removed. Then he was requested to tell all he remembered about the story printed on the cardboard.

All 16 Korsakoff patients and 16 control (A) subjects solved the puzzle without error, the former taking somewhat longer over it but none more than 150 seconds. Of the 11 units of content the Korsakoff patients recalled a mean of 1.75 (SD 1.69), the control group 3.69 (SD 2.12); the difference was significant ($t$=2.77). On questioning the subjects, it transpired that all but 3 in the control and 1 in the Korsakoff group had read only the words that provided clues. The highest recall score in the control group, 11, was attained by a subject who had read for content, but the best record in the Korsakoff group, 6, came from a patient who professed that he had not.

## Summary

The results present a wide spectrum of the Korsakoff patients' capacity to learn and retain information, diverse in form and content. While engaged in a repetitive activity, they seem able to follow instructions for relatively long periods, but cannot recover the set after an interruption. Like other men and women, they too are more likely to succeed in recognition than in unaided recall, but in all tests of memory their capacity and reliability are abnormally small. By the evidence of immediate tests, they acquire much less of the information presented to them than do normal persons, and the rate at which they forget that small amount is exceedingly fast.

Reproductions of figures by amnesic patients display the normal processes of distortion and omission in exaggerated forms, and also show two characteristics of other brain-damaged patients: perseveration and rotation. Tests of recall, recognition, and reproduction all point to the important part interrupted sets play in the forgetting of amnesic patients.

By the evidence of the foregoing experiments, Korsakoff patients are able to form new associations, but, once established, these dissolve very rapidly. Practice by repeated exposure or express repetition does not advance their learning, and neither does the correction of errors. Multiple associations with the same response create special difficulties; spatial cues can be helpful. While some verbal associations may last for an hour and even longer, conditioned responses extinguish almost instantly.

Interference as a cause of forgetting is more evident in the form of new task orientation than as new acquisition, of which little enough is achieved. If Korsakoff patients learn but little when expressly instructed to, their incidental learning is scarcer still. Neither old nor recent learning seems to transfer in their formal tests of learning, although they can apply old skills to novel situations and tasks, especially if these involve simple routine operations.

Comparing the Korsakoff patients' attempts to learn the solutions of such problems as were set by the puzzle, maze, and pegboards, and to learn skills by manipulating strange instruments, an obvious distinction emerges. One involves the acquisition and retention of a map and a related plan of action, the other proceeds with immediate proprioceptive cues. In the latter type of learning, Korsakoff patients may have started at some disadvantage, but seemed to improve with practice at much the same rate as the control group; or they fail alike to benefit from practice, possibly manifesting some general aging effect. In performances that depend for success on more extensive plans, amnesic patients do not improve with practice, even though the motor operations involved are well within their capacity. Very likely this is so because they cannot retain maps and plans of action for any length of time, whether in a visual, a kinesthetic, or a symbolic code.

All this agrees with the view that the learning and retention of mechanical skills and of problem-solving information involve different processes. For practical purposes, the results suggest that Korsakoff patients might be taught simple routine skills with reasonable success, but not the type of skill that involves the storage of information and its application in planned action. None of the patients studied in this project would have been able to emulate the man in Stern's (1935) report who, while totally amnesic for several years, learned to write shorthand and retained his skill subsequently.

*Chapter 9*

# REPRODUCTION AND DISTORTION OF NARRATIVE TEXTS

Rote learning of verbal material certainly tests a capacity of memory function, but it is not widely representative of normal remembering. It is a skill exercised in learning poetry, technical definitions, or magic formulae, but "accuracy of reproduction, in a literal sense, is the rare exception and not the rule" (Bartlett, 1932). Adult men and women normally aim at memorizing the content, not every word of a text or speech. Judged by clinical evidence, amnesic patients are as incapable of accomplishing this more lenient feat of reproduction as they are of rote learning. Some information, nevertheless, seems to make a lasting impression even on them, and re-emerges later, though often in an improper context. We have encountered this phenomenon before in a clinical discussion of confabulation. In this chapter it will be re-examined under the more standardized conditions of the experimental laboratory.

## Test Material and Procedure

In addition to Wechsler's (1945) Memory Scale, five narrative texts, each of paragraph length, were used for testing reproduction of connected verbal material under various conditions. The shortest two were employed once, the others in several experiments. Text A was Franz's (1919) "Cowboy" story which has done extensive service in psychological studies of neurological diseases:

(*A*) A *cowboy* / from *Arizona* / went to *San Francisco* / with his *dog*,/ which he *left* / at a *friend's* / while he *purchased* / a *new* suit of *clothes*./ Dressed finely,/ he *went back* /

to the *dog,*/ *whistled* to him,/ *called him* by name / and *patted* him./ But the dog would *have nothing to do* with him,/ in his new *hat* / and *coat,* / but gave a *mournful* / *howl.* / *Coaxing* was of no effect /: so the cowboy *went away* / donned his *old garments,*/ whereon the *dog* / *immediately* / showed his wild *joy* / on *seeing his master* / as he thought he *ought* to be./

Tendency toward symbolic distortion (cf. p. 85) was tested by one of Betlheim and Hartmann's own short stories (B) and a control text (C) matched for length and information but free from disturbing sexual content:

(*B*) "When the mother left the house,/ the father locked himself up in a room / with his daughter,/ threw her on the bed,/ and raped his own child."/

(*C*) "When the mother left the house, / the daughter stole into the pantry,/ took down a box of cookies from the shelf,/ and ate the lot,/ so that none was left."/

Last, the interference effect of redundant information was tested by two passages from a morning paper, the longer ones somewhat embellished, the shorter couched in a terser style than the reporter's.

(*D* / *Long*) Mailmen / are frequently asked questions that have little to do with postal matters./ Paul Callahan / was covering his route / in the Inman St. section /of Cambridge,/ and was stopped by a woman / in her twenties,/ wearing a brown dress,/ who had a worried expression on her face / when she asked him: "Can you tell me where I could borrow some money / without having to ask my husband to sign a paper?"/ "I don't know offhand" the mailman replied,/ "but I would not advise it,/ for he will find out about the loan / when the payments are due."

(*D* / *Short*) When a woman / asked a mailman / in the street / where she could borrow money / without her husband's knowledge,/ he replied he didn't know / and would not advise it / because the husband would find out / when the payments are due./

(*E* / *Long*) In a city / in India / several thousand school children / paraded in the main square / to celebrate the sixty-eighth birthday / of the prime minister./ While reviewing the parade / the prime minister released / a number of doves,/ the symbols of peace,/ from the cages in which they had been kept./ The white doves flew over the heads / of the young marchers./ One of them, however, perched atop the prime minister's head / while he took the salute./

(*E / Short*) The prime minister / of India / released white peace doves / over the heads of several thousand school children / who were parading / to celebrate / his sixty-eighth birthday,/ but one dove perched on his head / while he took the salute./

The strokes mark the units counted for quantitative measures of recall. For verbatim reproduction, the cowboy story was divided into 27 sections, following Franz's original design. When memorized for content, only the 24 words or phrases in italics were taken into account, and suitable synonyms or substitutes were accepted, e.g., "didn't recognize him" or "didn't know him" for "would have nothing to do with him"; "put on his old clothes" for "donned his old garments"; "happy" or "pleased" for "showed his wild joy." Three pairs of units were bracketed into single sections, so that, e.g., "mournful howl" counted as one point, as did "new suit" or "new clothes" but no credit was earned by a second mention of this phrase when the story read "dressed finely."

The same principle applied to the scoring of the other stories, i.e., the content of each unit counted, no matter how loosely phrased or how far out of its original position it occurred in reproduction, as long as the referent was unmistakably correct. A "lady" or merely "she" was accepted instead of a "woman" in the mailman story, "flew down on" "sat on," or "lit upon" in place of "perched atop" in the report on India, "crackers" or "candies" for "cookies" in story C. Texts C and D each divided into 5 sections, the short versions of D and E into 9, the long versions into 16 units.

Recall of the cowboy story was also tested by means of recognition, presenting the following 10 questions with a set choice of four answers to each:

| | |
|---|---|
| 1. About whom is the story? | Farmer Cowboy Carpenter Sailor |
| 2. Where was he from? | Chicago Mexico Arizona Florida |
| 3. What did he take with him? | His daughter His car His guitar His dog |
| 4. Where did he go to? | San Francisco New York Canada California |
| 5. What did he do with the dog? | Kept him with him all the time<br>Left him with a friend<br>Asked his wife to look after him<br>Locked him up in the kennel |
| 6. What did he go out to do? | Take a girl to a dance<br>Buy a new radio<br>Buy some clothes<br>See a movie |
| 7. What happened on his return? | Had he forgotten about the dog?<br>Did he pick up the dog?<br>Did he call the dog by name?<br>Had the dog disappeared? |
| 8. What did the dog do? | Did he jump up on him?<br>Did he howl mournfully?<br>Did he snap at him?<br>Did he growl at him? |
| 9. Why did the dog not recognize his master? | Because of the strange place<br>Because he wore new clothes<br>Because he was a very old dog<br>Because he was very hungry |
| 10. What did his master do to be recognized by the dog? | Coax the dog<br>Give him a bone to chew<br>Put on his old garments<br>Stroke the dog's neck |

In all tests but one the experimenter read the texts in a clear loud voice and at an even rate. This method of presentation was chosen in order to relieve the subjects of the burden of having to memorize while engaged in reading, normally a unitary task which, however, some pilot studies had shown, impaired the learning capacity of the Korsakoff patients. Only texts B and C were given them in print, in ¾-inch size type;

the subjects read these aloud, and the experimenter helped or corrected them if necessary.

The cowboy story was used on three occasions, first for verbatim memorization with 22 Korsakoff patients and a control group of the same size (14 A, 8 H),[1] who were tested by immediate unaided reproduction. After 18 to 20 months, 20 Korsakoff patients were given it a second time. The instruction was to reproduce the content; testing differed only in that the experimenter helped with a few prompting questions. Then followed a test of recognition with the ten four-choice questions. After intervals of 24 hours, and a week, recall was tested first by means of unaided reproduction and subsequently by recognition. Only 10 of the original 20 subjects were available for the 2 repeat tests.

Ten months later, the cowboy story was read once more to 16 members of the Korsakoff group and to 16 control (P)[1] subjects. Recall was tested by unaided reproduction of content, first immediately after presentation of the text, and then repeatedly after 1 hour, 2 and 3 hours. Finally, the forced-choice questionnaire was given. The first hour was occupied by a standard procedure of psychological experiments, most of the second hour by electroencephalograph recordings, and the third hour was a rest period. Twelve members of the control group were also tested for recall by reproduction a day later, and 10 after a week. In no instance were the subjects warned that further tests of recall would follow, whether an hour, a day, or a week later.

Stories B and C were given to 14 Korsakoff patients each on a separate day. Test of recall was by reproduction of content 5, 15, and 45 minutes after reading the story. Stories D and E were presented so that the longer version of one and the shorter version of the other were read on one occasion, the alternate versions several weeks later. The sequence of long and short version of the same story, and of the long and short story within one session, alternated across subjects.

---

[1]For identification of code letters A, H, X, and P used in conjunction with control groups see "Prefatory Note" at the beginning of Part 4.

Recall was tested by reproduction of content, a few seconds after the reading of each story; 17 Korsakoff patients formed the experimental group. Two years later 16 Korsakoff patients and a control group (X) of 16 were given the longer versions of texts D and E. Single presentations of one, and six repeated readings of the other alternated with the reverse arrangements. Testing was by unaided reproduction immediately after presentation and again an hour later.

No control groups were included in the earlier experiments with texts D and E, but a parallel procedure was conducted with 21 staff members of the writer's department, using the method of serial reproduction. This experimental device, also known as the telephone game, tests memory for messages by relay: one person writes down what he remembers, and then passes on his record to the next who does the same, until the reproduction of the last member of the chain is compared with the original text. Our chains consisted of three links, and subjects waited a full day before writing down their recollection of the text, to be read to the next member of the chain. Bartlett has demonstrated that the types of decay and distortion that occur in serial reproduction are similar to those to be found in a single person's memory, but occur on a larger scale and more rapidly. The method, as Paul (1959) has pointed out, capitalizes on the initial steep drop of the forgetting curve which is normally negatively accelerated. By forcing the extent of gaps in the texts in this manner, an opportunity was created for comparing the qualitative changes in normal recall with those characteristic of verbal reproduction in the Korsakoff syndrome.

## Amount of Acquisition and Retention

*Rate of Forgetting.* By verbatim recall the Korsakoff patients reproduced a mean of 3.97, the control group 8.32 from the 27 units of the cowboy story; the difference is significant ($t=5.51$). Both groups tended to report the first few items of the text more accurately, no doubt because these hardly lend themselves to changed phrasing. Such words as "donned," "coaxed," "howled," and the phrase "showed his wild joy" also recurred frequently in the records of the control group, though hardly at all in those of the Korsakoff patients. It seems that these units of content were either remembered verbatim or not at all, and this may account for the unexpected result that the two control groups performed about equally well, even though one was scored for verbatim reproduction, the other for the easier test of reproducing content.

In accordance with experiments in rote learning, the control group also did well with the final sentence in verbatim reproduction, but none of the Korsakoff patients reported the last five units. Indicating the frequencies of verbatim reproduction of the 27 divisions of the cowboy story, Fig. 21 shows a steeper rate of decline from beginning to end for the Korsakoff patients.

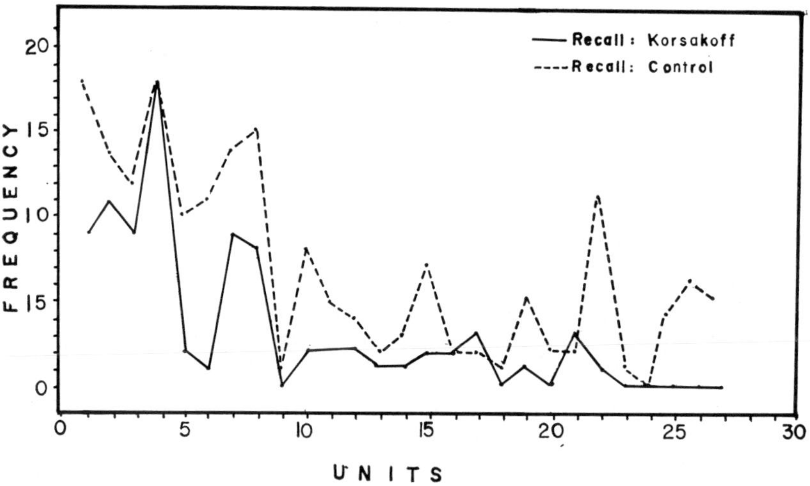


Fig. 21. Recall of units: verbatim reproduction.

Figure 22 illustrates the fluctuation in immediate recall of content across the 24 units of the same text. The relative position of the two groups remains as before, the main trend of the slopes is also similar, but the distance between the two curves has narrowed. The difference between the mean reproduction scores of the two groups, 5.82 and 9.56 was sig-

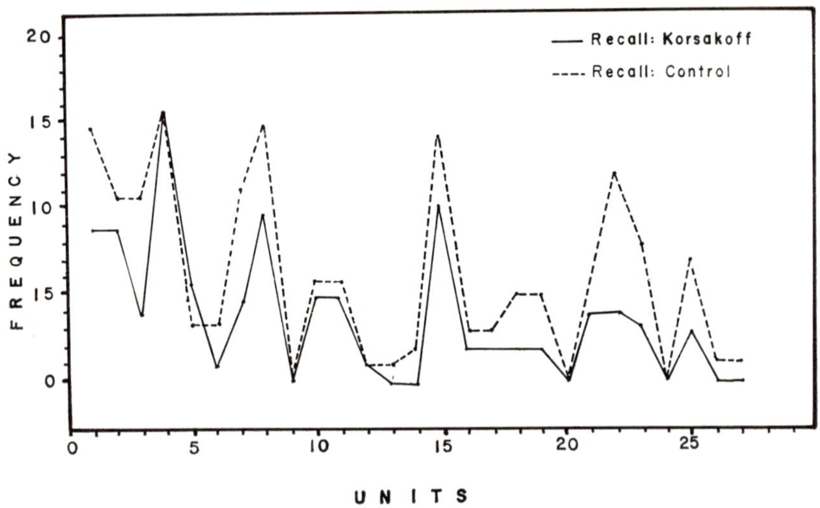


Fig. 22. Recall of units: reproduction of content.

nificant ($t$=5.22). Unlike the two control groups, the Korsakoff patients reproduced significantly ($t$=2.51, $p$<.02) more units when tested for content than in verbatim recall. Prompting questions, e.g., "Where did he come from?" "What did he do?" "Then what happened?" further increased their score to 9.30.

Figure 23 shows a composite forgetting curve for the Korsakoff patients, the first section representing the progressive decrement of content recalled in the third testing session. Their reproduction score dropped from 5.82 to 3.62 in the first hour, to 2.44 after the second hour, and to 1.81 after the third; the difference was significant in the first two instances ($t$=5.20, and 2.84), but not in the third. The other part of the Korsakoff group's curve is based on the results of the second session, when the patients were tested immediately, a day, and a week later. The group means in the two sections of the curve are not quite comparable, since only 10 of the 16 subjects tested at hourly intervals were available for delayed recall. After 3 hours, the mean reproduction score of this subgroup was 2.40—as compared with 1.81 for the entire

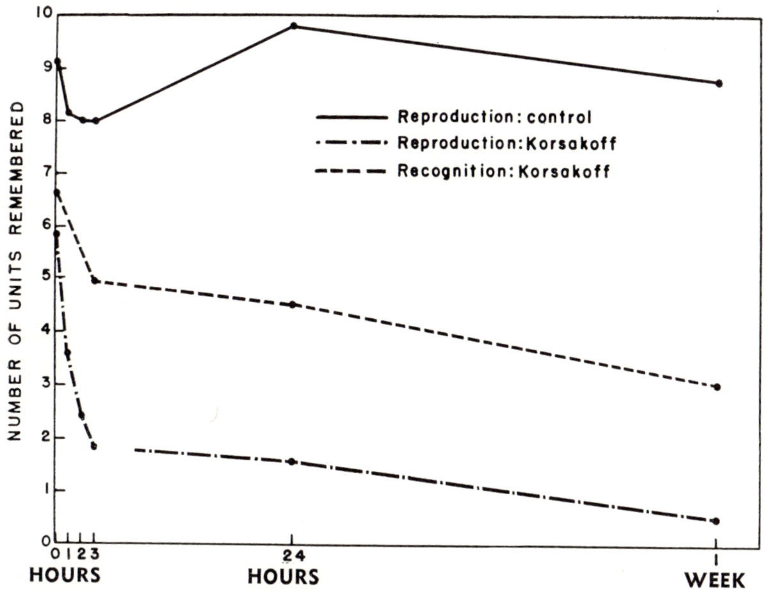


Fig. 23. "Cowboy" story: forgetting curves.

sample—two of its members scoring zero; a day later 5 patients recalled nothing of the text. At the end of the week only 3 of the 10 patients remembered anything about the story.

The control group dropped from 9.12 on immediate reproduction to 8.12 after the first hour, then to 8.00 after the second, and remained at this level after the third. After 24 hours their mean score rose to 9.75, and still reached 8.75 after a week. This paradoxical gain after a day's lapse is an example of *reminiscence* (Ballard, 1913), and also accounted in part for their slow rate of forgetting in the first 2 hours. In contrast to 25 instances of *reminiscence* in the control group, the total for the Korsakoff patients amounted to four.

Tests by recognition confirmed the findings made by reproduction, i.e., that in the Korsakoff syndrome the rate of forgetting is rapid in the first few hours and then tapers off. On immediate testing the patients' recognition score was 6.60; it dropped to 4.88 in 3 hours, and only a little further to 4.60 after a day. After a week, however, it was down to 3.10 which is not much better than the chance level of 2.50. The decrement over the first 24 hours ($t=3.04$) and again over the following 6 days ($t=3.00$) was statistically significant in the subgroup available for testing on every occasion.

*Reproduction of Text with Disturbing Content.* Betlheim and Hartmann's story, which combines incest and rape within its lexically narrow compass, was included in the research to replicate, if possible, their finding that in the Korsakoff syndrome sexually disturbing content tends to be distorted according to definite rules of symbolic transformation. It and control text C were considerably shorter and more unitary in content than the other prose passages. Although in number of words these texts exceeded the limits of accurate reproduction by Korsakoff patients, the content of either could be compressed within those limits. In fact 1 Korsakoff patient reported all five units of text B, another those of text C on first testing. The mean score of the group was 2.71 alike for B and C in immediate reproduction, and both were forgotten at about the same rate. Reproduction scores on subsequent testing were 2.00, 1.57, and 1.00 for B, 1.86, 1.43, and 1.07 for C. Prompting in several instances helped to recover some detail omitted in the spontaneous report, particularly in delayed recall. These are some examples: "When did it happen?"—"When the mother left the house"; "Who did it?"—"The father" in place of "he," "the daughter" instead of "she." Two instances of reminiscence occurred. After 5 minutes every subject remembered the gist of the stories; one completely forgot text B after 15 minutes, as did 4 others after 45 minutes; another patient could recall nothing of text C after 15 minutes, and still another could recall nothing after 45 minutes.

*Padding with Descriptive Details.* Judging by the ratio of units reproduced to the number of divisions in a passage, the Korsakoff patients recalled on immediate testing most of stories B and C. This outcome can be attributed to several properties of these texts; they were the shortest, had the fewest units to remember or forget even relative to their length, and contained no description or incident to detract attention from the principal action. Wechsler's (1945) test stories, although packed with information, were nevertheless remembered about as well as the cowboy story. Their mean reproduction scores, 7.31 (SD 2.60) and 4.50 (SD 2.28) represent 30 and 20 percent of the units, compared with 24 percent of the cowboy story and 54 percent of texts C and D on immediate reproduction.

The division of texts into items of content is, to some extext, an arbitrary matter and, even though Levitt (1956) has shown that the method employed does not affect the relative position of subjects, it is quite likely to favor or penalize one of the two principal styles in memorizing. Wechsler and Franz favored recall that, at the price of omission and condensation, retains some items of the original intact. Gomulicki (1956), modifying somewhat an older dichotomy proposed by Binet and Henri (1894), called the alternate type "changers," i.e., those who reconstruct the text around its theme rather than reproduce it in the original words. Both styles offer a solution when the material to be retained exceeds the retention capacity, although in normal memory and over longer terms the "changer's" style is likely to prevail. By analogy, the same trend might be expected to gain ascendance amidst the rapid decay of impressions in the Korsakoff syndrome, though Cameron (1943) held the opposite view when he suggested that amnesic patients remember stories better than other types of material because each detail serves as a cue for the next.

One purpose of our experiments with texts D and E was to examine the memory of Korsakoff patients for minor details in a narrative passage, and the effect of these details on their retention of the principal content. Being interleaved with the latter, such details could exert an interference effect, but this might be offset by their function in providing cues. Whatever the balance of interference and cue effects may be, incidental details lengthen the text; consequently more time elapses between the first major items of information and immediate reproduction, more words must be rehearsed before the essential elements are selected and structured. In view of these considerations it seemed quite likely that amnesic patients might reproduce more of a story thoroughly plucked of its unimportant details than of the same story when it contained them all.

Our experiment did not support this hypothesis. Texts D and E were both presented in a long and a short version, the former including seven additional items of little significance for the incident reported. Tested by immediate reproduction the Korsakoff patients recalled 4.1 units of both versions of the mailman story, 5.2 of the full and 4.8 units of the abridged report about the celebration in India. In the total record of 17 patients, the seven additional items accounted for a score of only one in text E, and for seven in D. Unimportant items were evidently neither remembered, nor did they noticeably interfere with the recall of the central theme. This finding agrees, in reverse, with Paul's observation that good memorizers in general also tend to retain more imagery.

Given the situation that the amount to be learned exceeds the subject's capacity, any descriptive detail would be expected to interfere with retention of the principal features of the narrative. With our amnesic patients this effect could barely be discerned. Presented with the longer and shorter variants of the mailman story, 15 and 16 of the group recalled its gist, i.e., that somebody wished to borrow money, 17 and 16 that it was a woman, 15 and 13 that a mailman was involved in the incident. The comical conclusion to the report of Nehru's birthday celebration made a mark on 15 patients with both versions of the account; 14 and 11 remembered that the central figure was a prime minister, 11 and 12 that doves were flying overhead; but only a few recalled the country or occasion of the event, who participated, or even that there was a parade or celebration of some sort. The relative unfamiliarity of the setting in this report did not reduce the amount recalled, probably because it was ignored.

*Rate of Acquisition.* A second hypothesis, tested by immediate and delayed reproduction of texts D and E, was that amnesic patients perform so poorly in tests of memorizing narrative material because they are not given adequate opportunities to learn it in the first place. No matter how carefully and articulately a text is being read, if the listener's attention strays he will miss some items of information, and these will be omitted from his immediate as well as delayed reproductions, or may be replaced by more or less successful reconstructions. If a text is presented to him several times in succession, the likelihood of his missing the same items repeatedly is slight; repetition, moreover, might strengthen the process of acquisition. Experiments presenting the texts, alternately once and six times in succession, failed to support the hypothesis.

**Table 37**

IMMEDIATE AND DELAYED RECALL OF 16 UNITS OF TEXT *III*

| | *Korsakoff (N=16)* | | *Control (N=16)* | |
|---|---|---|---|---|
| | *Immediate recall* | *Recall after 1 hour* | *Immediate recall* | *Recall after 1 hour* |
| One reading | 3.44 | 1.25 | 8.00 | 7.48 |
| Six readings | 4.44 | 2.25 | 8.78 | 7.22 |

As shown in Table 37, both groups reported more items after repeated than after a single hearing of the story, on immediate and delayed tests alike. Although the gain from repetition in immediate recall appeared to be larger for the Korsakoff patients, it failed to reach statistical significance ($t=1.55$), while the smaller mean difference shown by the control subjects exceeded the level of chance probability ($t=2.91$). The differential effect of single versus repeated presentation on reproduction after the lapse of an hour was in the same direction for the Korsakoff patients, but still not significant ($t=1.59$); for the control group it was reversed. The latter lost relatively little information in that time, while the amnesic patients showed the familiar steep rate of forgetting. In this experiment the Korsakoff group performed considerably less well than in the earlier test with the same material; the difference is almost fully accounted for by the replacement of three original members by others with a more severe memory disturbance. Successive presentation did not noticeably alter the content of the reproductions, except that 3 of 8 Korsakoff patients recalled the first sentence of the mailman story which does not form part of the narrative, while none of the other 8 did after a single reading. One member of the former group, in fact, recalled nothing but that general statement, on first and delayed testing alike.

## The Manner of Distortion

Unable to reproduce a story he has just heard, and very likely aware of his inability, the Korsakoff patient faces a situation not unlike that in the interview focused on his personal experiences. The omissions, distortions, embellishments, and elaborations introduced by amnesic patients into their reproductions of the experimental texts, and any progressive trend in these, are of interest in regard to confabulation.

Reproductions of Wechsler's stories by our patients in the early phase of the Wernicke-Korsakoff syndrome contained numerous examples of importation, rational condensation as well as quaint combinations of isolated details, perserveration, and an occasional instance of total incomprehension. In the protocols of the chronic amnesic patients, these features could not be found at all, or only rarely. Errors in names and numbers were not uncommon, condensation and elaboration also occurred, but omission was the typical cause of faulty recall.

In an attempt to investigate the changes our five texts underwent in subsequent reproduction, these have been classified under five headings, in addition to mere impoverishment of content. (a) *Levelling,* a transformation by loosening, toning down, generalization. (b) *Error* in fact. (c) *Elaboration:* a gratuitous embellishment of the original description or account. (d) *Comment* expressing the narrator's views on the incidents reported, including rationalization. (e) *Fabrication,* the insertion of an extraneous incident, that may be recognizably an importation from another context, and can indeed amount to the substitution of a self-contained and different narrative for the original.

*"Cowboy" Story.* Since most subjects, and especially the

Korsakoff patients, remembered best the first few items, much of the levelling occurred at the beginning of the story, e.g., by reporting that the cowboy or just "a man" went "to town," "to California," or "out west." The two groups differed little in levelling or in errors, for which between them they listed a fair sample of the southwestern states in lieu of Arizona. The opening words of a control subject, "A sailor from Wisconsin . . ." nicely matched those of a Korsakoff patient who began his story with "A sailor from Illinois . . ."

Examples of elaboration from the records of the control group are: "A cowboy left his ranch . . ."; ". . . the dog barked at him when he came out of the store"; ". . . the dog ran to him and licked him"; ". . . the dog yelped at him." Examples from those of the Korsakoff group included: "Nobody knew him he was so dressed up, even his neighbors did not recognize him . . ."; ". . . the man was very poorly dressed, so he bought . . ."; ". . . purchased new clothes, and then bought some food."

A glaring improbability of the cowboy story offered a very reasonable challenge for comment. Dogs are not at all likely to rely on visual recognition of their masters, and the fact that the story hinged on such an improbable contingency prompted some members of both groups to remark on it, either questioning the verisimilitude of the incident, or explaining it on the grounds that the new clothes had not yet absorbed the master's scent. One member of either group proposed this rather feeble explanation.

In fabrication, the two groups differed quite markedly. The control subjects provided a single example, but much variety could be found in the protocols of the Korsakoff patients. One instance led to a jesting comment: "The gentleman went to town to get himself some things and came back with a suit he had not intended to buy. At least he got himself a nice birthday present." A more imaginative example told about "A man from Texas went on a mission to visit some boys' schools. He took his dog with him, bought some new clothes, and then continued on his mission."

An interesting case of fabrication also exemplified the perseveration of an imported theme across experiments. A patient who had reproduced the barest skeleton of the story at the end of the first hour, after the second introduced a "fence" into her report, an hour later she appeared to have forgotten the cowboy altogether and produced this: "When the dog went near the fence someone tapped him on the shoulder—had to prevent him from going near the fence. He was afraid he might get hurt." The same concern emerged earlier in the testing session, when this patient was shown a picture of children leaving Sunday school and a line of cars at the edge of the road. The picture shows no fence, nor is there any likelihood of a child thoughtlessly rushing into the road, where the close line of stationary cars forms a solid barrier. Nevertheless, the patient introduced a nonexistent fence into the scene which had to be there to guard the children from the dangers of the traffic. As far as could be ascertained, she had had no personal experience to account for this theme, and her own children were certainly past school age at the time she was first hospitalized.

The most remarkable case of perseverative fabrication started with this recital on immediate testing: "A farmer went to the market with cows to sell, and to buy some finery for his wife. He sold the cows, shopped for the wife, built a new barn, bought cows. I forget the rest." The following day the same patient recalled what she had heard 24 hours earlier in these words: "Farmer story—went to market, did a lot of shopping, bought cows and some finery for his wife. Bought some paint for his barn which he was going to paint, to get ready for the spring." This much is not particularly striking, the patient evidently confused the text she was given to remember with some other story and slightly elaborated it after 24 hours. Ten months later she had the original story read to her again, and on immediate testing reproduced it with considerable embellishment, much omission, and a few errors, but it was still about a cowboy and his dog. After an hour, it became a story about a farmer who went to the market and left his dog behind, and was further elaborated by the time 2 hours had elapsed: "Farmer went to the market. Left his dog at home. Did not know he would be so long, he stayed in the market till the sun went down. When he went home the dog ran up to him barking, showing he was happy." Admittedly, this time a core of the original story carried through the reproductions, in a much distorted form; but without any detectable reason, again it set off the theme of the farmer going to the market. Nor was it a unique occurrence with this same patient who misidentified a tachistoscopically presented figure in the same manner on two occasions more than a year apart.

Another patient also twice distorted the cowboy story in much the same fashion on immediate testings, 10 months apart. Her reproductions were these: (a) "About a man and a dog; he took the dog for a walk, the dog ran off. The man kept calling, the dog ran off, and so the man would have to keep on calling." (b) "Fellow went out with the dogs, called them and whistled to them, but they would not come back, because he was dressed in different clothes. Dogs go by scent." In this instance again the second attempt retained more of the original text, but the same extraneous content crept into it as on the first occasion. These full quotations exemplify the most thoroughgoing distortion of the original story, and they also provide as good an instance of progressive embellishment as any of our records. Their main interest, however, is not so much in the extent to which they altered the original story, as in suggesting that a standard input of information can undergo much the same distortion in coding on repeated occasions, with the intervention of no other ascertainable agency than the patient's brain damage.

Betlheim and Hartmann, of course, have a psychological explanation for this phenomenon (see p. 85), although their own reference system would hardly regard a farmer as a stable symbol for a cowboy, a market for a clothing store, a skipping dog for a surly dog. Nonetheless, it is quite possible that the same mechanism that produces instances of symbolic reproduction also mediates these other distortions that recurred with such striking uniformity over long intervals of time.

*"Rape" Story.* Our Korsakoff patients furnished no evidence in support of Betlheim and Hartmann's thesis. They recalled

text B as accurately as the control text C, and on immediate testing every one of them reproduced the word "raped" and mentioned "father" and "daughter" as the parties involved. This was also true of the reproductions after 5 minutes, although 1 patient phrased it this way: "The father entered the room where his daughter lay and attacked her." However, when the experimenter remarked that attack was not quite the right word, the patient reproduced the original phrasing. There were very few instances of elaboration or distortion in the reproductions of either text B or C. One patient referred to a "little girl" in her first reproduction of the latter, though not in subsequent trials; another reported after 15 minutes that "some gentleman seduced his secretary—his daughter," and reverted to "man raped his daughter" on the last test. The only instances suggestive of symbolization were these: "When the mother left the home, the father threw his daughter on the bed, and she had a child by him," and "When the mother left home, father climbed the stairs and raped his own child." The former, however, is probably more a case of deliberate euphemism, and the latter hardly qualifies as symbolization, since the act which is supposed to be symbolized was named in full. The "rape" story visibly upset 2 or 3 women patients and seemed to embarrass a few others, but not to such an extent as to prevent their repeating it. Several of them, however, appended some censorious or exculpatory comments to their report, e.g., "ought to be shot" or "took advantage of her, did not know better." One comment of this kind also followed a report of the control story, a patient remarking on the girl's taking the cookies, "that was larceny."

*"Mailman" Story.* It was inevitable that the human interest of a person, whose predicament was so intuitively meaningful to many of our patients, should eclipse the generalization with which the editor prefaced the specific situation. Only a few subjects reproduced the opening sentence on immediate testing or in delayed recall. One remembered nothing else of the story but the overgeneralized moral: "Mailmen are often asked where to borrow money." The story provided some clear examples of levelling, e.g., the substitution of mere "man" or

"stranger" for the mailman, or the opinion that borrowing money without the husband's knowledge "wouldn't do," "couldn't be done." Crude errors of facts were rare; occasionally the episode was slightly misplaced, to Inman Square or Central Square, or the woman was reported to be from Dorchester or just South Boston—perhaps, exemplifying an attempt to translate the narrator herself into the story.

Some elaborations also served the purpose of providing the subject with a role in the action. In fact, they were comments, though spoken through the mouth of the mailman, advising the woman against borrowing without letting her husband know—"because it would get her into trouble," "it is bad policy," "husband would be awfully mad," "people who borrow without permission easily get into trouble," or suggesting "why not go to husband?" Some of the reasoning was of the *non sequitur* type, e.g., the counsel against proceeding in the manner proposed—as always, given in the mailman's reply—"because the husband would see the mail and know she borrowed it," or the mailman "didn't know because the husband would find out." A few patients radically misinterpreted the intention and words of the mailman's reply, believing he "thought it was a good idea," or suggested to the woman that "she should go and ask someone else." One patient was under the impression that the woman asked the mailman to tell her where her husband could borrow some money. These were about the most serious distortions of the original text, for the story did not give rise to any fabrication.

*"India" Story.* An account as exotic and colorful as this was fated to suffer drastic levelling. "A group went to India to see the prime minister. They had birds there." That was all a patient remembered about the carefully staged peace ceremony; and even less solemn was the report that "The prime minister took a walk with the kids." A few reduced the prime minister to a mere "leader" or "he." In one instance the parading schoolchildren were represented as "the populace," and "doves turned up" quite simply.

Errors occurred in greater abundance than in the parallel story, as would be expected in a setting so much further removed from the patients as is India than Inman Street. Some resulted from condensation, e.g., "minister responsible for children," or "a parade to celebrate peace," others from a precision unwarranted by the information given, as the mention of "5000 children," or from displacing the symbolic gesture to "the spectators who released doves."

Elaborations emerged with greatest facility in descriptions of the prime minister's part in the ceremony which, according to the original text, consisted of reviewing the parade, releasing a number of doves, and taking the salute. Several patients thought that he was delivering a speech, one of them making the specious though trivial remark that "he addressed them in his native tongue." Others believed he had told the children that "the doves were the symbols of peace," that "the prime minister was preaching," or that "he gave prayers over the children." The doves were reported to have "circled around" or "have gone out to spread peace. "In contrast, a somewhat homely elaboration started with the report of "a man and his wife were celebrating his 68th birthday."

One comment concerned the dove's felicitous choice of a landing stage: ". . . it lit on his head—to show appreciation, I suppose." Another contained some fabrication: "The assembly, especially the children, cheered. The prime minister thought they were cheering him, they were actually cheering the dove." Some examples of elaboration also bordered on fabrication, e.g., ". . . and the children watched the dove on the prime minister's head, until it flew away." More typical instances of fabrication, within a meager narrative span, were these two examples. "Maharajah of India came on a visit and brought some doves with him, one of which landed on the prime minister's head, thereby endowing peace on the world." "Prime minister had 68 doves to celebrate his birthday. When he went to count the doves, one was missing, as it was perched on his head."

*Serial Reproduction.* Since the characteristic defect of the Korsakoff patients' reproductions is the extent of the gaps, it is of interest to examine their distortions in relation to missing content. An experiment in serial reproduction, with seven chains of 3 intelligent and neurologically sound subjects, served the purpose of illustrating the manner of distortion that occurs as a result of gaps and consequent ambiguities. Because distortions tend to be cumulative, examples of only the final report in each chain will be listed.

In the mailman story, they mentioned a "William Connolly"; a woman who is "excited" and asks the postman to "help her steal some money"; "the woman's husband being sick"; "a young girl, married who lived in Inman Street"; and a "young blond 'dish' who walked up to a postman." They also included such reasoning as: "She somehow thought the postman could arrange it for her," and, as final comment, "The woman told him that he was right, she hadn't thought of that." This was an example of distortion: "A very anxious woman walked along a street in North Cambridge. She finally spotted a policeman by the name of Callahan. She proceeded to tell him her troubles and then felt much better."

The India story produced such exact data as "2000 pigeons," "64 white doves," and as many as "30,000 school children who were excused from classes to attend." The central figure appears as "a maharajah" as he did for one of the Korsakoff patients, or "the prime minister of Islam," the occasion a "large party for children," or a celebration which it is "customary for the prime minister of India to give"; "the people honor Nehru . . . with fireworks," who "makes a speech and is disturbed" by the final episode. One version retained no more than "A great crowd gathered in India. They all began to cheer. A flock of birds swooped down and then up again. This was a sign of good luck." In one instance there is the typical comment "must have looked amusing," in another an exact parallel of the Korsakoff group's most characteristic example of fabrication: "In honor of this occasion he released a flock of doves, 44 in number; 43 turned up, the 44th he couldn't find, for it was perched on his head." The Korsakoff patients, on the other hand, produced nothing to match this ending of the story: "During the course of the celebration one or more doves were released, and one of them laid an egg which hit Nehru on the head."

It seems unnecessary to examine in detail similarities and divergences between these distortions in serial reproduction and those found in the immediate recall of amnesic patients. Some parallels between omissions, textual alterations, and fabrications are evident. The serially reproduced stories, however, were more coherent and richer in words or items of information, in spite of their gradual shrinkage along the chain.

## Summary

In memorizing narrative texts, our Korsakoff patients showed the same defects as in other experiments of retention and learning. They are severely impaired in their capacity to absorb information in the first instance, and of that which they have taken in they forget more and at a faster rate than do control subjects. They retain very little, many of them retain nothing, after a period that is too short to show any decrement in normal remembering; their forgetting involves a sheer loss of information, not just a distortion of the content. They learn or retain emotionally loaded reports no better than neutral accounts, as might be expected on the strength of Clark's (1940) study with normal subjects.

The patients' poor retention of connected verbal material cannot be explained by their inability to grasp its content. They tend to reproduce a story in its barest outlines, retaining its gist rather than odd phrases, although the first few items are better remembered than the remainder. Of narratives crammed with incidents they remember only a few snatches, not enough to convey the principal theme; but if this is reasonably prominent, descriptive details do not interfere with its recall, and are virtually ignored. There is a marked propensity to shed all peripheral data, so that even the shortest texts (B and C), with a unitary theme and a bare modicum of descriptive frill, attenuated within 15 minutes or at most 45 minutes into such skeleton statements as "he raped her" or "she ate the cookies." The characteristic feature of the amnesic patients' reproduction of stories is reduction; their phrasing is starker, the content becomes sparser as well as shorter in extent.

In addition, amidst the ambiguity and indirection that follow from gaps in continuity, certain more or less predictable modifications of the text also occur in reproduction. Omission and levelling; the substitution of erroneous data; elaboration to make a tale more plausible, more dramatic, more rounded; rationalizations and comments; the importation of extraneous incidents are familiar features of normal remembering (Bartlett, 1932; Allport and Postman, 1947; Talland, 1956; Paul, 1959). Normally, in order to demonstrate these trends, ambiguity and breeches in coherence must be created by artificial means. With amnesic patients the sources of omission and distortion occur spontaneously—quite regularly, under objectively less severe strain, over very short intervals, and within the reference range of their personal experiences as well as of external events. It may be convenient to call this confabulation, but it should be borne in mind that these examples of misconstruction, like every attempt at recall, represent the one fundamental principle of remembering: a reconstructive effort after meaning.

*PART FIVE*

# THEORETICAL

*Chapter 10*

# MEMORY DISTURBANCE

A survey of the literature on the amnesic syndrome shows that the theoretical analysis of its psychopathology has proceeded at three levels. One approach is the neuropathological with its concomitant psychological models. Its point of departure is the locus of the lesion in the brain, from which it proceeds to examine the behavioral and experimental functions presumed to be associated with the damaged site or system. A second line of attack starts with psychological function, without reference to neuropathology. In some instances this approach involves and even hinges upon concepts that defy operational definition; more often their translation into testable operations has been neglected. A third order of contributions to the literature consists of observations of behavior, both clinical and experimental, and some attempt, more or less systematic, to order them within a conceptual frame of reference. The research outlined in the preceding section followed the third course, though undoubtedly certain theoretical biases determined both the design of the experiments and their interpretation. In the light of the findings presented, some controversial issues about the amnesic syndrome will be reconsidered, and a theory of its psychopathology will be outlined.

Although the salient defects in the Korsakoff syndrome are the patient's failure to learn new information and to recall much of that which he could remember before his illness, it has been evident to most observers that to call it simply a memory disturbance is an unsatisfactory description. The word unsatisfactory has been advisedly chosen in preference to the word incorrect, because memory as a function is not defined closely enough to allow for its absolute rejection. If the term comprises reproduction and recognition as well as registration, the context of recall as well as its content, a large component of the amnesic patients' disability can be ascribed to the memory disturbance. It still does not explain their poverty of initiative and affect, nor their inability to process certain types of complex perceptual information or motor response.

It seems even more misleading to say that the amnesic syndrome does not involve a memory disturbance, as some writers have been tempted to do. Of course, it is possible so to define memory as to leave it intact in all but the most deteriorated Korsakoff patient, but that would serve no good purpose beyond drawing attention to two important points of view. One is that a disease affects the patient and not just an autonomous function within the organism. This is a truism that it may be well to stress in the clinic but one that should not stand in the way of endeavors to discover functional mechanisms of the organism. The psychological derangement of the amnesic syndrome is not as predictable as is that which follows a specific lesion in the visual cortex, but neither is it entirely contingent on those innate and acquired dispositions that constitute the patient's personality, or on situational influences. If it were, we should hardly have found sufficient uniformity in our Korsakoff group to differentiate their performance from the control group on so many tests. There was no indication whatever that their personalities all differed in some systematic manner from the alcoholic control subjects or, for that matter, from those Korsakoff patients who were too demented to be studied—except in so far as their disease affects personality.

The second point of view to which a denial of the memory disturbances draws attention is the continuity and indivisibility of the various mental processes. Bartlett (1932) has shown that the processes involved in remembering are common also to other cognitive functions and interdependent with the affective. He also demonstrated that remembering—whether accurate or not—is an active accomplishment and, therefore, defective memory cannot be regarded simply as a loss of some property that was there once but is no longer. Against this background, the debate as to whether the amnesic syndrome consists of or involves a memory disorder has lost much of its erstwhile heat. The other traditional controversy concerns the processes in memory function that are and are not affected in the amnesic syndrome. It seems appropriate to restate the position on which the opposing arguments were based, even though it appears unlikely that the brain lesion characteristic of this disease should damage only one of several related processes and leave the others intact.

## The Processes of Memory Function

Efficient remembering involves at least three distinguishable operations or mechanisms: registration,[1] retention, and recall (or recognition). Any one of these can be impaired, although performance of the sequentially later process could hardly be faultless if an earlier one has been damaged. One difficulty in applying this general model arises from the fact that the intermediate stage is functionally so very different from the first and last. Registration and recall, whether they be unitary and clearly delineated processes or not, constitute a response of the organism to a situation. Very probably, these behavioral responses each correspond to a continuous neu-

---

[1]Registration is synonymous with acquisition, as long as it is understood that neither need involve reiterated trials or a cumulative process extended over time. Both terms are preferable to learning which often includes repeated or delayed performance. The term may also be interchangeable with fixation (e.g., Dugas, 1917), though Bernard (see p. 83) distinguished the two processes.

The word "registration" is not included in Warren's (1934) Dictionary, nor in Hilgard and Marquis's (1940) glossary, nor in the index of such standard American texts on learning as McGeoch and Irion (1952), Hilgard (1956), Deese (1958), and texts on experimental psychology such as Underwood (1949), Osgood (1953), and Woodworth and Schlosberg (1954). Why use it then? Because so much of the theoretical writing on the amnesic syndrome pivoted on the concept of *Merkfähigkeit* which Wernicke (1900) had introduced to distinguish a function from attention (*Aufmerksamkeit*). It refers to an ability to acquire memories, to put information into storage. It does appear as if an ability of this description might be affected in Korsakoff patients; also it is a function that can be tested in performance.

rophysiological process that runs its course and could leave some more or less lasting effect behind. Retention may be regarded as the lasting effect of registration. It is not likely to be an ongoing process but rather a structural alteration, since it is highly resistant to external disturbance though not to some processes originating within the organism itself (Bremer, 1953; Sperry, 1959).

A disease can, of course, just as well interfere with the integrity of structures as with the efficiency of mechanisms in the neuropsychological system. Since, however, neither is accessible to inspection except indirectly through the evidence of behavior, it is necessary to consider what functions can be so probed. Tests of behavior can determine the availability of a certain information or skill by reproduction in words or other performance, or by some token of recognition. A first evidence of such an accomplishment is known as the acquisition of a skill, or the registration of information. Repeated or delayed accomplishment by recall or recognition indicates retention: its presence, extent, and variability on successive occasions. Usually the change is one of gradual decline, i.e., forgetting. This offers an operationally practicable distinction between registration on the one hand and retention on the other. The operations involved in testing the two, however, are the same; consequently direct tests can only distinguish capacity to register and to recall (or recognize). Distinctions between recall and registration—even though, as Penfield (1954) holds, they involve two separate mechanisms—or between recall and retention rest on inference.

When recall is successful, by implication registration was efficient and—if some time has elapsed—retention too has been intact. When recall fails or is only partly accurate, there is no immediate clue for deciding whether the defect has occurred in that process, or previously in registration, or in retention. If immediate recall showed no fault but delayed testing does, by definition it did not occur in registration. If delayed recall fails but not recognition, if relearning is achieved more rapidly than original learning, the inference is made that there was some retention. Some retention, however, need not be the same as retention adequate for recall; success in recognition or saving in relearning does not prove that recall failed in spite of intact retention. It does happen, though, quite commonly and not only with amnesic patients, that some memory inaccessible on one occasion becomes available subsequently, often in a different context. Recall can fail even though enough information has been retained for its efficient function; the source of the failure must therefore be sought in some interfering effect of the momentary situation. A distinction between efficient recall and efficient registration or retention is indeed meaningful but cannot be tested with amnesic patients who forget so diffusely, instantly, and consistently.

## Registration

The historical controversy between writers who attributed the amnesic syndrome either to impaired registration or to defective retention and recall has gained renewed significance from current neuropsychological theory, and particularly in the context of dual trace models such as Hebb's (1949) that differentiate the mechanisms engaged in the establishment from those involved in the retention of memories, skills, or other information. In neurophysiological terms, registration may correspond to the activity cycle of a reverberating circuit as described by Lorente de Nó (1938) and proposed as a paradigm of conditioning by Hilgard and Marquis (1940). Although the model is no longer regarded as satisfactory for enduring traces of learning, it is compatible with the temporal range of immediate memory, and the operational test of registration is immediate recall or recognition. It is a process that is probably always subject to some fading and interference, and especially to interference by those intentional, selective, and classificatory operations that distinguish registration from the aftereffects of perception. Immediate recall can also serve as a test of the availability of after-images or echo sounds, if conditions favor such extensions of the perceptual process. Impressions carried over in this manner, i.e., without intent of retention, and messages held by some similar mechanism because they defy ordering into the categories of memory, tend to fade rapidly. The steep forgetting curves of Korsakoff patients suggest by analogy that their difficulties in remembering may be determined by a defect in registration.

If registration extends beyond perception, is it a process that should be equated with the fixation of memory traces? Bernard answered in the negative, because he regarded fixation as an undirected process outside any cognitive context. By implication, the course and direction of fixation is determined by a prior process, i.e., by registration. Both registration and fixation, or the consolidation of traces, are hypothetical constructs, supported by evidence from different types of experiments, and viewed as progressing over somewhat different temporal spans. Behavioral observations prompted the first theories that it takes some time for memories to become established: by the perseveration of neuronal processes activated in perception (Müller and Pilzecker, 1900), or as a "secondary function" of the neural event that has its correlate in consciousness (Gross, 1902). Sherrington's (1906) discovery of the after-discharge offered a convenient physiological analogue for these theories of learning (DeCamp, 1915). A process of consolidation extended in time seems to be compatible with the findings of neurophysiological experiments, and more so if viewed as limited in duration than as the unending process of neuronal stabilization proposed by Russell and Nathan (1946).

Psychological experiments, however, have failed to confirm certain implications of the consolidation hypothesis, in that retention is not disrupted more by interference that occurs while the traces are supposed to consolidate than at a later time (e.g., Postman and Alper, 1946). Evidence in support of the theory has come chiefly from studies in electric shock therapy (Zubin, 1948), traumatic amnesias (Burnham, 1904; Russell, 1948), and also from ablation studies with animals (e.g., Boycott and Young, 1955). On the strength of animal experiments, Stellar (1957) concluded that it may take about an hour before the memory process ceases to be vulnerable to interference by electric shock. Stellar's fixation process may account for the memory loss Burnham called retroactive amnesia, loss of memory for the events immediately preceding a trauma, as distinct from the more extensive retrograde amnesia characteristic of Korsakoff patients. A derangement of this fixation process could hardly explain the extremely rapid memory loss of Korsakoff patients, since this happens before the initially labile traces might become stabilized.

While registration should be distinguished from the more protracted process of consolidation, it is also distinct from perception. Empirically, the latter two processes can be separated (Fraisse and Florès, 1956), and theoretically I have proposed a distinction in terms of intent (see p. 132). Accordingly, perception accomplished with an intent to retain the information develops into registration. This transition may be viewed as one of consolidation, though it is not necessarily further extended in time than is perception. The interdependence between the two processes is close and unidirectional; registration cannot be successful unless perception has been, and perceptual defects carry over into registration. Others may arise subsequently, e.g., in several experiments our Korsakoff patients failed in immediate tests of memory, in spite of their capacity to make accurate perceptual discriminations. The most cogent example was furnished by the experiment in successive recognition of the winged figure, in which every patient but one successfully matched the model displayed, yet almost half their number selected a different pattern in a recognition test after a moment's delay. The steep increase of errors in Benton's visual design test between copying and memory after 10 seconds is another example in point, and so are several experiments in verbal reproduction. Some of the latter also showed that defects in immediate recall could not be attributed to an insufficient opportunity to perceive the information, since repeated presentation did not improve performance.

While most tests of immediate recall and some of immediate recognition showed the Korsakoff patients to be, more or less, impaired in the process of registration, in no instance did they all fail completely. Their normal digit span, forward and in reverse, formed a notable exception to their short-term memory disorder; they could also reproduce verbatim sentences of ten or twelve words. If, however, their task was to repeat the last five of a string of digits of indefinite length, or to report a few units of content in a short prose passage, their performance fell far below the control norm.

The impairment manifested in tests of registration is not restricted to this process; it affects the patients' perceptual function as well. Amnesic patients were found to be defective in perceptual tests that required the temporary storage of some information while additional information was added to it. The same happens in memorizing a text or the last few digits in a string. Both tasks require continuous integration of items; the second moreover demands that some information be continuously discarded. It is quite likely that the short-term storage mechanism is impaired in the Korsakoff syndrome. Following Miller's (1956) analysis of this mechanism, the defect could be either in a narrower storage capacity or in a diminished efficiency in coding. Tests of the memory span argue against the former explanation; very likely amnesic patients do not have available the devices by which information in excess of storage capacity can be recoded into shorter lists of items that are within that capacity, a probable and important mechanism[2] in both short-and long-term remembering, as Oldfield (1954) has demonstrated schematically.

Alternatively, it is not the availability of the codes that distinguishes amnesic patients from normal persons but their lack of flexibility, their inability to see the same information in more than one pattern. This deficiency is a component of the concrete attitude Goldstein (1942) observed in brain-injured patients, and was the conclusion to which several of my own experiments with Korsakoff patients have pointed. Their inability to utilize more than one perceptual set at a time furnished the most direct evidence for the argument.

---

[2]For example, the number sequence 101001001101001100 can be remembered quite easily by recoding into CAACAB with this code: 001 = A, 100 = B, 101 = C.

The virtual absence of any incidental learning, the patients' failures with such construction tasks as Arthur's stencil test, their sluggishness in changing hypotheses in tests of concept formation can all be traced to the same underlying disturbance. The difficulty posed to amnesic patients by the requirement to transpose information from one sensory modality to another may also be a problem in recoding. Perhaps the most direct examples of faulty coding were those reproductions of stories and descriptions of pictures in which the same extraneous content re-emerged even after long intervals.

## Attention

The amnesic patients' impairment in perception and registration could be attributed to derangements other than deficient coding of information. Insufficient attention has been advanced as an explanation. Attention refers to several directional properties of behavior or experience. In one sense (cf. Broadbent, 1958), attention is equated with or closely related to the perceptual scanning, filtering, and storage mechanisms that determine the content and extent of immediate memory. This concerns the span and the capacity to refocus attention, both of which are abnormally limited in Korsakoff patients. Another aspect of attention, sometimes qualified as primary, is the startle reaction which may indeed be slowed down in amnesic patients, but that would hardly exercise a direct influence on their memory function. In contrast to this type of attention, aroused without or contrary to expectation, is attention in the sense of directedness, maintenance of a set, anticipation of the next moment. Our experiments have shown that in this aspect of attention Korsakoff patients are signally deficient, that their impairment restricts their efficiency in perception and inevitably also in registration.

If attention is judged by the capacity to stick to a task and to resist distraction, Korsakoff patients could attend to repetitive jobs as well as anybody, even over the long empty intervals in the vigilance situation. On the other hand, if attention involved continuous shifts in focus, e.g., when following the narrative of a story, they quickly lost its thread and were not apt to pick it up again. They could listen to and follow instructions, and proved to be exceptionally impervious to distraction by noise or unscheduled incidents in their surrounding. Controlled attempts to protect them from distraction, e.g., blindfolding during auditory or tactual tests, failed to improve their performance, presumably because they were immune to visual distraction even without such aid. In tests of divided attention, Korsakoff patients performed poorly because those tasks demand rapid shifts in orientation, the maintenance of multiple sets.

Most of our experiments in the retention of connected verbal material employed auditory presentation, because empirically this proved the most favorable method for Korsakoff patients, except for very short tests. An interesting conflict between the influences of distraction and transposition occurred in an experiment that tested immediate and delayed recall of ten-word sentences, some read by, others read to the subject. In immediate recall the Korsakoff group's performance was about the same following the two methods of presentation, but after 5 minutes they reproduced more of the sentences they had read themselves. Possibly they had registered more of the sentence in print, but in the first test this advantage was offset by the requirement to transpose the message from the visual to the auditory-vocal mechanism. Once this transposition had been accomplished, however, the advantage in registration manifested itself without hindrance, and this accounted for the difference in recall after a short interval. This explanation, of course, rests on the assumption that the consolidation of memory traces extends in time beyond the test of immediate memory and of such interferences as may exert their effects on registration.

Apart from attention, defective registration could also be attributed to insufficient intention. If intention refers to a general attitude toward the situation, it certainly did not account for the inferior performance of the Korsakoff patients whose cooperation was always adequate or better. Another meaning of intention is ability to program action, to adopt an appropriate orientation toward each subsequent event. In this regard, a general program or task-set was provided for the patients by the experimental instructions and situation; they did not have to decide whether to look or listen for some signal, whether merely to observe and report a message or to remember it for later.

In certain experiments, the Korsakoff patients did depend on their own initiative to search for relevant cues, and in those they notably failed. This search may indeed form part of attention; it is also an instance of those scanning operations that enter into various cognitive processes, into registration and recall as well as perception or judgment. The perceptual defects of Korsakoff patients were attributable to unavailable memory images no more than to faults in the peripheral sensory apparatus. Familiar, immediately fitting templates for sorting the incoming information were readily accessible to the patients. Their troubles began when the obvious template did not quite fit. In view of their inability to sort according to other criteria and their extraordinary difficulties in dealing with meaningless or unfamiliar messages, it seems that the source of their ineffective coding operations is a low rate of search for appropriate categories of classification.

## Retention: Interference or Fading

Registration, as tested by immediate reproduction or recognition, indicates the approximate limits of the information that can be retained. Memory traces probably take longer to stabilize. Whether this is under or over an hour has not been decided; undoubtedly the length of the process varies with person and situation, with the objective and subjective properties of the material. Cameron (1947), in order to avoid the connotation of fixity, prefers the term integration to retention, and believes that repetitions of the same neural events may help to stabilize the process underlying memories by relating them to a wide range of settings of the organism. Ribot (1881) proposed that repetition helped stabilization by preventing the reversal of "dynamic" neuronal connections that occur with new learning. The two views correspond to the interference and fading trace theories of forgetting. Both attribute the consolidation of memories to repeated firing along the same neuronal circuit, whether triggered by sensory stimuli or—as current neurophysiology allows us to assume—by a self-perpetuating program. Adrian (1936) demonstrated that repeated excitation diminishes synaptic resistance, and further evidence that it facilitates activitation along specific neuronal circuits has come from Burns (1958). It should be noted, though, that Burns questions the direct relevance of his findings to the neural process of remembering.

Theoretical arguments against the hypothesis of an exact topographical replication of neuronal discharges have been advanced by Koffka (1935) and by Russell (1948), on the ground that it would blur the original trace. Hypotheses about the part of exact repetition in the process of consolidation are closely tied to assumptions about specific pathways subserving specific memories. Those who are chiefly interested in the acquisition of habits and skills have little use for a brain model of specific pathways; others concerned with man's capacity to remember individual events are more receptive to the construct, even though only as a supplement to the general schemata of memories (Oldfield and Zangwill, 1943; Gomulicki, 1953). Students of the amnesic syndrome cannot help but note the unavailability of specific memories against a background of adequate retention of skills and habits.

The process of stabilization is the active phase of retention, and must either be continuous with perception and registration or be accomplished within the course of the latter. It is unlikely to be a neural activity that goes on indefinitely, though it may be revived from time to time. In retention there is a second phase of indeterminate length, the period that intervenes between registration and recall or recognition. During that phase memories are supposed to persist passively, i.e., not as continuous neurophysiological processes, but rather as structures in the brain. Adrian (1947) and Hebb (1949) hypothesized that these structures consist of plastic changes at the synapses, and Eccles (1953) has furnished empirical evidence for the theory. Biochemical processes have also been proposed as the mechanism of memory storage. Psychologists for a long time have known that retention during this passive phase is not stable, information undergoes both quantitative diminution and certain more or less predictable qualitative changes. The latter are similar in type to distortions that occur in immediate memory, and tend to be progressive in accordance with personal experiences (Bartlett, 1932), new perceptions as well as certain formal properties (Koffka, 1935), inferential substitution (Postman, 1954), or normalizing toward modal values (Bruner, 1957). Distortions arising from any of these tendencies—excepting those of gestalt theory—could as well occur in reproduction or recognition as in retention.

Whether the long-term phase in retention is active or passive is relatively unimportant in studying the amnesic syndrome, quite apart from the doubtful reliability of the operations that would test the distinction. Either way, the loss and distortion of information must occur principally in the early phase. This is not only shown by tests of registration but is even more evident from the patients' comparatively intact retention of much information registered in the more remote past. Their inefficient retention may be attributed to a rapid fading of traces or to their excessive susceptibility to obliteration by subsequent impressions, but either or both must take place before any process of stabilization could be completed.

In psychological theory, decay and interference have been the two major explanatory principles of forgetting, and the latter has all but completely ousted the other. McGeoch and Irion (1952), for example, categorically deny that forgetting can occur as a result of passive decay. Discussing the decay theory, Brown (1958) remarked that it has been unpopular as an explanation of forgetting, except where this was studied over very short periods, as e.g., by Hull (1940). It implies that memories, unless rehearsed or otherwise revived, lapse spontaneously and apart from any interference. In a descriptive sense this theory perfectly fits the amnesic patients; at the explanatory level it is closely tied to the hypothesis that these patients are abnormally limited in their use of the short-term storage mechanism. *Prima facie,* it seems preferable to the alternative explanation of interference which, at least in its retroactive variety, depends on some activity intervening between registration and remembering, more especially upon interpolated learning. Now, amnesic patients show pronounced signs of forgetting long before any normal interfering activity could intervene with the consolidation of their memories; they also engage in considerably less activity than do normal persons, and in virtually no new learning.

Unlike the theory of autonomously fading traces, interference is usually treated as occurring in recall or recognition (Underwood, 1945; Osgood, 1953), and will therefore be discussed in that context. Proactive interference originates in learning prior to the experiment, and would consequently exercise its influence on registration rather than on retention. Underwood (1957) demonstrated that in rote learning experiments more forgetting is caused by proactive than by retroactive interference, and subsequently Underwood and Postman (1960) stated that whatever forgetting cannot be attributed to formal interference, proactive and retroactive, must be due to extraexperimental sources of interference of the same types. How far conclusions drawn from memorizing lists of syllables are to be generalized is not clear, but it seems safe to assume that proactive interference of one sort or another could account for a large share of normal forgetting. Proactive interference occurs when unlearning of inappropriate responses fails, and is manifested by the substitution of such incorrect responses.

It seems improbable that the trouble of amnesic patients should be that of unlearning. Although it is generally believed that their failures in recall result in the substitution of incorrect information, this is actually the exception rather than the rule. It happens when they believe they have the information available, though in fact they do not, and is therefore the consequence rather than the cause of their forgetting. It could, however, be the cause of their failure in registration, of the unavailability of appropriate codes. Those Korsakoff patients who, over the years, kept on calling me Talbot, provide an example of inability to unlearn.

Judging from their performance in every test of successive or delayed recall, amnesic patients forget much of the information they originally registered. If their retention were not affected, it would be thought that they should remember the little they had registered better than do control subjects who register more. In fact, amnesic patients register less and retain a smaller portion of that which they had registered. If Underwood (1957) is right in concluding that individual differences are manifested only in learning (i.e., acquisition) and never in forgetting, it follows that Korsakoff patients not only register less but register less solidly in some sense. The apparent decay of memories is a direct function of their registration; their abnormally rapid decay is an effect of abnormally weak registration.

The alternative theory regards decay as an autonomous process, and is quite compatible with known facts and hypothetical models in neurophysiology. Psychological findings in support of it have been marshalled by Broadbent (1958) and by Conrad and Hille (1958). In many respects the experiments designed to demonstrate that memory traces fade in time without any external interference are very similar to those demonstrating interference effects, and perhaps none has succeeded in isolating the two effects. Broadbent, who is the spokesman of the decay theory, assumes that memory traces fade very rapidly unless the message is rehearsed or recirculated between a limited capacity system concerned with perceptual processing and a separate storage system. This mechanism provides for the tenability of the decay theory, in spite of the fact that amnesic patients tend to retain best the earliest items in a text or list. If these are rehearsed at a very slow rate they may occupy both systems, so that additional items cannot be registered. Presumably if the information received does not fit any available code it will not be rehearsed at all, and will decay instantly; hence the amnesic patient's inability to memorize even for a few seconds an unfamiliar address or proper name, and the futility of repeating it for his benefit.

The decay theory is entirely consonant with the steep forgetting curves obtained from our Korsakoff patients in various experiments, with the absence of reminiscence effects, and also with their ability to follow instructions and maintain task-sets for relatively long periods. They could rehearse a simple unit of information—like the positions of the adjectives in the spatial word-association test—or an instruction while performing in accordance with it. With a change in set, however, the instruction ceases to circulate, is lost beyond recovery, and nothing is gained by practice or by the correction of errors.

While a message is being rehearsed, more stable memory traces can be established. This may account for the successes of Korsakoff patients in learning new word associations or items in a list, or in identifying examples within a collection, although even these traces fade fast. Whether fading implies the annihilation of traces, the reversion of neural structures within the brain to their previous condition, or merely an increasing inaccessibility, is a matter of conjecture. Most observations do not rule out the former alternatives but some are compatible only with the latter, i.e., that the memory derangement is in recall.

## Recall

Three reasons led most students of the amnesic syndrome to place the memory defect in the process of recall. One was retrograde amnesia, i.e., the unavailability of memories that had been soundly established previously; another was the errors in verbal reconstruction described as confabulation; a third was the inference from latent dispositions and overt behavior to the operation of memories that could not be consciously elicited. Some experiences undoubtedly make more lasting impressions on certain amnesic patients than would appear from direct tests of recall or recognition, but they do not justify a generalization to all experiences of every Korsakoff patient. The same caution applies to the statements that, as amnesic patients improve, they recall events they never seemed to register or remember during the more severe phase of their illness. Careful examination would surely prove that the amount of information lost to these patients, even at that later stage, far exceeds the boundaries of normal forgetting. For all that, their capacity to recall is undoubtedly damaged, and this impairment may indeed be reversible within limits.

Inhibitory influences on recall have been traced to several diverse sources: emotional, motivational, and more directly cognitive. Of the latter, proactive and retroactive interference have been most carefully explored. Following Müller and Pilzecker (1900), an extensive literature based on laboratory experiments has covered the various parameters of retroactive interference that contributes more or less to forgetting. Although the term, if interpreted literally, would imply that subsequent events exerted their influence backward on memory traces, i.e., on retention, in fact the effect is commonly attributed to the competition of responses in recall or in recognition, i.e., to a failure in discrimination (Gibson, 1940; Underwood, 1945). To make this point explicit, McGeoch (1936) proposed the term reproductive inhibition. Even so, as Brown (1958) has pointed out, it is not clear whether retroactive inhibition should be regarded as the cause or the result of forgetting. This ambiguity has not been resolved by the admission of unlearning as a second factor in retroactive inhibition (Melton and von Lackum, 1941). Osgood (1953, p. 551), who considers reciprocal inhibition as a third of possibly several more factors in retroactive interference, resolves the dilemma by divesting the concept of its explanatory function and treats it as a measure of the processes that jointly account for forgetting. Accordingly, retroaction only provides an analogy from which to infer the causes of forgetting in every day life and, *a fortiori*, in the amnesic syndrome.

Operationally, the evidence for retroactive interference is the substitution of some later acquired response or information for that which was originally learned. Korsakoff patients do that even more rarely than they substitute earlier acquired information. Formal tests of retroactive interference showed that its effect—as well as that of proactive interference—could not be detected in Korsakoff patients, when tested by savings in relearning. Since, however, the method of relearning without interference also failed to demonstrate any retention, the negative results for interference effects cannot be regarded as decisive. There was not enough learning to be subject to interference. In another experiment that tested memorization of short sentences immediately following presentation and again 5 minutes later, the amnesic patients showed both learning and some retroactive interference effects. In line with other findings, however, this experiment also suggested that the interruption of the original task-set contributed more to this effect than the competition of rival contents or responses.

Recall and recognition can fail, not because some alternative interferes with the correct response, but because the subject cannot adopt the set that will make the appropriate response available to him. As a general rule, tests of recognition show more retention than tests of recall, and this is also true of Korsakoff patients. The usual explanation of this difference (e.g., Postman and Rau, 1957), that a lower degree of learning is sufficient for recognition than for recall, does little more than restate the observation. More probably the difference lies in the burden of the task in the two tests. Recognition is literally a response to a situation which forces the subject to act; recall demands that he initiate the process of recovery and set a limit to the alternatives from which to choose. That these additional requirements overload the capacity of Korsakoff patients is evident from their considerable gain by prompting questions.

A failure to adopt the appropriate set in recall or recognition, however, need not arise from the immediate situation in which retention is tested. Katona (1940), Reed (1946), Postman and Jenkins (1948), and Brown (1954) have demonstrated in various ways how the set adopted at the time of learning can influence recall and, in more formal terms, Miller, Galanter, and Pribram (1960) trace failure in recall to the stage of registration when plans are constructed that will guide subsequent recall. Bartlett, who holds that remembering depends on the persistence of the original orientation or attitude, also stresses the importance of the set at the time of learning or registration. Since, however, remembering is itself a constructive act, he regards recall and recognition as only partly determined by the mode and conditions of the prior perception (Bartlett, 1932, p. 188). Bruner (1957), discussing the manner and degree in which new learning is coded, pointed out that a person's attitude toward learning can be an enduring disposition, not merely a transient set.

It hardly needs restating that the degree of learning, no matter how that be defined, directly influences remembering. The question at issue here is not that some insufficiency in registration impedes recall but whether, for the lack of an appropriate set in recall, information is inaccessible in spite of the prior successful completion of the learning process. It is quite common to register some information with the intention of retaining it, but of retaining it only for a short while—as I might do with directions for finding a short cut that will take me around a town I wish to avoid and do not anticipate seeing again. If at some later date I happen to be on the same road, and that time without any one in sight to ask for directions, I shall regret my mistake in judgment, although errors in coding or lack of capacity would land me in the same predicament.

Defects of this type, i.e., in judgment or set at the time of registration, might explain the occurrence of anterograde amnesia, but not the associated defect of retrograde amnesia. In view of the latter memory dysfunction, it would appear that the attitudinal derangement must occur on the occasion of recall or recognition, and that it is independent of the set or intention that was operating at the time of registration.

The manner in which amnesic patients reshuffle the chronological order of their memories cannot be explained by such constructs as Bartlett's schemata or the neurophysiological models of learning that follow the paradigm of conditioning. These errors in remembering point to the influence that context or connections exert on the availability of the appropriate content. Students of retroactive interference (e.g., Newman, 1939; Deese and Hardman, 1954; King and Cofer, 1960) have noted the importance of that influence. The contextual isolation—relative rather than absolute—of memory traces would explain the amnesic patients' confusions in the sequential ordering of events and in the chronological placement of memories; it could also account for the unavailability of effective sets in recall. Isolation that occurs in registration or possibly in retention, however, cannot be the sole source of the amnesic defects, as it would not allow for the patient's ability to overcome those defects in time. Some measure of recovery from the disability can be attained, and with it the restoration of previously inaccessible information. This could happen only if the amnesic disturbance originated in recall or recognition.

There is also direct evidence that retrograde amnesia, and to a lesser extent anterograde amnesia too, stem from an inaccessibility of memories or information rather than from their complete absence. The missing information may emerge on other occasions or in a different context. Whether through lack of control or some other derangement, the operations of recall and recognition seem to be impaired in Korsakoff patients, and there is hardly one of our experiments that does not support this conclusion. Nevertheless, failure of recall or recognition, in the sense of a function or ability, is not a sufficient explanation of the amnesic disorder. In several instances the Korsakoff patients' performance in recall was quite successful, e.g., for certain autobiographical data. It could even reach the population norm of attainment, as in the test of the digit span. Furthermore, their recall of newly acquired information steadily deteriorated with the distance from the time of registration. Apparently, the anomalies manifest in the recall and recognition of amnesic patients are determined to some extent at the stages of initial registration and of the subsequent processing or storage of memories.

*Chapter 11*

# TEMPORAL SIGNS AND SELF-REFERENCE

Those who have outlined theoretical analyses of the amnesic syndrome were tempted by global constructs in order to fit the various associated symptoms into a unitary model. Several attempts have also been made to derive all the defects characteristic of Korsakoff's psychosis from a disturbance in a mental function more specific than perception or learning, intention or recall. Because of their influence as well as their inherent interest, two such theories will be examined in some detail, those expounded most notably by van der Horst (1932) and by Claparède (1911).

## The Sense of Time

The core of the Korsakoff patient's psychopathology, according to van der Horst, in his inability to comprehend the flow of time. The object of intuitive awareness that is so deficient in the amnesic syndrome is neither time as conventionally measured nor a subjective apprehension of duration; it is independent of the perception of events that delimit its divisions or fill its spans. It is time sensed in its flow; that which continuously elapses. Time, thus substantiated, manifests itself in two effects: (a) it impresses personal experiences with temporal signs, and (b) it orders events into sequences.

Quite apart from theoretical predilections, explanations derived from this concept are apt to appeal to the clinician who observes the collapse of the amnesic patients' time scale, their tendency to telescope oft-repeated occurrences into one or a few occasions, and their frequent confusion of the order of events. Although temporal disorientation is not complete, and its severity varies within as well as between patients, from one occasion to the next, from one context to another, it is a characteristic feature of the amnesic syndrome. To attribute errors of this type to a separation of the experience—clearly perceived, registered, and responded to on each occasion—from its temporal mark, seems a convenient solution. It does, however, suffer from the weakness of *ad hoc* constructions. Do we normally attach temporal signs to all our experiences? If we do so register them, from what source are the temporal signs drawn? Advocates of this theory propose an autistic frame of reference rather than the Gregorian calendar and the clock, but translation from one to the other, or even simultaneous coding in both should be possible, Gillespie's (1937) denial notwithstanding.

In psychology, the concept of temporal marks leans on the authority of Bartlett (1932, p. 208) who attributed them to all that is remembered. What are then the implications for the amnesic syndrome of the proposition that every memory or, as van der Horst puts it more cautiously, every experience is impregnated with a temporal sign? It would quite definitely explain failures in the formation of sequences, reduplicative paramnesias, and most of the behavior that is generally described as confabulation. By equating the mechanism which impresses temporal signs with that of sequencing or planning, the defect may also explain the patients' lack of spontaneity. It would account for their anterograde amnesia assuming—and, advocates of the theory do make this assumption—that sequential classification is the only principle by which discrete experiences are organized into a mnemonic system.

Van der Horst staked his theory on its capacity to explain all the psychopathological signs of the Korsakoff syndrome, retrograde amnesia included. This he attempted by reasoning that, when continuity ceases to be experienced, the need for the primary chronological ordering of past experiences is also weakened, and therefore gradually that order will dissolve. This argument implies (a) that the collapse of the temporal frame of reference is a gradual process, extending from the present to the past, and (b) that the hypothetical "primary order" determining the registration of experiences is itself dependent on a need. Clinical observation does not support the view that the patients' confusion of the order of events unfolds gradually along a retrospective gradient. Moreover, a principle of categorization can hardly be regarded as primary if it operates in response to some unspecified needs. These may indeed interfere with recall, but cannot affect retroactively a process completed in the past.

Probably a stronger case could be made for explaining retrograde amnesia by van der Horst's theory than his own argument. At the same time, the defects it proposes to explain can be derived as well by reversing the theory, and treating temporal disorientation as an effect secondary to the memory disturbance. Correct temporal judgments need not be formed by some immediate apprehension of their object, they could be based on the perception of cues. For all that, they are no less immediate experiential processes than judgments of size, brightness, or speed. To be sure, accurate assessments of these properties must be relative to some learned standards, but then every amnesic patient has acquired appropriate standards for making temporal judgments prior to his illness, even though he may no longer be able to apply them effectively.

Van der Horst postulates a primary category of mnemonic organization, the temporal. His proposition, that man possesses a faculty for the intuitive perception of the flow of time, is not amenable to direct scrutiny. Psychopathological evidence of pure temporal agnosia—i.e., for duration, sequence, and recurrence—along with intact memory for content might prove it true, but has not been furnished by Korsakoff patients. The corollaries of the key concept are more easily testable, and as readily on normal as on brain-damaged men and women. Do we in fact mark our experiences with temporal signs? Does our remembering of events, supposedly so marked, follow laws different from remembering other information? In what sense is the chronological a primary principle of mnemonic organization; is failure to register duration, sequence, and recurrence a necessary condition or concomitant of general amnesias?

Introspection can hardly answer these questions. Undoubtedly it would furnish examples of temporal signs: one may remember a toothache at Easter or meeting somebody at a first coming-out party. Because of some meaningful association the events remain inseparable in memory from their temporal signs. It is not obvious that every personal experience is so marked; on the other hand, just as certain experiences are indelibly impressed with a temporal sign, others are impregnated with the character of location, mood, affect, sensory quality, or some other significant parameter of the subject's cognitive structure. It is quite normal to forget both personal memories and impersonal information, to make errors about the temporal attributes of events as well as about their content. Granting that experiences are somehow registered in a sequential structure, the primacy or uniqueness of this principle or organization is not self-evident. Rather do we appear to file information under multiple headings, and the temporal signs belong to one category of classification, but are not our only frame of reference.

## Clinical Observations

Amnesic patients notably underestimate the extent of the time that has passed since the onset of their illness; they often err in other temporal judgments, more commonly by underestimation but not infrequently in the opposite direction. They are conspicuously inaccurate in recalling the order of past events, and at times quite astoundingly imperceptive of the recurrence of similar occasions. While noting all these anomalies in our Korsakoff patients, I have also been impressed with the many instances in which they judged correctly the duration of periods, the sequence of events, and even their recurrence. Van der Horst attributed similar examples to chance or to the mediation of associated experiences, more precisely to situational cues. In fact, their incidence far exceeds chance expectancies, and the effective utilization of cues would demand an exceptional keenness of observation and speed of reasoning, neither of which distinguishes amnesic patients.

Several examples of errors in the judgment of time spans and in the order and recurrence of events made by our Korsakoff patients were listed, and group trends indicated in Chapter 2. Here some extracts will be given from an interview with a woman who had, until a few weeks before, lived in her home which, in its economic and cultural standards, was typical of a successful professional man. She herself had had a university education, and was in her 68th year, hospitalized after a prolonged history of drinking which had become gradually more intensive. When questioned in 1959, she believed that the last war had been between 1914 and 1918, and distorted her not inconsiderable store of information about public events so as to conform with the chronological frame of reference set by those dates. She knew that Eisenhower was the President at the time and, though somewhat confusedly, could also report on his current activity which was figuring prominently in the headlines of the papers. She was also aware that he had first made his name as "commander-in-chief of the army at the end of the last big war," that Franklin D. Roosevelt was the President at that time, and she could place Hitler and Stalin with fair accuracy. She correctly recalled what had happened at Pearl Harbor, and was able to define the meaning of Prohibition and the Great Depression. Asked for dates, she placed those of Eisenhower's command, Roosevelt's Presidency, and Hitler in the 1910's with 1920 as an upper limit, and the beginning of the Depression—correctly—before Franklin D. Roosevelt's first term.

Here is an example of events recorded without their temporal signs, or of their being displaced from their proper chronological setting. The events, however, were not personal experiences, and their sequential order was correct within the wrong temporal frame. Moreover, the patient accurately remembered the interviewer's name, the length of her hospitalization, her previous visit to the laboratory, old and quite recent events in her personal life, and even the principal contents of a story she had been reading in a magazine prior to the interview. She was invariably mistaken about the day's date—though the extent of the error was barely a few months

—and was occasionally wrong about her own age as well, but she dated events in her personal life up to the actual calendar year.

When asked to list the ages of her four children, the patient was as likely to place them at equal intervals between 20 and 14 as between 40 and 34. Once, when I interrupted her in the process of listing their ages, she had begun by giving these correctly as 40, 38 and then, asked the age of the youngest, answered 15. She was not visibly perturbed when I pointed out that this would mean a gap of 25 years between her oldest and youngest child, but as a concession raised the age of the latter to 21. Obviously, her point of reference for the entire series was very unstable, yet she never erred in naming the children in chronological order, nor would she mistake the 2 years' gap between each one and the next younger, if allowed to work her way down from the oldest. The source of her errors, therefore, could not be primarily in the detachment of temporal signs nor in a disturbance of sequential ordering.

It would be even more contrived to attribute to these defects the same patient's response to a question about her grandchildren. She correctly said she had five, three by her eldest and two by another daughter. When asked to name them, the patient started by listing Carol's children as Marilyn, John, Billy, and Marilyn. I repeated these names and asked her to check whether I had heard correctly, and she gave a confirmatory reply. Thereupon I remarked that Carol would hardly have christened both her daughters Marilyn, and besides she was supposed to have only three children. The patient, nevertheless, insisted that both Marilyns were Carol's daughters, but now called them cousins. She also gave the names of her second daughter's children, and neither of them as Marilyn.

The last example of confusion is similar to certain errors amnesic patients make by chronological displacement, except that it did not occur on a temporal scale. It may be taken as an example of that "incapacity to respond to identity" that Zangwill (1941) recognized as the cause of reduplicative paramnesia. In this patient, however, as probably in Zangwill's too, the incapacity was by no means general. She did not fail to recognize identity in her husband whom she had known for several decades, in her other grandchildren whom she had known for a few years, or in her doctor, her nurse, and me, whom she had known only a few days or weeks. The patient also correctly observed that a research assistant who appeared for the first time in her third testing session was not the same who had been present on the previous occasions, and recognized her the next time as one familiar from her last visit to the laboratory.

Our observations on this patient are significant for an evaluation of van der Horst's theory on three scores. Her case demonstrates that: (a) pathological errors in recognizing identity do not necessarily stem from a failure to keep apart the repeated occurrences of an event; (b) extensive mistakes in attaching temporal marks to events can be made without a corresponding confusion about the order of those events; (c) these mistakes can be limited to one area of reference. She only placed more recent public events before 1920, but correctly assigned incidents in her private life to later dates.

On all three scores the case contradicts van der Horst who concluded from his theory that Korsakoff patients would fail to recall personal experiences—events impregnated with temporal signs—but be able to remember events not so marked. In making this prediction, or rather so generalizing from a few observations, van der Horst came close to formulating an operational test of his hypothesis. In fact, he did not define the conditions in which Korsakoff patients should show no memory impairment, but he did propose that information imparted in experimental tests would be of this type and should certainly be less vulnerable to their amnesic disturbance than experiences of personal significance. Empirical evidence does not support this thesis, for all our Korsakoff patients tended to forget impersonal information as rapidly and completely as their personal experiences.

An interesting, though atypical, case was that of a patient who will be discussed again in the second part of this chapter.

Unlike the members of our chronic Korsakoff group, this was a professionally trained young man whose disease was of a viral encephalitic origin. His amnesic derangement was extraordinarily severe in respect to events of the preceding 2 months but relatively mild retroactively. He made strenuous efforts to learn from others current information concerning himself, and to retain this. Such events as he could recall from the immediate past, as well as more remote memories, he placed in accurate chronological order, but his judgments of time spans between events were uncertain and often incorrect. He had much difficulty in learning new names and little confidence in attaching the right name to the two or three persons he had come to know in the hospital, though in fact he rarely mistook one for another. Like other amnesic patients, he could follow experimental instructions as long as these were required and forgot information imparted to him in experiments as fully as he did personal experiences. Neither could he recall at the end of an hour's session in the laboratory the tasks he had been occupied with.

During the period of his illness with which we are concerned—the second and third months—this man was unable to recall anything of short prose passages read to him or by him, even though their content was from the technical literature of his own profession. He tended to forget all items in a list of ten meaningful or meaningless three-letter words within 90 seconds, and could not reliably carry out the instruction to count slowly from 1 to 23; as a rule he went beyond the limit set. On the other hand, he was able to discover and memorize a relatively difficult sequential concept combining double and single alternation: the playing cards stacked in series of B-B-R-B-R-R, described in Chapter 7. He also succeeded in completing the following two sequential tasks, for which all the instructions were given once only and in advance of the first move:

(a) Drawing a ship, measuring its length, memorizing the size, then going to another desk, measuring the size of another drawing of a ship which was lying there, and reporting the difference between the two sizes.

(b) Taking a box of colored (Kohs) blocks from a drawer, then collecting a book of block designs from a shelf, turning up design number 8, starting a stop watch which was lying on the bench, constructing the block design, and reporting on the time taken for the construction task.

In both these tasks, the initiative for each operation in the series was provided by the instruction, but none of the moves was automatically activated by the previous one, either by means of motor cues or of long established habits. The patient had to remember at every stage what was required of him next; he had to carry a plan for sequential performance, and did so without losing track of or omitting any of the constituent operations. Although this patient's success in these tests despite his severe amnesia is of considerable interest, it may not seriously damage van der Horst's theory which is restricted to sequencing of past, not future, events. Let us, therefore, consider some experiments testing the registration of sequence and of other temporal parameters of completed tasks.[1]

## Experimental Findings

A corollary of the sense for the continuity of time is the apprehension of a sequential order. According to van der Horst, Korsakoff patients cannot remember the sequence of events even though they remember the events themselves, and if they forget their content that happens because of the absence of the "primary order" imposed by the flow of time. If van der Horst's reasoning is correct, amnesic patients should either be unable to register as well as retain information about sequential order, or at least their memory of this should dissipate more rapidly than their memory of discrete items. This hypothesis was tested in several experiments with our group of chronic Korsakoff patients. It will be recalled

[1]Tests in estimation of time intervals are not directly relevant to the thesis under consideration, because they were conceived in the absolute units of scaled time. Others involving the reproduction of spans and rhythms may have confounded short-term memory effects with the apprehension of temporal relations.

that its test by a somewhat informal procedure requiring the memorizing of four objects (see p. 207) was inconclusive, though certainly not in support of the hypothesis.

*Word List.* The same list of ten meaningful words was used as in several experiments described in Chapter 8. In one test no restriction was placed on the order in which the words were to be reproduced after a learning period of 3 minutes, in another test the instruction was to report them in the original order. In both tests the words were presented simultaneously, printed in a column. The mean reproduction score of the 13 Korsakoff patients who took part in both tests was 5.00 (SD 2.34) without the restrictive instruction, 4.7 (SD 2.23) when required to observe the sequence, and of the latter 3.9 (SD 1.52) words were reported in the correct order. Mean differences between the two latter scores and the first were not statistically significant. In a control (X) group of 16, the corresponding mean scores were 7.1 (SD 1.53), 7.0 (SD 1.37), and 5.6 (SD 1.73); the last of these was significantly below the others ($t=3.26$ and 4.98). These results would indicate that, relative to their diminished capacity to register, the amnesic patients remembered the order of the items better than the control group. In fact, the difference between the two groups' differential scores was not significant.

All that can be concluded from this experiment is that the requirement to follow the sequence of events, and thus presumably to attach temporal marks to each, did not reduce the achievement of the amnesic patients in registration, and that they could learn a list of items in a fixed order about as well as in random assortment. Experiments in rote learning have suggested that a standard sequence may facilitate the retention of discrete items by strengthening bonds on either side of each (Deese, 1958). Although this effect was not evident with either of our groups, it does seem probable that associations are the medium by which serial order is established in a chain of items. If that were so, the sense of temporal continuity would lose its uniqueness as a source of the sequential principle.

Our experiment has shown that amnesic patients are quite

able to register information of a sequential order; it could not determine whether the same conclusion is applicable to their retention or delayed recall. Since, even after an interval as brief of 5 minutes, their recall scores were between one and three words, not much information could be drawn from the order in which so few items were reported.

*Overlapping Signals.* A second experiment investigated the capacity of amnesic patients to register duration in relative terms, as well as sequence, by four complementary procedures. Two of these presented them with visual, to with auditory information: (a) pictures of two different animals; (b) a red and a green light; (c) the recorded voices of a man and of a woman, one listing names of colors, the other those of food; (d) a buzzer and a bell. There were four experimental treatments which, for the sake of clarity will be described for material (a): (*i*) both pictures shown simultaneously for 1 minute; (*ii*) both pictures shown together, but one removed after 30 seconds and the other after 60 seconds; (*iii*) one picture presented alone for 30 seconds, and along with the other picture for 30 seconds more; (*iv*) one picture shown for 30 seconds, then removed and the second picture presented for 30 seconds. The lights and sounds were also continuously presented for periods of 30 or 60 seconds, the human voices with as little interruption as compatible with a steady rate of speech. Each subject was presented with all four materials under the four treatments in balanced order on four separate occasions.

Before each experiment the subject was told what he would see or hear, and was asked to observe carefully which of the two figures (lights, voices, sounds) came first, which second, and which was in view (sounded) longer than the other in any one presentation. In experiment (c) he was also advised that he would not be asked the words listed, and was to take notice of the voices only. After presentation he had to answer three questions in this order: "What did you see (hear)?" "Which did you see (hear) longer?" "Which came first, which second?" The last two questions were asked after an answer had been given to the previous one.

**Table 38**

IMMEDIATE RECALL OF SEQUENCE AND RELATIVE DURATION OF TWO SIGNALS

| | *Sequence* | | | | | | | |
|---|---|---|---|---|---|---|---|---|
| | *i* | | *ii* | | *iii* | | *iv* | |
| | *A. 1–60 sec.* *B. 1–60 sec.* | | *A. 1–30 sec.* *B. 1–60 sec.* | | *A. 1–60 sec.* *B. 30–60 sec.* | | *A. 1–30 sec.* *B. 30–60 sec.* | |
| | *Correct answers* | *Errors* | *Correct answers* | *Errors* | *Correct answers* | *Errors* | *Correct answers* | *Errors* |
| a. Two pictures | 13 | 2 | 11 | 5 | 14 | 2 | 15 | 1 |
| b. Two lights | 14 | 2 | 13 | 3 | 16 | 0 | 13 | 2 |
| c. Two voices | 15 | 1 | 12 | 4 | 15 | 0 | 12 | 0 |
| d. Two sounds | 9 | 2 | 10 | 4 | 13 | 1 | 14 | 1 |
| | *Duration* | | | | | | | |
| a. Two pictures | 14 | 1 | 14 | 2 | 13 | 3 | 12 | 3 |
| b. Two lights | 16 | 0 | 13 | 3 | 13 | 3 | 10 | 3 |
| c. Two voices | 15 | 1 | 13 | 3 | 15 | 0 | 11 | 1 |
| d. Two sounds | 10 | 1 | 14 | 0 | 11 | 3 | 12 | 2 |

Table 38 summarizes the performance of a group of 16 Korsakoff patients, listing correct answers and errors. The latter include both reversals and failures to make the required distinction; the balance between the sum of the two scores and 16 represents instances in which a subject was unable to recall both signals. No statistical tests were calculated, since it is quite evident that with each type of signal and with each method of presentation the correct answers far exceeded alike the errors and the number of successes that could be theoretically attributed to chance. Amnesic patients seem to be quite able to register the duration and sequence of such events as were presented to them in this experiment.

*Serial Slides.* In both the preceding experiments the subjects were instructed in advance to observe and remember the sequence of the events and, in the latter, their relative duration as well. In a third experiment which tested registration of recurrence, as well as of duration and sequence, the subjects were asked to watch the screen of a projector without advice about what they would see or what would be asked of them. They were shown drawings of six objects (umbrella, bell, clock, etc.), once or repeatedly for 5 or 10 seconds, in a standard sequence. Systematically varying the initial item from one subject to the next, the schedule of presentation was the following:

| Figure: | A | B | C | A | D | A | C | A | E | E | F |
|---|---|---|---|---|---|---|---|---|---|---|---|
| Exposure time (in seconds): | 5 | 10 | 10 | 5 | 5 | 5 | 10 | 5 | 5 | 5 | 5 |

The slides were shown without interruption, and at the end the subject had to answer three questions in turn: "What are the pictures you have seen?"; "Which were shown longer?"; "Which were shown more than once?" He was not instructed to list the items in the original sequence, but they were recorded in the order reported. After 30 minutes of further activity in the laboratory, but no repeated presentation

**Table 39**

Immediate and Delayed Recall of Six Figures Shown in Series

| | *Recall* | | *More than once* | | *Longer* | | *Mean rank* | |
|---|---|---|---|---|---|---|---|---|
| | *Immediate* | *Delayed* | *Immediate* | *Delayed* | *Immediate* | *Delayed* | *Immediate* | *Delayed* |
| Korsakoff Group ($N$=16) | | | | | | | | |
| A. (4 x 5 sec.) | 15 | 6 | 13 | 3 | 3 | 1 | 1.13 | — |
| B. (1 x 10 sec.) | 9 | 1 | 0 | 0 | 0 | 0 | 2.33 | — |
| C. (2 x 10 sec.) | 13 | 4 | 5 | 1 | 3 | 1 | 2.60 | — |
| D. (1 x 5 sec.) | 7 | 0 | 1 | 0 | 0 | 0 | 3.00 | — |
| E. (2 x 5 sec.) | 8 | 3 | 2 | 2 | 1 | 0 | 3.50 | — |
| F. (1 x 5 sec.) | 9 | 2 | 1 | 0 | 0 | 0 | 3.67 | — |
| Control Group ($N$=16X) | | | | | | | | |
| A. (4 x 5 sec.) | 16 | 16 | 16 | 14 | 7 | 3 | 1.25 | 1.00 |
| B. (1 x 10 sec.) | 12 | 13 | 3 | 3 | 10 | 9 | 2.75 | 2.54 |
| C. (2 x 10 sec.) | 15 | 15 | 10 | 9 | 7 | 3 | 2.87 | 2.80 |
| D. (1 x 5 sec.) | 7 | 3 | 0 | 1 | 0 | 1 | 4.14 | 4.00 |
| E. (2 x 5 sec.) | 16 | 15 | 7 | 8 | 2 | 4 | 3.81 | 3.73 |
| F. (1 x 5 sec.) | 14 | 12 | 4 | 2 | 0 | 1 | 4.36 | 4.75 |

of the slides, he was asked the same questions over again. The results of this experiment are set out in Table 39, and represent the number of subjects naming each item in response to the three questions. Mean rank represents the ordinal position of the items as they were reported. Owing to the very incomplete answers Korsakoff patients gave in delayed recall, no meaningful rankings could be assigned to these.

The results are of interest on several counts. First, they suggest that such a temporal attribute of the input as duration does influence registration in amnesic patients, and may do so to a greater extent than with other persons. Within the limits of the experiment, their registration of duration was extremely poor, but it was by no means negligible for recurrence. Most notable, however, is their observation of the original serial order, which remained accurate in spite of the fact that not one of the patients gave a complete list of six, and that it was not required of them. Evidently it is either unnecessary to postulate a special need for sequential ordering, or this need is present in amnesic patients as much as in other persons.

This experiment has furnished no more information about the capacity of amnesic patients to retain a record of the sequence of events over a period of time than did their recall of the word list. In absolute terms, the order of events is necessarily more fully forgotten than their content—one cannot rank more items correctly than one remembers. However, comparisons can be made in relative terms. The Korsakoff group recalled after 30 minutes just over one-quarter of the items reported immediately after presentation, and reproduced about the same proportion of its first correct reports on recurrence and on duration, listing four items in the correct sequential order, four incorrectly; the remaining eight responses all consisted of answers of one item. The corresponding proportions for the control group, with a much higher baseline, were .92, .92, .81, and 7 items listed in the incorrect serial order. These data suggest that both groups retained information on recurrence and duration about as well as on content, and that the amnesic patients forgot relatively more about the serial order than the control. This latter effect may, however, be due entirely to the greater difficulty these patients had in recalling anything.

## Summary

Clinical observations showed that amnesic patients fail to remember all kinds of impersonal information imparted to them, that they can be mistaken about their temporal references without losing the sequence of events, that their errors of identity need not result from missing the recurrence of events. By the evidence of our experiments, they are capable of registering the serial order and the relative duration of events and forget this information at about the same rate as the content of the same events. All these findings are contrary to van der Horst's theory.

It seems that amnesic patients are quite capable of registering the passage of time, but lose the information necessary for making temporal judgments as rapidly as they forget other information, and often miss the cues for noting the temporal properties of events. Even when they register the duration, serial order, and possibly the repetition of events, they cannot connect these records with subsequent relevant information. In addition to their low retentive capacity, they may be abnormal also in spending long stretches of time without engaging in any activity, real or symbolic. In order to underestimate the distance of a past event it is enough that the intervening range be empty or only partially filled. When that happens the subjective time scale becomes distorted or completely collapses, and objective chronological references may follow its course. If they do not follow, that experience of contradiction arises when a span of time feels different from what it must be according to an external authority. Since a normal and reliable time scale is anchored, not in the subject's birthday or some other past event, but in the present, in amnesic patients the temporal frame of their pre-morbid experiences must also undergo distortions.

Accordingly, the temporal frame of reference is indeed disrupted and misshapen in the amnesic syndrome, but the patients' inability to recover so many previously well-established memories cannot be attributed to this anomaly. The temporal is not the only category within which information is registered and stored; neither is it the only frame of reference to suffer distortion and dissolution in Korsakoff patients. Their failures in sequential ordering are as notable in the forward as they are in the retrospective direction, in developing percepts and concepts, and in planning for the immediate and more distant future. Temporal marks and a sense of continuity are hardly the necessary conditions of pursuing those prospective operations, but are more likely the products of their completion; the same conclusion applies to the reconstruction of the past.

## Self-Reference

A more concrete extension through time than the sense of continuity is a person's notion of himself. Whatever the content of the self may be, it is derived from actual events and experiences that took place in objective time and have accumulated into some structure. To Gamper and other students of the amnesic syndrome it appeared that Korsakoff patients could no longer add to that structure, could not relate their experiences to it. Allowing for exceptions to the rule, the formula sounds true intuitively. It could be quoted to explain many examples of memory loss in content, temporal misplacements, and above all those remarkable misjudgments of familiarity that occur in the amnesic syndrome. Examples of its varieties are: the experience of *déjà vu,* mistaking the novel as familiar and its opposite, a sense of familiarity divorced from its knowledge; unconscious plagiarism and its reverse, the conscious communication of a message without awareness of being an agent in its transmission.

Claparède's classic case must be cited again (see p. 73) in this context, that of a Korsakoff patient who, after a few minutes, failed to recall an incident as a personal experience, while behaving in a manner entirely determined by that experience. The woman had quickly forgotten that, when shaking hands with the doctor, she had been jabbed with a pin hidden between his fingers. She did, however, refuse to shake hands with him again and, when asked her reason, explained that he might hide a pin in his hand. She justified her suspicion merely as a thought that had crossed her mind, for people sometimes do hide pins in their hands, and apparently completely failed to relate the notion to a personal experience of her own. Claparède quoted this example as evidence for his thesis that Korsakoff patients lost their capacity of self-reference, of a disturbance in the "feeling of me-ness."

A striking example of this phenomenon was provided by our young postencephalitic patient who had a few months earlier lost a brother in a car crash, and whose younger brother was about to get married. His amnesia had apparently so completly deleted all memory of the fatal accident that only a couple of days before his interview he had attributed a letter that had just arrived from his surviving brother to the other brother who was dead. Nevertheless, when asked to tell me about his older brother, though first questioningly rather than affirmatively, the patient reported that he was dead. He gave accurate answers to my questions relating to the circumstances of his death, the time and place of the accident, and knew that his brother's wife too had been killed, but that their little child was safe at the home of her maternal grandparents in a foreign country. Likewise, the patient reported in reply to my question that his younger brother was to be married next week, knew the name of his fiancée, the place of the wedding, and correctly named those members of the family who had flown there for the occasion. However, when subsequently I pointed out to the patient that his memory for recent and current events was not as blank as he had thought, for he could recollect these two occasions accurately and in some detail, he looked incredulous and answered: "But wasn't it you who has just told me?" When apprised that he himself, not I, was the source of all this information, the patient appeared unconvinced. About half an hour later the same procedure was repeated; I asked the same questions, received the same answers, and again the patient believed that I had imparted to him all the information he had given me.

Clearly, the sense of familiarity can be disturbed while the content is available; self and other can be confused as the source of information. Errors of this type do occur with normal persons, but not after so brief a lapse of time, nor about events as personally significant and affect-laden as those on which I questioned this patient. His disturbance was rather like some perceptual anomalies Penfield (1954, p. 298) observed following epileptic discharge or electrical stimulation of the cortex. They seem to stem from an absence of awareness that a process has been initiated by the subject himself. Quite possibly our patient would have been unable to present all the information that was available to him if he had been asked in general terms to report about his family. The specific details may have become accessible in response to my questions, uninformative though these were; and it may have been for that reason that he attributed their content to me.

It is hardly surprising that, even more so than other amnesic patients, this young man always felt insecure about the accuracy of his recollections and diffident in his ability to recall events correctly. He often expressed astonishment when told that he had already said previously that which he was currently reporting. Are these unusual instances of faulty recognition, of failure to note familiarity, to register one's own acts and experiences as bygone rather than as potential, central to the amnesic symptom complex? Hardly so, for they were observed only rarely in our Korsakoff group, nor were they ubiquitous in the one patient who provided the examples quoted. They are more characteristic of the early confusional stage of the disease, but carry over to the chronic amnesic phase no more regularly than do confabulation or the neurological signs of Wernicke's encephalopathy. Neither do amnesic patients tend to mistake memories for current impressions; that which they remember may be displaced in its temporal context but is unmistakably referred to the past.

Failure to remember significant personal experiences is so

much less common and puzzling than the forgetting of impersonal information that this derangement has occupied a position of unwarranted prominence in writings on the amnesic syndrome. Van de Horst (1932), Gantt and Muncie (1942), Kral (1956), and Mouren and Felician (1958) reported that Korsakoff patients remember impersonal data much better than those concerning their own experiences. Comparisons between the two kinds of memories are difficult to make and difficult to dispute, for there is no common scale on which to measure them. In spite of occasional confusion and errors, our Korsakoff patients were likely to remember much better who the experimenter was and what he did than a news item read to them from their *Hospital News,* though that too had some bearing on their lives. No matter how monotonous their daily routine, they were almost certain to report more accurate information about what they had done the day before than about the book they had read or the television play they had watched the same day. So would probably most healthy men and women, and therefore no particular conclusion can be drawn from these observations. Sometimes, amnesic patients remarked on the familiarity of objects or texts or procedures but failed to recall their own previous encounter with these. Conversely, they might relate a false recognition to themselves, but most often they identified the item correctly and in relation to their past experience.

At the moment of an event, amnesic patients relate it to themselves much as do other men and women. Indeed, against a background of apparent withdrawal, it is remarkable how promptly they respond when addressed. This suggests that their failure in establishing connections between current experiences and those accumulated in the past may not be a cause but rather an effect of their poor retention. One reason for attributing their disorder to a disturbance in the sphere of personality has been their weirdly detached attitude to events that would normally arouse emotional effects. This may be due to the fact that emotions have to build up over short spans of time and, though their initial reaction may be proper to the occasion, Korsakoff patients fail to sustain and develop it into a full-fledged affective response. Another reason for supposing that the amnesic syndrome hits the personal more than the impersonal is that those overlearned skills, such as dressing, eating, or writing, which are apparently unaffected, belong to the latter sphere. It is a matter of practice rather than acquisition in early life, judging by Liepmann's (1910) mathematician chess player and also by our young engineer who, vague though he may have been on other topics, spoke with complete confidence about affairs concerning his own professional interests. He sketched with great facility models of the machines his own and rival concerns were producing, and did not fail to attach the proper temporal signs to them, in that he drew with assurance the models brought out during the preceding 12 years as well as those current at the time of testing. Yet the same patient could recall after an hour a short text drawn from a technical journal of his specialty no better than a control passage culled from a textbook in sociology.

It is only a short step to pass from theories about disturbed self-reference to questions about the state of consciousness in amnesic patients, or to compare their memories, impressions, and responses with dream experiences (e.g., Gamper, 1928; Scheid, 1934; Bernard, 1951; Wieck, 1955). Sollier (1900) who likened amnesic patients to somnambulists, thought that they gained consciousness at each moment but, unable to synthesize successive impressions, they could not attain a notion of their continuous personality. It is this isolation of their experiences—which occurs with a high probability rather than of absolute necessity—that suggests the analogy with dream states. The analogy, however, is only partly true. In dreams, the scanning operations by which their content is selected and processed are extremely rapid, and control by sensory input is relatively weak. In the waking function of Korsakoff patients the balance is tilted in the opposite direction. Unless an imbalance either way is thought to have the same effects, the analogy rests entirely on such criteria as a lack of conviction and a precarious chronological anchorage of memories. These could be the effects of the rapid fading of registered information. At any rate, amnesic patients are perfectly conscious in the sense of being aware of their surroundings, of making appropriate perceptual discriminations and responses within their repertory based on established skills; nor are they mistaken about their personal identities—seldom so even in the early confusional state of the disease—although in content these tend to be abnormally sparse.

*Chapter 12*

# PREMATURE CLOSURE OF ACTIVATION

Perception and registration, retention, and recall, are all impaired in the amnesic syndrome, but none can be regarded as the ultimate source of its psychopathology. These functions are diminished in capacity, more in some, less in other patients, and to an extent varying between occasions and situations. Some patients function quite consistently farther below the normal level than others. This is particularly marked when the deleterious effects of aging, and possibly of some other disease, interact with those that are more typical of the Korsakoff syndrome, e.g., when gross errors in reasoning are superimposed on the amnesic disorder. Still, not one of our Korsakoff patients performed consistently within the range of the control group, nor did any one of the control subjects perform regularly at the level of the Korsakoff group.

Within our sample of Korsakoff patients no stable hierarchical order emerged, according to which certain members would reliably occupy a high or a low rank. Correlations between test scores rarely reached the level of statistical significance; patients who achieved the control norm of performance in two or three discriminatory tests fell below it in the others. It is tempting to view the amnesic syndrome as determined by several factors or functional disturbances, and those as being correlated to an extent less than unity. This may, indeed, prove to be the correct explanation, but such a resolution of the dilemmas presented by the amnesic syndrome would be contrary to the law of parsimony, and would also intuitively appear as inconclusive.

Just as memory defects are not caused by the dropping out of discrete items of information from storage, so the more general derangements in the amnesic syndrome need not be conceived as a disturbance in several, more or less interdependent, functions that can be meaningfully isolated in behavior. The alternative conceptualization is that of a change in the level of function, implicit in Hughlings Jackson's (1884) principle of dissolution of function and also in Goldstein's (1934) theoretical gradient of concreteness. The solution here proposed follows the Jacksonian canon in general terms, but not in certain of its specific implications. More particularly, in the Korsakoff syndrome the disintegration of function does not proceed along a scale of complexity or difficulty; the patient may retain skills such as playing the piano or solving mathematical problems, while the simple task of counting up to 23 and stopping at that point, or to resume counting after a brief interruption, is beyond his capacity. Furthermore, his more efficient performance of automatic acts can be explained without resort to the concept of volition. That the course of dissolution does not coincide entirely with a gradient of abstractness to concreteness has already been pointed out in Chapter 7. It hardly needs stating that a theory of reduced level of function need not, and is not in this instance, based on a phylogenetic or architectonic hierarchy of cerebral anatomy. By now it has become a commonplace to include in the highest integrative system those brain structures that are thought to be damaged in the Korsakoff syndrome.

*Searching Cycles.* In examining the mnemonic defects of amnesic patients, so far little attention has been paid to their notorious anomalies in affect and initiative. Since my aim is to arrive at a unitary construct from which to derive the diverse derangements of the Korsakoff syndrome, the patients' passivity, lack of spontaneity, must be functionally related to their cognitive disturbance. With this end in view, it is reasonable to regard the normal condition of organisms as one of search—whether to satisfy needs, or for solutions in the execution of plans. This search proceeds at several levels, and its direction changes after longer or shorter intervals; some of it is periodic and all of it progresses by stages, each phase being terminated by some implicit act of recognition. In motor performance kinesthetic cues provide the necessary information for closing a phase in search; in perception it is given with an articulate percept; in problem solving and learning it is reached when the task is mastered; in remembering it is achieved with the recovery of the information sought. At times these searching operations conclude with errors; as a rule they are so rapid that neither objective nor subjective records on their progress can be obtained. Most of the time, however, they are correct, and often enough we are aware of them, e.g., when faced with some ambiguous image, a difficult problem, or with a name which is "at the tip of one's tongue."

Recognition, in the sense of closing a searching cycle, implies an act of matching; the establishment of identity or of a close fit. This can be an instantaneous achievement in a single trial, but as a rule it involves repeated attempts for which function must be sustained. In Korsakoff patients this operation tends to be defective, even though it does not depend on memory function, as several of our experiments in perception and concept formation have shown. Our patients were apt to terminate their search with an incorrect match instead of pursuing it until their performance became faultless. Premature closure occurs quite commonly in normal persons too; in fact, all errors in perception, problem solving, and remembering could be cited as examples, whether they occur by missing the goal or by stopping short of it, for in searching tasks missing the target is tantamount to halting before completion.

In amnesic patients, premature closure seems to be the rule rather than the exception. A direct experimental instance in point is their inability to develop (microgenetically) percepts as fully and in such detail as can be done in the course of repeated brief exposures. The same anomaly can also be discovered at the root of their difficulties in visual scanning tasks, in sampling their vocabulary without close directives, in finding cues for perceptual discrimination or criteria for concept formation, and—as Pick and Grünthal proposed—in their reasoning. In their memory function, the most immediate examples of insufficient search are faulty recognition and confabulatory responses to questions, i.e., answers that just happen to come to hand, irrespective of their veracity or consistency with prior statements. According to this model, the amnesic anomalies originate in a failure to sustain the searching operations that are involved in normal remembering, and all the psychological defects of the Korsakoff syndrome can be traced to a premature termination of an activating function.

A deficiency of this kind has already been considered in accounting for certain perceptual impairments in Korsakoff patients. The reasoning advanced was that they failed or fell short of the normal standards in those tests of perception, because they could not hold preceding items of input long enough to integrate them with those that arrived later, and success depended on their summation, on the progressive development of a percept. It was furthermore proposed that the mechanism of short-term storage on which those perceptual accomplishments depend is also involved in registration. The consolidation theory of memory traces implies a neural process sustained over time; but so does also the microgenetic principle of perception and, by implication, of registration. If function is not sufficiently sustained, perception will not lead to registration since, in order to achieve that, the neural events initiated in perception must extend further, in time or in another dimension. This extended brain activity depends either on repeated cycles triggered by the same stimuli or by reverberations of the original impulse, or both. If the extension is in time, i.e., traces are consolidated, fading rate of function would account for the rapid decay in immediate and short-term memory, but not for the patients' continued loss of retention.

## Anterograde Amnesia

Hebb's (1949) neuropsychological theory proposes a functional relationship between such lasting changes in the brain as would subserve long-term memories and the dynamic short-term storage process. The latter involves the continuous and reiterated propagation of neural impulses, a process that extinguishes within a few seconds or minutes, but may leave lasting effects behind by modifying, in the course of its reverberations, the excitatory and inhibitory properties of the synapses along its track. Long-term memory thus has the same neurophysiological pattern as the activity subserving immediate memory, and depends for its articulation on the reverberatory process being sustained long enough to produce the necessary enduring changes. If it declines and lapses precociously, it may fail to bring about those modifications in the synapses—or wherever they take place—that are necessary for successful learning.

*Filing Systems.* In amnesic patients, if the short-term process fades fast, the synaptic changes either do not occur at all or do but are less "plastic" than in normal brain function, and consequently the newly acquired fund of information is not lost, but is less than normally accessible. Learning in adult man, as Hebb proposed, involves not so much the formation of new bonds as the reorganization of pre-existing associations. Information is presumably stored within a hierarchy of structured systems in the brain, one or more of which become modified whenever learning occurs. In the course of normal registration, it would follow, an item or complex of incoming information becomes embedded in several mnemonic systems simultaneously. In Korsakoff patients, however, registration not being sustained long enough, it is filed only in one system, or in a very few. This hypothesis implies that multiple filing requires a wider extension of the registration process, either in time or in brain space, or in both, and that accordingly restriction in extent also reduces the number of contexts in which the message is recorded. At its narrowest, the only context is that which includes every aspect of the learning situation and is continuous with it; this would allow for a single reproduction or immediate recognition only.

Theories that derive the amnesic syndrome from a disruption in consciousness, in self-reference, or in the sense of temporal continuity, allow for but a single category of coding. My alternative is that information properly registered is simultaneously filed in several systems of mnemonic storage—conceptual, attitudinal, affective, contigual, etc.—and becomes available for recall by means of these coding systems. Other things being equal, the more filing categories that embed an experience, a unit of information, the more probable is its recovery in remembering. In order to persist as a distinct event or item, it must fit into more categories than one; indeed, it differs from other similar events or data in the unique combination of its embedding structures. It is characteristic of amnesic patients that they recognize many times repeated occurrences as familiar, but as if they had encountered them only once or twice before. They do not register their observations with the distinctive marks necessary for memorizing specific, as contrasted with generic, instances. Temporal marks may serve the purpose of investing memories with their uniqueness, but so could impressions from a different stamp, in fact any codable association.

*Prospective Range of Retention.* Registration, operationally defined by immediate recall or recognition, has also been invested with the properties of a hypothetical process by which the incoming information is first sorted for retention, and then filed under appropriate headings. That some disposition for remembering is involved in registration was implicit in the distinction of this process from perception. We observe certain events or cues—such as traffic signals or hyphens at the end of printed lines—that are necessary for making the correct response or for the immediate processing of the information, but not beyond that moment. Other information we note with an intention to have it available for a limited time or indefinitely. We usually remember a telephone number after closing the directory until we have dialed it and have made contact; if the line is busy we often remember it for a few minutes but not for hours or months. This is the memory range that could be subserved by reverberating neural impulses or, in terms of information processing, by rehearsal.

Examples of retention for limited periods can be found at almost every range of the time scale. The food we had for lunch we usually remember for hours, the characters in a novel we are reading, or the reigns of monarch we shall be examined on, for days or a few weeks. These spans are certainly outside the limits of reverberating neuronal processes, yet they are limited and not randomly so. It is not at all obvious that information of this type is forgotten in accordance with the interference of external inhibitory influences or with some general laws of fading traces. More probably the duration of such memories is determined, within limits, at the time of registration. Internal inhibition, as the term is used in learning theory, does not explain this process. It can be conceived only as an intentional choice based on previous experience and, presumably, on probabilistic judgments derived from past experience. It could fail, therefore, if records of the past or of probabilities are not available, or if errors are made in their application, or if the capacity to apply the decision is defective. Since the errors in amnesic patients are not random but always reduce the memory span below its normal range, it seems most probable that the source of the error is in capacity rather than in judgment.

This aspect of registration by which prospective limits for retention are set is closely related to its other, classificatory, function. The argument here advanced is that registration is not sustained long enough or does not extend sufficiently to embed the process in all the appropriate systems of information storage and, either as a consequence or as a concomitant effect, to provide for its endurance. If Korsakoff patients fail to register information with lasting effect because of a low capacity to complete this operation, the question of their intent or judgment need not arise. In test and real life situation alike, their assessment of probabilities was usually quite sound, and they showed no gross defects in intention, such as would be revealed by poor motivation or a habit of breaking down in the continuous execution of tasks. It is, of course, debatable, whether intent to learn or remember is analogous to these propensities, and there is also the question whether we intend to forget.

*Storage Capacity.* Intention to forget need not be traced to such affective-motivational influences as are implied in the psychoanalytic construct of repression. Simple economic considerations, derived from the premise that the storage capacity of the brain is limited, led Ribot (1881) to the conclusion that the total obliteration, i.e., forgetting, as well as the momentary suppression of a vast store of information are necessary conditions of remembering. Quite possibly the amnesic patient's capacity is exceptionally small, so that he must clear the registers at frequent intervals and, to that extent, he intends to forget. The few examples of new learning by our Korsakoff patients, however, conflict with this explanation. If no residual trace of the map or the phonemes were left each time they sought their way about the hospital grounds, each time they read or heard the experimenter's name, they would never learn either. If the trace were but hard of access, being isolated from other filing systems, repeated trials could strengthen it by establishing new functional bonds. Why this should happen with some information that is or seems important for the patient's welfare but not with stories or syllables presented in the laboratory can be explained in more ways than one. The significant fact is that affective involvement, interest, and repetition are neither sufficient nor necessary conditions of retention in the amnesic syndrome. Registration on first trial, and without strong motivation, can be sustained sufficiently to embed information in accessible storage systems. Very likely, though, it will not be entered in as many files as it would in a healthy person, and therefore if available for recall it will not be reliably so. Remembering for a Korsakoff patient is a matter of probability; success is possible, failure more probable.

Apart from lack of intention and insufficiently sustained function, registration could fail because appropriate mnemonic systems are not available for embedding, or because information is so inefficiently filed that it cannot be recovered by the normal processes of search. The first hypothesis extends to recall the argument that attributes defects in registration to the unavailability of proper coding templates (cf. 268). To be sure, in Korsakoff patients the coding devices and files are inaccessible, but not because the organism has not been furnished with them. Those patients could hardly function so close to the normal standards in tests of reasoning and judgment if an ordered stock of past experience were no longer at their disposal or, for that matter, if they were no longer able to check and test the fit of specific designs or propositions against a generic rule. They fail in these operations because they do not persist long enough in their search for the closest fit or for all suitable matchings.

*Scanning Operations.* After examining several hypothetical, but behaviorally circumscribed, functions we thus return to the proposition that anterograde amnesia originates in a rapid decay of the initial response. This deficiency can be detected in the Korsakoff syndrome, as in other examples of brain damage, in observable behavior as well as at the level of hypothetical neural function. It is most immediately evident from the patients' abnormal slackness in initiating action, and from their rapidly flagging interest in the absence of repetitive or response-triggered arousal. The patients' inability to initiate action, while in fairly effective command of the mechanisms necessary for executing actions set into motion by an external agency, demands the postulation of a general activating function that, in fact, has been attributed to the ascending reticular formation (Lindsley, 1951; Hebb, 1955). Subsequent elaborations of its functions, and more especially of its thalamic nuclei (Lindsley, 1956; Samuels, 1959), have attributed to this system a cardinal part in focusing attention on differential signals, in perceptual processing, in learning, and in those processes that effect the continuity of consciousness. Lindsley (1956) intimated that this neural system may also be involved in processes of coding, decoding, storage, and recovery of information. Gearing it to Hebb's (1949) dual-process model of learning, Milner (1957) proposed that more rapid firing in the nonspecific systems promotes learning by raising the rate of cortical activity, and consequently also of the processes by which associations between cells are established. The system can exert its influence alike by suppressing and by facilitating neural events in the brain, and by the pattern no less by the quality of discharge (Malmo, 1959). Its topography as well as its functional properties qualify it for the role of Penfield's (1938, 1958) subcortical integrating system. It has been invested with all the functions hypothesized here to account for the psychopathology of the Korsakoff syndrome.

Its anatomical pathology, however, furnishes no immediate support for this hypothetical formulation. The cerebral damage most reliably associated with the amnesic syndrome is in the mammillary and hippocampal zones, in the medial parts of the thalamus and hypothalamus (Brierly, 1961; Adams, Collins, and Victor, 1962; Barbizet, 1963), not in the reticular formation. Moreover, the severe behavioral derangements observed in man with known reticular lesions do not occur in the Korsakoff syndrome. The implication of the nonspecific activating system in the dysfunction of a subcortical integrating system in the Korsakoff syndrome is, therefore, entirely inferential. Any effect originating in an activating system must be mediated through a mechanism that is involved, not in consciousness and momentary perception, but in the more intricate operations of sequential integration, search and set.

Lindsley (1957) has proposed a model of a brain mechanism that would determine flexibility of set, the rate of perceptual scanning, capacity to pay attention to more than one thing at a time; in short, the central integration of information received through multiple channels. This model is based on a suggestion that the alpha rhythm and its cycle might operate like the shutter of a movie projector, alternately passing and blocking information. In fact the EEG records of our Korsakoff patients have failed to show any characteristic abnormality, and moreover the model of a neuronic shutter may not fit comfortably into that of a scanning mechanism.

Jamming of the shutter would, of course, provide a convenient image of the Korsakoff patients' arrest with one set, with their first interpretation of a pattern or situation, and their apparent resistance to changing it. At that stage, however, jamming is not the only conceivable impediment in that scanning operation which selects and structures the incoming signals. This hypothetical scanning mechanism need not correspond in detail to any known electronic model or fully described neural system. It corresponds to the psychological notion that the organism is normally in a state of activity that is not random but follows programs—conditional and unconditional—and every so often reaches a momentary pause with an event of completion, matching, recognition. Defects in such a complex and hierarchically ordered mechanism could occur in one or more of several operational phases. The dysfunction characteristic of the amnesic syndrome seems to arise from the most general activating operation that determines the rate, range, and persistence of scanning. Very probably, this operation is controlled to a considerable measure by corticofugal impulses that could be obstructed by the subcortical lesion in the Korsakoff syndrome.

An activating mechanism would thus determine the extent or power of the scanning operations, while their direction follows the varying goals and programs of the organism, and changes with those events of recognition that terminate each successive phase of search. Closure of a cycle redirects the operation but, if the function is insufficiently sustained, closure occurs prematurely and no new direction will be set. It is at these junctures that the organism alters its set which is then confirmed or negated during the next phase of scanning. Continuity of experience is provided by the chain of expectancies, their subsequent confirmation or negation, and their appropriate continued maintenance or modification. With amnesic patients this entire cycle becomes stunted. The scanning operation is inadequate, phases are not completed, and no new expectancies are directed toward the ensuing events. If the set happens to be appropriate for the information of the moment then perception, response, and experience will be appropriate too, but only for the moment; they will remain isolated.

All this attempts to explain the anterograde amnesia of Korsakoff patients, and to relate that disability to their personality malfunction characterized by lack of spontaneity and flat affect. It does allow for occasions of successful learning and recall of even recently encountered information, in that the mechanism is probabilistic, and the functions involved in these operations are assumed to be reduced in capacity and unreliable rather than completely abolished. It needs further elaboration to account for the patients' retrograde amnesia and those errors in reproduction that constitute the bulk of confabulation.

## Retrograde Amnesia

Much practiced, overlearned skills are relatively unaffected in the amnesic syndrome, and so is usually a fair amount of autobiographical information, particularly that which dates back to childhood, though it may extend well into adult life and indeed as far as the patient's first confusional breakdown. Ribot's laws of regression hold up with all their puzzling implications that demand some such resolution as a model of gradually consolidating traces can provide. Consolidation alone, however, does not offer a sufficient explanation, since a good many old memories decay in time, and even amnesic patients are capable of reactivating some traces that have had relatively little time to consolidate. Heuristically, memory structures can be differentiated and ranked according to their autonomy as systems. A skill like tieing a shoe lace or signing one's name is highly autonomous, because it has been performed so often and also because it regularly follows the same situational cues and consists of a stable succession of moves. These are the automatic memories with no temporal sign attached to them, reactivated without the experiential quality that accompanies the recovery of a unique autobiographical item. The sequence of operations that constitute such an automatic response is very close to the ideal model of the conditional reflex. Once established, it remains accessible to the amnesic patient, though he may not be able to acquire new skills in the same manner.

*Unique Memories.* Most singular items of information have multiple bonds, and to extract one from storage involves an extensive search. To illustrate the difference in difficulty between the two operations, let us compare these two questions: (a) What is the year of the Declaration of Independence? (b) What important events occurred in 1776? To the former question there is only one correct answer, and the two form a close bond. To the second there are a good many correct answers, and their appropriateness depends on various situational criteria; therefore, not only must the search extend further but its termination too involves a more complex decision. Now, this is the task amnesic patients face when they entirely fail, or make mistakes in recalling personal experiences or other information imparted to them in the past.

The occasion when they confabulate or show signs of retrograde amnesia is typically one that confronts them with a question probing for some specific item of information. The cycle of events is thus initiated by an external agency, the patient must sustain it until the phase allotted to him is completed. Usually he does not keep searching thoroughly enough to recover the information required, either because his ongoing scanning operation does not reach the file which stores that information or, more probably, because it does not sufficiently explore that file. Owing to its reduced rate, range, or persistence, the search only reaches the closest target, and misses all but the most immediate approaches. The result is either a complete failure to answer the question, or the substitution of some likely enough information for the correct one; but at times the correct reply can be given.

*Errors in Substitution.* His difficulty in recapturing the proper information does not of itself explain why an amnesic patient should so unhesitatingly respond with an incorrect substitute. Some defect in checking and verifying his response must also exert an influence; recognition as well as retrieval is at fault. There are two leads in the theoretical model outlined here that could account for this additional detriment in amnesic patients. One is an extension of the principle of reafferent stimulation (von Holst, 1957; Held, 1961) that attributes stability in perceptual orientation to spontaneuosly initiated motor acts against which afferent signals are checked. These are quite likely to be wanting in Korsakoff patients, and by analogy so are the operations necessary for checking the accuracy of all cognitive responses.

A second reason why amnesic patients do not correctly identify memories of unique events is that these could not retain their specificity if they were defined by a single category of mnemonic storage. Within any one category a trace is generic; its individuality is determined by the combination of the files in which it is recorded. This condition of the singularity of a memory is most obvious in respect to its temporal context. A control subject is more exact than a Korsakoff patient in recalling the number of occasions on which he has met the experimenter, not because the latter appears to him as a different person on each occasion, marked with a different temporal sign, but because his every visit to the laboratory occurred within a different series of other events, and may have been distinguished by a different battery of experimental tasks. Man's brain undoubtedly is equipped to scan an ordered file of these memories very rapidly, and can thus provide the correct answer to a question "How many times have you . . .?" It is unlikely to keep special ledger entries for the emergence of any possible question of this type, and to bring its record up to date continuously in the form of so many discrete traces.

Errors in chronological placement of actual events can thus occur if the memory of each is determined by the intersection of several trace systems. They cannot be explained if the temporal is the only category of memory filing, nor do Bartlett's schemata offer a model for the recovery or misplacement of unique events in recollection. Rote learning theories allow for inter-serial intrusions as well as for intra-serial transpositions but, as Conrad (1959) pointed out, no neurophysiological explanation has yet been advanced for these occurrences.

Neither should the hypotheses presented here be regarded as other than purely formal. They imply a brain model in which: (a) specific memories are filed under generic headings but entered plurally, so that their uniqueness depends on cross-indexing; (b) that any item on file is accessible, although such properties as recency or frequency, interest or affective coloring influence the degree of accessibility; (c) the items are surveyed by a rapid scanning operation, and the process of selection fits a matching test. In amnesic patients the scanning process fades before completing its course, thus the information sought is not recovered from the files. Furthermore, scanning proceeds entirely or mainly across a single file, and therefore the identity of individual memories cannot be properly established.

## Defective Activation

The theory advanced here thus traces retrograde amnesia and confabulation to the same disturbance in function as anterograde amnesia and lack of spontaneity. Although the pursuit of single causation has its attraction and is sanctioned by the law of parsimony, it is neither necessarily the clearest nor the only right course to follow. Habitual lack of initiative is not invariably accompanied by defects in memory and learning; the two symptoms—in spite of their close association—could be caused by two distinct disturbances in brain function. Some recent neurophysiological experiments with animals, however, suggest that aesthetic pleasure and economic virtue are not the only arguments for deriving the two sets of disorder from one functional derangement. Cerebral ablation and stimulation experiments have demonstrated a functional connection between the initiation of responses, new learning, and the exercise of incompletely established skills (Buchwald *et al.*, 1961); and Cobb (1958, p. 71) remarked about mammals whose cortex had been removed but whose basal ganglia were intact that "all they lack is initiative and spontaneity, as well as memory."

That the anatomical areas investigated in these experiments are not those associated with the Korsakoff syndrome seems to be a matter of minor significance, for neither are the operations testing memory function in man and animal closely comparable, nor do cerebral systems necessarily subserve identical functions at higher and lower grades of the evolutionary scale. Nevertheless, if in subhuman species the Papez circuit is primarily associated with emotions, and if in man the same system is implicated in memory function, there is good case for hypothesizing a mechanism involved in both these aspects of behavior. A mechanism that sustains activity until an event of closure is reached is precisely such a construct, and one that can be related to observable events.

Adey (1962) noted that the initiation and execution of goal-oriented responses are associated with a characteristic (6 c.p.s.) electrophysiological pattern in the hippocampus, the *theta* rhythm. Grastyán and Karmos (1962) associate the *theta* rhythm of the hippocampus with an inhibitory function which, in effect, provides for the maintenance of an excitatory process. This process could indeed be involved in the establishment of memories, in their retrieval, and in the execution of specific action patterns; it does in fact influence learning at the level of conditioning, in the phase of stabilization and in delayed reaction. Hippocampal lesions result in failure to complete goal-oriented responses, to sustain specific "excitatory" processes in the brain. They, or functionally equivalent disruptions of cerebral systems, could also result in the diffuseness of message processing in the brain. The orderly operations of matching and information filing would be disrupted by the invasion of messages that are normally suppressed.

Arnold (1960), who regards the hippocampus as the source of impulse for action, explains the behavioral defect that ensues from lesions in it or in its efferent pathways, as a defect in matching or appraisal. She reasons that, before its execution, every action is appraised against the memory of the pleasurable (or the contrary) outcome of similar action in the past. While such a simple hedonistic formula may be appropriate for the interpretation of animal behavior in the experimental laboratory, it obviously does not fit the amnesic syndrome. Within its limits, the behavior of Korsakoff patients is much too orderly and adaptive to suggest any detachment of the hedonic tags from the actions with which they should be associated. Furthermore, as has been pointed out, their amnesic disorder is not systematically related to the affective loading of memories. Observations of the amnesic syndrome agree with conclusions drawn from animal experiments that the cognitive processes involved in learning and remembering share certain subcortical neural systems with the conative processes of initiative and spontaneity, and probably also with certain intensive properties of affection. They do not bear out the primacy of the cognitive, i.e., of the memory defect.

The view that argues the dependence of memory function on motivation and persistence rests on firmer evidence. Lashley (1950) gave it expression when he stated the belief that amnesias resulting from brain injury are not caused by the destruction of specific memory traces, "but represent a lowered level of vigilance, a greater difficulty in activating the organized patterns of traces, or a disturbance of some broader system of organized functions." Russell (1959, p. 75) put forward this functional relationship quite unequivocally when he suggested that patients recovering from concussion regain their memories by an effort at piecing them together. In my own research his hypothesis gained convincing support from the case history of the young encephalitic man presented in the preceding chapter.

This puts the conative before the cognitive disturbance in the amnesic syndrome. A colleague paraphrased this conclusion when he declared that Korsakoff's psychosis is a disease of morale. No doubt, a case could be made for deriving the character of Korsakoff patients from their amnesic derangement. Very likely such a derivation would employ arrested self-development or a disturbed temporal sense as a mediating construct. From either point of departure the logical progress would lead to some general activating or dispositional function of the brain.

Setting up plans for action, their hierarchical ordering, testing, and modification, are all included in this function. Such plans can originate from outside only within a limited scope. By means of instruction, by steering the interview, plans of action were imposed on our Korsakoff patients, and their responses indicated the extent to which they could exercise their abilities. If the instruction was to perform a much rehearsed skill, to discriminate signals, or to execute some simple reasoning, it usually proved effective. If, however, the instruction specified alternates contingent on the outcome of events, or asked for the memorization or recall of a recent message or event, it almost invariably failed in execution. Since Korsakoff patients have no difficulty in comprehending such an instruction, their failure must be attributed to an inability to carry it out. Their plans to register information for future recall or recognition must evidently be initiated from outside. Even the recovery of information that was once memorized may involve so many choices and sub-plans that it falters in the absence of sustained direction.

This study of the amnesic syndrome started out by raising the question of memory. After examining my own observations and those of others, I am concluding it with speculations about a general activating function, and by proposing premature closure of this function as an answer to the psychological derangement under investigation. The loss of static traces of memory content and the corresponding disruption of cortical associations have at no time provided an adequate explanation of the derangements characteristic of this syndrome. Disturbances in one or another more specific function of the organism, and in the neural mechanisms that correspond to them, can account for some or all of its psychopathology. They provide the material for a pluralistic explanation that is also subject to certain qualifications, so as to allow for examples of efficient function retained by Korsakoff patients. The paradigm of reduced activation and premature closure of function has the advantage of being both comprehensive and probabilistic. Its drawbacks are that it may not be specific enough, and that it does not stand out clearly within our current conceptual system of behavior. But the need to revise our concepts of man's neuropsychology is precisely one of the lessons to be learned from the study of such diseases as the Korsakoff syndrome.

# REFERENCES


Adams, R. D. (1959). Nutritional diseases of the nervous system. (Gordon Wilson Lecture.) *Trans. Amer. Clin Climatol, Assoc.*, 71:59-93.

Adams, R. D., Collins, G. H., and Victor, M. (1962). Troubles de la mémoire et de l'apprentissage chez l'homme. Leurs relations avec des lésions des lobes temporaux et du diencéphale (pp. 273-294). *Physiologie de l'hippocampe.* Paris: Centre National de la Recherche Scientifique.

Adey, W. R. (1962). EEG studies of the hippocampal system in the learning process and Discussion (pp. 236-237). *Physiologie de l'hippocampe.* Paris: Centre National de la Recherche Scientifique.

Adrian, E. D. (1936). The spread of activity in the cerebral cortex. *J. Physiol.*, 88:127-161.

Adrian, E. D. (1947). *The physical background of perception.* London and New York: Oxford Univer. Press (Clarendon).

Ajuriaguerra, J. de, Hécaen, H., and Sadoun, R. (1954). Tumeurs de la région mésodiencéphalique. *Encéphale* 5:399-473.

Allport, G. W., and Postman, L. (1947). *The psychology of rumor.* New York: Holt.

Ames, A. (1951). Visual perception and the rotating trapezoidal window. *Psychol. Monogr.*, No. 324.

Angelergues, R. (1958). *Le syndrome mental de Korsakow.* Paris: Masson.

Arnold, Magda B. (1960). *Emotion and personality* (Vol. II: Neurological and physiological aspects). New York: Columbia Univer. Press.

Arthur, G. (1943). *A stencil design test.* New York: Psychological Corp.

Babilée, W. (1886). *Des troubles de la mémorire dans l'alcoolisme, et plus particulièrement de l'amnésie alcoolique.* (Doctoral Thesis.) Paris: A. Parent.

Ballard, P. B. (1913). Obliviscence and reminiscence. *Brit. J. Psychol. Monogr.*, No. 2.

Barbizet, J. (1963). Etudes cliniques sur la mémoire. *Semaine des Hopitaux,* 20:931-950; 21:983-995. Translated in part as: (1963). Defect of memorizing of hippocampal-mammillary origin: a review. *J. Neurol. Neurosurg. Psychiat.* 26:127-135.

Bartlett, F. C. (1932). *Remembering.* London and New York: Cambridge Univer. Press.

Belbin, E. (1950). The influence of interpolated recall upon recognition. *Quart. J. Exp. Psychol.*, 2:163-169.

Bender, L., Curran, F. J., and Schilder, P. (1938). Organization of memory traces in the Korsakoff syndrome. *A.M.A. Arch. Neurol. Psychiat.*, 39:482-487.

Benedek, L. and Juba, A. (1941). Korsakow-Syndrom bei den Geschwülsten des Zwischenhirns. *Arch. Phychiat. Nervenheilk.*, 114: 366-376.

Benton, A. L. (1955). *The revised visual retention test.* Iowa City: State Univer. Iowa.

Bergson, H. (1896) *Matière et mémoire.* Paris: Alcan. (Transl. *Matter and memory.* London: Allen, 1911).

Bernard, P. (1951). Essai psycho-pathologique sur le comportement dans le syndrome de Korsakoff. *La Raison*, 2:93-101.

Bessière, R. (1948) : Presbyophrénie et psychose polynévritique de Korsakoff. *Encéphale*, 37:313-342.

Betlheim, S., and Hartmann, H. (1924). Über Fehlreaktionen bei der Korsakowschen Psychose. *Arch. Psychiat. Nervenheilk.*, 72:275-286. (Transl. On parapraxes in the Korsakow psychosis. *In* Rapaport, D. (1951), pp. 288-307, listed below.)

Binet, A., and Henri, V. (1894. La mémoire des phrases. *Anneé psychol.*, 1:24-59.

Bleuler, E. (1922). *Das autistisch-undisziplinierte Denken.* Berlin: Springer.

Bleuler, E. (1924). *Textbook of psychiatry.* New York: Macmillan.

Bonhöffer, K. (1901). *Die akuten Geisteskrankheiten der Gewohnheitstrinker.* Jena, Germany: Fischer.

Bonhöffer, K. (1904). Der Korsakowsche Symptomenkomplex in seinen Beziehungen zu den verschiedenen Krankheitsformen. *Allg. Z. Psychiat.*, 61:744-752.

Bouman, L., and Grünbaum, A. (1929). Eine Störung der Chronognosie und ihre Bedeutung im betreffenden Symptomenbild. *Mschr. Psychiat. Neurol.*, 73:1-40.

Boycott, B. B., and Young, J. Z. (1955). A memory system in octopus vulgaris Lamarck. *Proc. Roy. Soc.*, 143:440-480.

Bremer, F. (1953). Aspects physiologiques de la mémoire. *Centre Belge de Navigation.* 9:25-38.

Brierley, J. B. (1961) Clinico-pathological correlations in amnesia. *Geront. Clin.*, 3:97-109.

Broadbent, D. E. (1958). *Perception and communication.* New York: Pergamon Press.

Brodmann, K. (1902, 1904). Experimenteller und klinischer Beitrag zur Psychopathologie der polyneuritischen Psychose. *J. Psychol. Neurol.*, 1:225-247; 3: 1-48.

Brown, J. (1954). The nature of set to learn and of intra-serial interference in immediate memory. *Quart. J. exp. Psychol.*, 6:141-148.

Brown, J. (1958). Some tests of the decay theory of immediate memory. *Quart. J. exp. Psychol.*, 10:12-21.

Bruner, J. S. (1957). Going beyond the information given. *Contemporary approaches to cognition*, pp. 41-70. Cambridge, Massachusetts: Harvard Univer. Press.

Bruner, J. S., Goodnow, J. J., and Austin, G. A. (1956). *A study of thinking*. New York: Wiley.

Buchwald, N. A., Wyers, E. J., Carlin, J., and Farley, R. E. (1961). Effects of caudate stimulation on visual discrimination. *J. exp. Neurol.*, 4:23-36.

Bürger, H. (1927). Zur Psychologie des amnestischen Symptomenkomplexes. *Arch. Psychiat. Nervenheilk.*, 81:348-352.

Bürger-Prinz, H., and Büssow, H. (1943). Über das amnestische Syndrom. *Allg. Z. Psychiat.*, 121:195-215.

Bürger-Prinz, H., and Kaila, M. (1930). Über die Struktur des amnestischen Symptomenkomplexes. *Z. Neurol. Phychiat.*, 124:553-595.

Burnham, W. H. (1904). Retroactive amnesia: illustrative cases and a tentative explanation. *Amer. J. Psychol.*, 14:118-132.

Burns, B. D. (1958). *The mammalian cerebral cortex*. London: Arnold.

Cameron, D. E. (1943). Impairment of the retention phase of remembering. *Psychiat. Quart.*, 17:395-404.

Cameron, D. E. (1947). *Remembering*. New York: Nerv. ment. Dis. Monogr.

Cameron, N., and Magaret, A. (1951). *Behavior pathology*. Boston: Houghton Mifflin.

Carmichael, E. A., and Stern, R. O. (1931). Korsakoff's syndrome: its histopathology. *Brain*, 54:189-213.

Charcot, P., (1884). Les paralyses alcooliques. *Gazette des Hopitaux*, 57: 785-787.

Chaslin, P. (1912). *Eléments de clinique et de séméiologies mentales.* Paris: Asselin.

Claparède, E. (1911). Recognition et moiïté. *Arch. Psychol. Genève*, 11:79-90.

Clark, K. B. (1940). Some factors influencing the remembering of prose material. *Arch. Psychol.*, No. 253.

Clarke, F. B. (1912). Korsakow's syndrome with synopsis of cases. *Amer. J. Insan.*, 69:323-336.

Cobb, S. (1958). *Foundations of neuropsychiatry*. Baltimore, Maryland: Williams & Wilkins.

Colella, R. (1894). La psicosi polineuritica. *Ann. Neurol.*, 12:1-66, 151-225, 449-521.

Collins, G. H., Victor, M., and Adams, R. D. (1961). A neuropathological study of Wernicke's Disease and Korsakoff's psychosis. *J. Neuropath. Exp. Neurol.*, 20:289-291.

Conrad, K. (1953). Zur Psychopathologie des amnestischen Symptomenkomplexes. Gestaltanalyse einer Korsakowschen Psychose. *D. Z. Nervenheilk.*, 190: 471-502.

Conrad, K. (1953b). Über einen Fall von "Minuten Gedächtnis." *Arch. Psychiat. Z. Neurol.*, 190:471-502.

Conrad, K., and Ule, G. (1951). Ein Fall von Korsakow Psychose mit anatomischen Befund und klinischen Betrachtungen. *D. Z. Nervenheilk*, 165:430-445.

Conrad, R. (1959). Errors of immediate memory. *Brit. J. Psychol.*, 50: 349-359.

Conrad, R., and Hille, B. A. (1958). The decay theory of immediate memory and paced recall. *Canad. J. Psychol.*, 12:1-6.

Crahay, S. (1957). Les épreuves de mémoire immédiate dans la maladie

Czechmanek, K. von (1954). Ein Korsakow syndrom bei traumatischer Schädigung des Hypothalamus durch Granatsplitter. *Nervenarzt*, 25:158-160.

de Korsakow d'origine alcoolique. *Acta Neurol. Belg.*, 57:570-581.

Davidson, G. M. (1948). Psychosomatic aspects of the Korsakoff syndrome. *Psychiat. Quart.*, 22:1-17.

DeCamp, J. E. (1915). A study of retroactive inhibition. *Psychol. Monogr.*, No. 84.

Deese, J. (1958). *The psychology of learning*. New York: McGraw-Hill.

Deese, J., and Hardman, G. W. (1954). An analysis of errors in retroactive inhibition of rote verbal learning. *Amer. J. Psychol.*, 67: 299-307.

Delay, J. (1942a). *Les dissolutions de la mémoire*. Paris: Presses Univer. de France.

Delay, J. (1942b). *Les maladies de la mémoire*. Paris: Presses Univer. de France.

Delay, J., and Brion, S. (1954). Syndrome de Korsakoff et corps mamillaires. *Encéphale*, 43:193-200.

Delay, J., Brion, S., and Elissalde, B. (1958). Corps mamillaires et syndrome de Korsakoff: Etude anatomique de huit cas de syndrome de Korsakoff d'origine alcoolique sans alteration significative du cortex cérébral. I. Etude anatomo-clinique. *Presse Médicale*, 66: 1849-1854; II. Tubercules mamillaires et mécanisme de la mémoire. *ibid.*, 66:1965-1968.

Delay, J., Boudin, G., Brion, S., and Barbizet, J. (1958). Etude anatomo-clinique de huit encéphalopathies alcooliques. (Encéphalopathie de Wernicke et syndromes voisins.) *Encéphale*, 47:99-142.

Döblin, Alfred (1905). *Gedächtnisstörungen bei der Korsakoffschen Psychose.* (Dissert., Univ. of Freiburg.) Berlin: O. & E. Klett.

Dugas, L. (1917). *La mémoire et l'oubli.* Paris: Flammarion.

Dupré, E. (1906). Encéphalites aigues diffuses histologiques. Psycho-polynévrites. *Traité de patholigie de Gilbert Baillet*, Vol. I, pp. 1122-1160. Paris: Doin.

Ebbinghaus, H. (1885). *Über das Gedächtnis.* Leipzig: Duncker.

Eccles, J. C. (1953). *The neurophysiological basis of mind.* London and New York: Oxford Univer. Press (Clarendon).

Ehrenwald, H. (1931). Über den Zeitsinn und die gnostische Störung der Zeitaufassung beim Korsakow. *Z. Neurol. Psychiat.*, 134:512-521.

Ewald, G. (1940). Zur Frage der Lokalisation des amnestischen Symptomenkomplexes. *Allg. Z. Psych.*, 115:220-237.

Finzi, J. (1901). Zur Untersuchung der Auffassungfänhigkeit und Merkfähigkeit. *Psychologische Arbeiten* (E. Kräpelin, Ed.), Vol. III, pp. 289-384. Leipzig: Engelmann.

Fisher, R. A. (1934). *Statistical methods for research workers.* (5th ed.) Edinburgh and London: Oliver & Boyd.

Flament, J. (1957). La fabulation dans le syndrome de Korsakow d'étiologie traumatique. *Acta Neurol. Belg.*, 57:119-161.

Flavell, J. H., and Draguns, J. (1957). A microgenetic approach to perception and thought. *Psychol. Bull.*, 54:197-217.

Florès, C. (1958). Études sur les processus d'utilisation de la trace mnésique. Le rappelle, la reconnaissance et le réapprentissage. *Anneé psychol.*, 57:25-43.

Förster, O., and Gagel, O. (1934). Ein Fall von Ependymcyste des III Ventrikels. *Z. Neurol. Psychiat.*, 149:312-344.

Fraisse, P. (1963). *The psychology of time.* New York: Harper and Row.

Fraisse, P., and Florès, C. (1956). Perception et fixation mnémonique. *Anneé psychol.*, 56:1-11.

Franks, C. M., and Withers, W. C. R. (1955). Photoelectric recording of eyelid movements. *Amer. J. Psychol.*, 68:467-471.

Franz, S. L. (1919). *Handbook of mental examination.* New York: Macmillan.

Freund, K., and Srnec, J. (1956). Zum Problem der allgemeinen Merkschwäche. Ein Modellversuch. *Mschr. Psychiat. Neurol.*, 131:226-246.

Gál, P. (1955) Agyrázkodas utáni amnesticus tünetegyüttes. *Ideggyógy. Szemle*, 8:49-55.

Gamper, E. (1928). Zur Frage der Polyencephalitis haemorrhagica der chronischen Alcoholiker. *Dtsch. Z. Nervenheilk.*, 102:122-129.

Gamper, E. (1929). Schlaf-Delirium tremens-Korsakowsches Syndrom. *Z. Neurol. Psychiat.* 51:236-239.

Gantt, W., and Muncie, W. (1942). Analysis of mental defect in chronic Korsakov's Psychosis by means of the conditioned reflex method. *Johns Hopkins Hosp. Bull.*, 70:467-487.

Gibson, E. J. (1940). A systematic application of the concepts of generalization and differentiation to verbal learning. *Psychol. Rev.*, 47:196-229.

Gillespie, R. D. (1937). Amnesia. *Arch. Neurol. Psychiat.*, 37:748-764.

Glaze, J. A. (1928). The association value of nonsense syllables. *J. genet. Psychol.*, 35:255-267.

Glees, P., and Griffith, H. B. (1952). Bilateral destruction of hippocampus (cornu Ammonis) in case of dementia. *Mschr. Psychiat. Neurol.*, 123:193-205.

Goldstein, K. (1934). *Der Aufbau des Organismus.* The Hague: Nijhoff. Transl. *The organism.* (1939). New York: Amer. Book.

Goldstein, K. (1942). *Aftereffects of brain injuries in war.* New York: Grune & Stratton.

Goldstein, K., and Scheerer, M. (1941). Abstract and concrete behavior. *Psychol. Monogr., No.* 239.

Gomulicki, B. R. (1953). The development and present status of the trace theory of memory. *Brit. J. Psychol. Monogr. Suppl.*, No. 29.

Gomulicki, R. (1956). Individual differences in recall. *J. Pers.* 24:387-400.

Gottschaldt, K. (1926). Über den Einfluss der Erfahrung auf die Wahrnehmung von Figuren. *Psychol. Forsch.*, 8:261-317; and (1929) 12:1-87.

Grastyán, E. (1959). The hippocampus and higher nervous activity. In *The central nervous system and behavior* (M. A. B. Brazier, Ed.), Trans. 2nd Conf., pp. 119-205. New York: Josiah Macy, Jr. Foundation.

Grastyán, E., and Karmos, G. (1962). The influence of hippocampal lesions on simple and delayed instrumental conditioned reflexes. *Physiologie de l'hippocampe*, pp. 225-234. Paris: Centre National de la Recherche Scientifique.

Gregor, A. (1909).Beiträge zur Psychopathologie des Gedächtnisses. *Mschr. Psychiat. Neurol.*, 25:218-255; 330-386.

Gregor, A., and Römer, H. (1907). Beiträge zur Kenntnis der Gedächtnisstörung bei der Korsakowschen Psychose. *Mschr. Psychiat. Neurol.*, 21:19-46; 144-167.

Gross, O. (1902). *Die cerebrale Sekundärfunction.* Leipzig: Vogel.

Grünthal, E. (1923). Zur Kenntnis der Psychopathologie des Korsakowschen Symptomenkomplexes. *Mschr. Psychiat. Neurol.*, 53:85-132.

Grünthal, E. (1924) Über das Symptom der Einstellungestörung bei exogenen Psychosen. *Z. Neurol. Psychiat.*, 92:255-266.

Grünthal, E. (1939). Über das Corpus Mammillare und den Korsakowschen Symptomenkomplex. *Conf. Neurol.*, 2:64-95.

Grünthal, E. (1947). Über das klinische Bild nach umschriebenem beiderseitigen Ausfall der Ammonshorn-Rinde, ein Beitrag zur Kenntnis der Funktion des Ammonshorns, *Mschr. Psychiat. Neurol.*, 113: 1-16.

Grünthal, E. (1954). Zur psychophysiologischen Deutung "isolierten" dauernden Merkfähigkeitsverlustes von extremen Grade nach initialer Kohlenoxydschädigung eines Unfallversicherten. *Schweiz. Arch. Neurol. Psychiat.*, 74:179.

Grünthal, E. (1959). Über den derzeitigen Stand der Frage nach den klinischen Erscheinungen bei Ausfall des Ammonshorn. *Psychiat. Neurol.*, 138:145-159.

Grünthal, E., and Störring, G. E. (1930a). Über das Verhalten umschriebener, völliger Merkunfähigkeit. *Mschr. Psychiat. Neurol.*, 74:254-269.

Grünthal, E., and Störring, G. E. (1930b). Erganzende Beobachtungen und Bemerkungen zu dem in Band 74. (1930) dieser Zeitschrift beschriebenen Fall mit reiner Merkunfähigkeit. *Mschr. Psychiat. Neurol.*, 77:374-382.

Grünthal, E., and Störring, G. E. (1956). Abschlieszende Stellungsnahme zu der vorstehenden Arbeit von H. Völkel und R. Stolze über den Fall B. *Mschr. Psychiat. Neurol*, 132:309 311.

Gruner, E. (1956). Sur la pathologie des encéphalopathies alcooliques. *Rev. Neurol.*, 94:682-689.

Gudden, H. (1896). Klinische und anatomische Beiträge zur Kenntniss der Multiplen Alkoholneuritis nebst Bemerkungen über die Regenerationsvorgänge in peripheren Nervensystem. *Arch Psychiat. Nervenkrankh.*, 28:643-744.

Halstead, W. C. (1947). *Brain and intelligence.* Chicago: Univer. of Chicago Press.

Hanawalt, N. G. (1937). Memory trace for figures in recall and recognition. *Arch Psychol.*, 31, No. 216, pp. 1-89.

Hartmann, H. (1927). Zur Frage: Organische Amnesie und Hypnose. Versuche an Korsakoffkranken. *Wiener Klin. Wschr.*, 40:1507-1508.

Hartmann, H. (1930). Gedächtnis und Lustprinzip. Untersuchungen an Korsakoffkranken. *Z. Neurol. Psychiat.*, 126:496-519.

Hartmann, H. (1935). Das Korsakowsche Syndrom. *Wien. Klin. Wschr.*, 1:457-459.

Hartmann, H., and Schilder, P. (1925). Zur Psychologie der Schädelverletzter. *Arch. Psychiat.*, 75:287-300.

Hebb, D. O. (1949). *The organization of behavior.* New York: Wiley.

Hebb, D. O. (1955). Drives and the C.N.S. (Conceptual nervous system.) *Psychol. Rev.*, 62:243-254.

Heimann, A., and Heimann, H. (1952).Nachuntersuchung des Falles B. mit "umschriebener völliger Merkunfähigkeit." *Mschr. Psychiat. Neurol.*, 124:272-303.

Held, R. (1961). Exposure-History as a factor in maintaining stability of perception and coordination. *J. nerv. ment, Dis.*, 132:26-32.

Henderson, D., and Gillespie, R. (1937). *A textbook of psychiatry* (4th ed.) London and New York: Oxford Univer. Press.

Hilgard, E. R. (1956). *Theories of learning.* New York: Appleton.

Hilgard, E. R., and Marquis, D. G. (1940). *Conditioning and learning.* New York: Appleton.

Holst, E. von (1957). Aktive Leistungen der menschlichen Gesichtswahrnehmung. *Studium Gen.*, 10:231-243.

Horányi, B. (1945). Az amnestikus syndroma kórlélektani szerkezetéröl. *Orvosok Lapja,* 1:4-7.

Holst, E. von (1957). Aktive Leistungen der menschlichen Gesichtswahrnehmung. *Studium Gen.*, 10:231-243.

Hull, C. L. (1940). *Mathematico-deductive theory of rote learning.* New Haven, Connecticut: Yale Univer. Press.

Huss, M. (1852). Cronische Alcohols Krankheit. Stockholm: Fritze.

Jackson, J. Hughlings (1884). Evolution and dissolution of the nervous system. (Croonian lecture). *Lancet,* I:555-558, 649-652, 739-744. Reprinted in *Selected writings of John Hughlings Jackson.* (J. Taylor, Ed.), Vol. II, pp. 45-75. New York: Basic Books.

Janet, P. (1928). *L'évolution de la mémoire et la notion du temps.* Paris: Chahine.

Jasper, H. H. (1949). Diffuse projection systems: the integrative action of the thalamic reticular system. *EEG. clin. Neurophysiol.*, 1:405-419.

Jenkins, J. G., and Dallenbach, K. M. (1924). Obliviscence during sleep and waking. *Amer. J. Psychol.*, 35:605-612.

Joliffe, N., Wortis, H., and Fein, H. D. (1941). The Wernicke syndrome. *A.M.A. Arch. Neurol Psychiat.*, 46:569-597.

Jolly, F. (1897). Über die psychischen Störungen bei Polyneuritis. *Charitéannalen,* 22:579-612.

Jones, E. E., and Bruner, J. S. (1954). Expectancy in apparent visual movement. *Brit. J. Psychol.*, 45:157-165.

Kant, F. (1933). Die Pseudoencephalitis Wernicke der Alkoholiker. *Arch. Psychiat. Nervenkr.*, 98:702-768.

Katona, G. (1940). *Organizing and memorizing.* New York: Columbia Univer. Press.

Katzaroff, D. (1911). Contribution a l'étude de la récognition. *Arch. Psychol. Genève,* 11:2-78.

Kauffmann, A. F. (1913). Zur Frage der Heilbarkeit der Korsakowschen Psychose. *Z. Neurol. Psychiat.*, 20:488-510.

Keehn, J. D. (1956). A modified interpretation of Thurstone's flexibility of closure factor. *J. soc. Psychol.*, 44:215-222.

Kerschbaum, P. (1953). Untersuchungen zur psychologischen Struktur der Merkfähigkeitsstörung bei traumatischer Schädigung des Hypothalamus. *Z. exp. angew. Psychol.*, 1:244-264.

King, D. J., and Cofer, C. N. (1960). Retroactive interference in meaningful material as a function of the degree of contextual constraint in the original and interpolated learning. *J. gen. Psychol.*, 63: 145-158.

King, H. E. (1954). *Psychomotor aspects of mental disease.* Cambridge, Massachusetts: Harvard Univer. Press.

Klein, G. S., and Krech, D. (1952). Cortical conductivity in brain injured. *J. Pers.*, 21:118-148.

Klein, R., and Kral, V. A. (1933). Zur Frage der Pathogenese und Psychopathologie des amnestischen Symptomenkomplexes nach Schädeltraumen. *Z. Neurol. Psychiat.*, 149:134-175.

Kleist, K. (1934). *Gehirnpathologie.* Leipzig: Barth.

Körner, G. (1935). Zur Psycho-pathologie des amnestischen Syndroms. *Mschr. Psychiat. Neurol.*, 90:177-216.

Környey, S., and Saethre, H. (1937). Die hypothalamische Lokalisation der histologischen Befunde in Korsakowfällen, *Acta Psychiat. Neurol.*, 12:491-498.

Koffka, K. (1935). *Principles of gestalt psychology.* New York: Harcourt-Brace.

Kohnstamm, O. (1917). Über das Krankheitsbild der retro-anterograden Amnesie und die Unterscheidung des spontanen und des lernenden Merkens. *Mschr. Psychiat. Neurol.*, 41:373-382.

Korsakoff, S. S. (1889). Étude médico-psychologique sur une forme des maladies de la mémoire. *Rev. phil.* 28:501-530.

Korsakoff, S. S. (1889). Über eine besondere Form psychischer Störung, combiniert mit multiplen Neuritis. *Arch Psychiat.*, 21:669-704.

Korsakoff, S. S. (1890). Eine psychische Störung combiniert mit multipler Neuritis (Psychosis polyneuritica seu cerebropathia psychica toxaemica). *Allg. Z. Psychiat.*, 46:475-485.

Korsakoff, S. S. (1892). Erínnerungstäuschungen (Pseudoreminiscenzen) bei polyneuritischer Psychose. *Allg. Z. Psychiat.*, 47:390-410.

Kräpelin, E. (1896). *Psychiatrie* (5th ed.) Leipzig: Barth.

Kräpelin, E. (1900). Über die Merkfähigkeit. *Mschr. Psychiat. Neurol.*, 8:245-250.

Kral, V. A. (1956). The amnesic syndrome. *Mschr. Psychiat. Neurol.*, 132:65-80.

Kral, V. A. (1959). Amnesia and the amnestic syndrome. *Canad. Psychiat. Assoc. J.*, 4:61-68.

Kral, V. A., and Durost, H. B. (1953). A comparative study of the amnesic syndrome in various organic conditions. *Amer. J. Psychiat.*, 110:41-47.

Krauss, R. (1904). Über Auffassungs- und Merke-Versuche bei einem Falle von polyneuritischer Psychose. *Psychol. Arbeiten* (E. Kräpelin, Ed.), Vol. IV, pp. 513-534. Leipzig: Engelmann.

Krauss, S. (1930). Untersuchungen über Aufbau und Störung der menschlichen Handlung. I. Die Korsakowsche Störung. *Arch. Psychol.*, 77:649-692.

Lanceraux, E. (1864). Alcoolisme. *Dictionnaire encyclopédique des sciences médicales.* Paris: Masson.

Lashley, K. S. (1950). In search of the engram. Physiological mechanisms in animal behavior. *Symp. Soc. exp. Biol.*, 4:454-483.

Latscha, R. (1953). Tests of significance in a 2 $\times$ 2 contingency table: Extension of Finney's table. *Biometrika*, 40:74-86.

Levitt, E. E. (1956). A methodological study of the preparation of connected verbal stimuli for quantitative memory experiments. *J. exp. Psychol.*, 52:33-38.

Lewin, K. (1935). *A dynamic theory of personality.* New York: McGraw-Hill.

Lewis, A. (1961). Amnesic syndromes. *Proc. Roy. Soc. Med.*, 54:955-961.

Lhermitte, J., Doussinet, P., and Ajuriaguerra, J. (1937). Une observation de forme Korsakovienne de tumeurs du 3e ventricule. *Rev. Neurol.*, 68:709-711.

Lidz, T. (1942). The amnestic syndrome. *Arch. Neurol. Psychiat.*, 47: 588-605.

Liepmann, H. (1910). Beitrag zur Kenntnis des amnestischen Symptomenkomplexes. *Neurol. Zbl.*, 29:1147-1161.

Lindberg, B. J. (1946). On the question of psychologically conditioned features in the Korsakow syndrome. *Acta Psych. Neurol.*, 21:497-542.

Lindsley, D. B. (1951). Emotion. *Handbook of experimental psychology* (S. S. Stevens, Ed.), pp. 473-516, New York: Wiley.

Lindsley, D. B. (1956). Physiological psychology. *Ann. Rev. Psychol.*, 8:323-348.

Lindsley, D. B. (1957). Psychophysiology and motivation. *Nebraska symposium on motivation* (M. P. Jones, Ed.), pp. 44-105. Lincoln: Univer. of Nebraska Press.

Linskii, V. P. (1954). On the formation of conditioned reflexes in patients exhibiting Korsakoff's syndrome. *Zh. vyssh. nervn. Deiatel'.*, 4:791-798. Quoted in (1956). *Psychol. Abstr.*, 30, 128.

Lorente de Nó, R. (1938). Synaptic stimulation of motoneurones as a local process. *J. Neurophysiol.*, 1:195-206.

Lotmar, F. (1954). Zur psycho-physiologischen Deutung "isolierten dauernden Merkfähigkeitsverlustes von extremen Grade nach initialen Kohlenoxydschädigung eines Unfallversicherten. *Schweiz. Arch. Neurol. Psychiat.*, 73:147-205.

Lotmar, F. (1958). Über die abschliessende Stellungnahme Grünthals und Störrings zu der auf den Fall B. Sekundegedächtnis bezüglichen Arbeit von Völkel und Stolze (1956) *Schweiz. Arch. Neurol. Psyciat.*, 81:203-225.

Lückerath, M. (1900). Beitrag zu der Lehre von der Korsakowschen Psychose. *Neurol. Zbl.*, 19:341-347.

Luh, C. W. (1922). The conditions of retention. *Psychol. Monogr.*, No. 142.

Lum, P. (1951). *Fabulous beasts.* New York: Pantheon.

Mabille, H., and Pitres, A. (1913). Sur un cas d'Amnésie de fixation post-apoplectique ayant presisté pendant vingt-trois ans. *Rev. Med.*, 33:257-279.

MacCurdy, J. T. (1928). *Common principles in psychology and physiology.* London and New York: Cambridge Univer. Press.

McGeoch, J. A. (1936). Studies in retroactive inhibition. VII. Retroactive inhibition as a function of the length and frequency of presentation of the interpolated lists. *J. exp. Psychol.*, 19:674-693.

McGeoch, J. A., and Irion, A. L. (1952). *The psychology of human learning*. New York: Longmans, Green.

Malamud, N., and Skillicorn, S. A. (1956). Relationship between the Wernicke and the Korsakoff syndrome. *Arch. Neurol. Psychiat.*, 76: 585-596.

Malmo, R. B. (1959). Activation: A neuropsychological dimension. *Psychol. Rev.*, 66:367-386.

Mann, H. B., and Whitney, D. R. (1947). On a test of whether one of two random variables is stochastically larger than the other. *Ann math. Statist.* 18:50-60.

Marcus, H. (1932). Morbus Korsakow. *Dtsch. Z. Nervenheilk.*, 124:165-170.

Melton, A. W., and von Lackum, W. J. (1941). Retroactive and proactive inhibition in retention: evidence for a two-factor theory of retroactive inhibition. *Amer. J. Psychol.*, 54:157-173.

Mettler, F. A. (1955). Perceptual capacity, functions of the corpus striatum and schizophrenia. *Psychiat. Quart.*, 29:89-111.

Meyer E., and Raecke, J. (1903). Zur Lehre vom Korsakow'schen Symptomencomplex. *Arch. Psychiat.*, 37:1-44.

Miller, G. A. (1956). The magical number seven, plus or minus two: some limits on our capacity for processing information. *Psychol. Rev.*, 63:81-97.

Miller, G. A., Galanter, E., and Pribram, K. H. (1960). *Plans and the structure of behavior*. New York: Holt.

Milner, B., and Penfield, W. (1956). The effect of hippocampal lesions on recent memory. *Trans. Amer. Neurol. Assoc.*, 1955:42-48.

Milner, P. M. (1957). The cell assembly: Mark II. *Psychol. Rev.* 64:242-252.

Moeli, O. (1883). Casuistische Mitteilungen. 1. Acute hallucinatorische Verwirrtheit bei chronischer Bleivergiftung. *Charité-Ann.*, 8:538-539.

Moll, J. M. (1915). The "Amnestic" or "Korsakow's" syndrome with alcoholic etiology: an analysis of thirty cases. *J. Ment. Sci.*, 61:424-443.

Mönkemöller, O. (1898). Casuistischer Beitrag zur sogenannten polyneuritischen Psychose. (Korsakoff's Krankheit.) *Allg. Z. Psychiat.*, 54:806-874.

Moruzzi, G., and Magoun, H. W. (1949). Brain stem reticular formation and activation of the EEG. *EEG Clin. Neurophysiol.*, 1:455-473.

Mouren, P., and Felician, J. (1958). Le syndrome de Korsakow posttraumatique. *Ann. Med. Psychol.*, 116:665-691.

Müller, G. E., and Pilzecker, A. (1900). Experimentelle Beitrage zur Lehre vom Gedächtniss. *Z. Psychol. Ergbd.* 1:1-288.

Müller-Suur, H. (1949). Beitrag zur Frage des Korsakow-Syndroms und der Analyse der amnestisch-strukturelle Demenz. *Arch. Psychiat. Nervenheilk.*, 181:683-711.

Neubürger, K. (1931). Über Hirnveränderungen nach Alkoholmisbrauch. *Z. Neurol. Psychiat.*, 135:159-209.

Newman, E. B. (1939). Effect of crowding of material on curves of forgetting. *Amer. J. Psychol.*, 52:601-609.

Nyssen, R. (1926). Psychose polynévritique de Korsakow. *J. Neurol. Psychiat.*, 26:419

Nyssen, R. (1956). Des capacités de definition et d'évocation des mots dans la psychose de Korsakow alcoolique. *Evolut. Phychiat.*, 1:303-314.

Nyssen, R. (1957). Contribution experimentale a l'étude de l'amnésie de fixation dans la maladie de Korsakow d'origine alcoolique. *Acta Neurol. Psychiat. Belg.*, 57:639-666.

Ohkuma, T. (1930). Zur pathologischen Anatomie des chronischen Alkoholismus. *Z. Neurol. Psychiat.*, 126:94-128.

Oldfield, R. C. (1954). Memory mechanisms and the theory of schemata. *Brit. J. Psychol.*, 45:14-23.

Oldfield, R. C., and Zangwill, O. L. (1943). Head's concept of the schema and its application in contemporary British psychology. Part III. Bartlett's theory of memory. *Brit. J. Psychol.*, 33:113-29.

Orthner, H. (1957). Pathologische Anatomie der vom Hypothalamus ausgelösten Bewusstseinsstörungen. *Actes du Ier Congrès international des Sciences Neurologiques* Vol. II, pp. 77-96. Bruxelles: Acta Medica Belgica.

Osgood, C. (1953). *Method and theory in experimental psychology.* London and New York: Oxford Univer. Press.

Ovsiankina, M. (1928). Die Wiederaufnahme unterbrochener Handlungen. *Psychol. Forsch.*, 11:302-379.

Papez, J. W. (1937). A proposed mechanism of emotion. *Arch. Neurol. & Psychiat.*, 38:725-743.

Paul, I. H. (1959). *Studies in remembering.* (Monograph 2 in psychological issue.) New York: Internat. Univer. Press.

Pavlov, I. P. (1927). *Conditioned reflexes.* (Engl. transl.) London and New York: Oxford Univer. Press.

Pemberton, C. (1952). The closure factors related to other cognitive processes. *Psychometrika,* 17:267-288.

Penfield, W. (1938). The cerebral cortex in man. I. The cerebral cortex and consciousness. *A.M.A. Arch Neurol. Psychiat.*, 40:417-442.

Penfield, W. (1954). Studies of the cerebral cortex of man. *Brain mechanisms and consciousness* (E. D. Adrian, F. Bremer, and H. H. Jasper, Ed.), pp. 284-309. Oxford: Blackwell.

Penfield, W. (1958). Centrencephalic Integrating System. *Brain,* 81:231-234.

Pick, A. (1903). On reduplicative paramnesia. *Brain,* 26:260-267.

Pick, A. (1905). Zur Psychologie der Confabulation. *Neurol. Cbl.,* 24:509-516.

Pick, A. (1915). Beiträge zur Pathologie des Denkverlaufes beim Korsakow. *Z. Neurol. Psychiat.,* 28:344-383.

Ploog, D. (1955). Über den Abbau des Gedächtnisses und seine Beziehungen zum Umbewussten. *Schweiz. Arch. Neurol. Psychiat.,* 76:259-297.

Popov, E. A. (1954). K. psikhopatologii Korsakovksogo sindroma. *Nevropatologii i Psikhiatrii,* 54:127-130. (Quoted by Angelergues, 1958.)

Postman, L. (1954). Learned principles of organization in memory. *Psychol. Monogr.* No. 68.

Postman, L., and Alper, T. G. (1946). Retroactive inhibition as a function of the time of interpolation of the inhibitor between learning and recall. *Amer. J. Psychol.,* 59:439-449.

Postman, L., and Jenkins, W. O. (1948). An experimental analysis of set in rote learning: The interaction of learning instruction and retention performance. *J. exp. Psychol.,* 38:683-689.

Postman, L., and Rau, L. (1957). Retention as a function of the method of measurement. *Univer. Calif. Publ. Psychol.,* 8:217-270.

Pribram, K. H. (1960). A review of theory in physiological psychology. *Ann Rev. Psychol.,* 11:1-40.

Purdy, D. M. (1934). The theory of forgetting. *Amer. J. Psychol.,* 46: 339-340.

Ranschburg, P. (1911). Das kranke Gedächtnis. Leipzig: Barth.

Ranschburg, P. (1939). Les bases somatiques de la mémoire. *Volume jubilaire du Centenaire de Th. Ribot.* pp. 513-531. Agen: Imprimerie Moderne.

Rapaport, D. (1942). *Emotions and memory.* Baltimore: Williams & Wilkins.

Rapaport, D. (1951). *Organization and pathology of thought.* New York: Columbia Univer. Press.

Raven, J. C. (1956). *Progressive matrices and the coloured progressive matrices.* (Revised order 1956). London: Lewis and Harrap.

Reed, H. B. (1946). Factors influencing the learning and retention of concepts. I. The influence of set. *J. exp. Psychol.,* 36:71-87.

Régis, E. (1913). *Précis de psychiatrie* (4th ed.) Paris: Doin.

Remy, M. (1942). Contribution à l'étude de la maladie de Korsakow. *Mschr. Psychiat. Neurol.,* 106:128-144.

Ribot, T. A. (1881). *Les maladies de la Mémoire.* Paris: Germer Baillere.

Righetti, R. (1920). Contributo allo studio delle amnesie lacunari. *Riv. patol.,* 25: 261-284.

Rizzo, E. M. (1955). Sulla sindroma di Korsakoff. *Rassegna di Stud. Psychiat.,* 44:800-816.

Rosenbaum, M., and Merritt, H. H. (1939). Korsakoff's Syndrome. Clinical study of the alcoholic form with special regards to prognosis. *A.M.A. Arch. Neurol. Psychiat.*, 41:978-983.

Ross, J. (1890). On the psychical disorders of peripheral neuritis. *J. Ment. Sci.*, 36:156-172.

Ross, J., and Bury, J. S. (1893). *On peripheral neuritis. A treatise.* London: Griffin.

Russell, W. R. (1948). Studies in amnesia. *Edinburgh Med. J.*, 55:92-99.

Russell, W. R. (1959). *Brain-memory-learning.* London and New York: Oxford Univer. Press.

Russell, W. R., and Nathan, P. W. (1946). Traumatic amnesia. *Brain*, 69:280-300.

Samuels, I. (1959). Reticular mechanisms and behavior. *Psychol. Bull.*, 56:1-25.

Sander, F. (1928). Experimentelle Ergebnisse der Gestaltpsychologie. *Ber. 10. Kongr. Exp. Psychol., Bonn.* (E. Becher, Ed.) Jena: Fischer.

Scheele, H. (1951). Organische Merkunfähigkeit oder Hysterie? Neuere Untersuchungen zu dem von E. Grünthal unde G. E. Störring beschriebenen Fall völliger isolierter Merkunfähigkeit. *Mschr. Psychiat. Neurol.*, 121:345-363.

Scheid, W. (1934). Zur Pathopsychologie des Korsakow-Syndroms. *Z. Neurol. Psychiat.*, 151:246-369.

Scheller, H. (1950). Völliger isolierter Verlust der Merkfähigkeit; organische CO-Schädigung oder hysterische Verdrängung? *Nervenarzt*, 21:49-56.

Schilder, P. (1925). Zur Psychologie epileptischer Ausnahmezustände (mit besonderer Berücksrhtiguing des Gedächtnisses). *Allg. Z. Psychiat.*, 80:33-79.

Schilder, P. (1942). *Mind: Perception and thought in their constructive aspects.* New York: Columbia Univer. Press.

Schneider, H. (1901). Über Auffassung und Merkfähigkeit beim Altersblödsinn. *Psychol. Arbeiten* (E. Krapelin, Ed.) Vol. III, pp. 458-481. Leipzig: Engelmann.

Schneider, K. (1912). Über einige klinisch-pathologische Untersuchungsmethoden und ihre Ergebnisse. Zugleich ein Beitrag zur Psychopathologie der Korsakowschen Psychose. *Z. Neurol. Psychiat.*, 8:553-616.

Schneider, K. (1928). Die Störungen des Gedächtnisses. *Handbuch der Geisteskrankheiten* (O. Bumke, Ed.), Vol. I, pp. 509-529. Berlin: Springer.

Scoville, W. B., and Milner, B. (1957). Loss of recent memory after bilateral hippocampal lesions. *J. Neurol. Neurosurg. Psychiat.*, 20: 11-21.

Seashore, C. E. (1919). *Psychology of musical talent.* Boston: Silver-Burdette.

Seashore, R. Buxton, C., and McCullom, I. (1940). Multiple factorial analysis of fine motor skills. *Amer. J. Psychol.*, 53:259-261.

Selz, O. (1913). *Über die Gesetze des geordneten Denkverlaufs.* Bonn: Cohen.

Sherrington, C. S. (1906). *Integrative action of the nervous system.* New Haven, Connecticut: Yale Univer. Press.

Sollier, P. (1895). Un cas de psychose polynévritique. *Rev. Neurol.*, 3: 433-437.

Sollier, P. (1900). *Le problème de la Mémoire: Essai de psycho-mécanique.* Paris: Alcan.

Sperry, R. W. (1959). Post-Pavlovian development in conditional reflexes. *The central nervous system and behavior* (M. A. B. Brazier, Ed.), Trans. 2nd Conf. New York: Josiah Macy, Jr. Foundation.

Sprofkin, B. E., and Sciarra, D. (1952). Korsakoff's psychosis associated with cerebral tumors. *Neurology,* 2:427-434.

Steinthal, E. (1921). Ein eigenartiger Fall Korsakowscher Psychose. *Z. Neurol. Psychiat.*, 67:287-310.

Stellar, E. (1957). Physiological psychology. *Ann. Rev. Psychol.*, 8:415-436.

Stern, W. (1935). *Allgemeine Psychologie.* The Hague: Nijhof. Transl. *General psychology from the personalistic standpoint.* New York: Macmillan, 1938.

Störring, G. E. (1931). Über den ersten reinen Fall eines Menschen mit volligen isoliertem Verlust der Merkfähigkeit. *Arch. Psychol.*, 81: 257-384.

Stransky, E. (1905). Zur Lehre des Korsakoffschen Symptomenkomplex. *Jahrb. Psychiat. Neurol.*, 26:422-444.

Street, R. F. (1931). *A Gestalt completion test.* New York: Teachers College.

Strümpell, A. (1883). Zur Kenntnis der multiplen degenerativen Neuritis. *Arch. Psychiat.*, 14:339-358.

Sweet, W. H., Talland, G. A., and Ervin, F. R. (1960). Loss of recent memory following section of the fornix. *Trans. Amer. Neurol. Assoc.*, 1959:76-82.

Syz, H. (1936). Posttraumatic loss of reproductive memory and its restoration through hypnosis and analysis. *Med. Rec. N. Y.*, 144: 313-317.

Talland, G. A. (1956). Cultural differences in serial reproduction. *J. soc. Psychol.*, 43:75-81.

Talland, G. A. (1957). Criteria in conceptual transposition. *Amer. J. Psychol.*, 70:263-267.

Talland, G. A. (1958a). Psychological studies of Korsakoff's psychosis: II. Perceptual functions. *J. nerv. ment. Dis.*, 127:197-219.

Talland, G. A. (1958b). Perception of apparent movement in Korsakoff's psychosis. *J. Pers.* 26:337-348.

Talland, G. A. (1959a). Age and the effect of expectancy on the accuracy of perception. *J. Geront.*, 14:202-207.

Talland, G. A. (1959b). Psychological studies of Korsakoff's psychosis: III. Concept formation. *J. nerv. ment. Dis.*, 128:214-226.

Talland, G. A. (1961). The effect of aging on the formation of sequential and spatial concepts. *Percept. motor skills*, 13:210.

Talland, G. A. (1962a). The effect of age on speed of simple manual skill. *J. Genet. Psychol.*, 100:69-76

Talland, G. A. (1962b). Cognitive function in Parkinson's disease. *J. nerv. ment. Dis.*, 135:196-205.

Talland, G. A., and Cairnie, J. (1961). Aging effects on simple, disjunctive and alerted finger reaction time. *J. Geront.*, 16:370-374.

Teuber, H. L. ((1960) Perception. In *Handbook of physiology* (J. Field, Ed.), Sect. 1: Neurophysiology, Vol. III, pp. 1595-1668. Washington, D. C.: Amer. Physiol. Soc.

Teuber, H. L. (1961). Sensory deprivation, sensory suppression and agnosia: notes for a neurologic theory. *J. nerv. ment. Dis.*, 132:32-40.

Thurstone, L. L. (1944). *A factorial study of perception.* Chicago: Univer. of Chicago Press.

Tiling, T. (1890). Über die bei alkoholischen Neuritis multiplex beobachtete Geistesstörung. *Allg. Z. Psychiat.*, 46:233-257.

Tiling, T. (1892). Über die amnestesche Geistesstörung. *Allg. Z. Psychiat.*, 48:549-565.

Ule, G. (1958). Pathologisch-anatomische Befunde bei Korsakow-Psychosen und ihre Bedeutung fur die Lokalisationslehre in der Psychiatrie. *Aerzt. Wschr.* 13:6-13.

Underwood, J. B. (1945). The effect of successive interpolations on retroactive and proactive inhibition. *Psychol. Monogr.*, 59: No. 3.

Underwood, J. B. (1949). *Experimental psychology, an introduction.* New York: Appleton.

Underwood, J. B. (1957). Interference and forgetting. *Psychol. Rev.*, 64: 49-60.

Underwood, J. B., and Postman, L. (1960). Extraexperimental sources of interference in forgetting. *Psychol. Rev.*, 67:73-95.

van der Horst, L. (1932). Über die Psychologie des Korsakowsyndroms. *Mschr. Psychiat. Neurol.*, 83:65-84; also: Le sens de la temporalization pour la memoire et pour l'orientation. *Evolut. Psychiat.*, 1: 189-205, 1956.

Vernon, M. D. (1957). Cognitive inference in perceptual activity. *Brit. J. Psychol.*, 48:35-47.

Victor, M., and Adams, R. D. (1953). The effect of alcohol on the nervous system. *Proc. Assoc. Res. nerv. ment. Dis.*, 32:526-573.

Victor, M., and Yakovlev, P. I. (1955). S. S. Korsakoff's psychic disorder. *Neurology*, 5:394-407.

Victor, M., Talland, G. A., and Adams, R. D. (1959). Psychological studies of Korsakoff's psychosis: I. General intellectual functions. *J. nerv. ment. Dis.*, 128:528-537.

Völkel, H., and Stolze, R. (1956). Nachuntersuchüng und Versuch einer epikritischen Deutung des Falles B von E. Grünthal und G. E. Störring. *Mschr. Psychiat. Neurol.*, 132:291-309.

Walker, E. E. (1957). Recent memory inpairment in unilateral temporal lesions. *A.M.A. Arch. Neurol. Psychiat.*, 78:543-552.

Walton, J. N. (1953). The Korsakov syndrome in spontaneous subarachnoid haemorrhage. *J. ment. Sci.*, 99:521-530.

Warren, H. C. (1934). *Dictionary of psychology.* Cambridge, Massachusetts: Houghton Mifflin.

Wechsler, D. (1917). A study of retention in Korsakoff psychosis. *Psychiat. Bull. N. Y. State Hosp.*, 2:403-451.

Wechsler, D. (1944). *The measurement of adult intelligence* (3rd ed.) Baltimore: Williams & Wilkins.

Wechsler, D. (1945). A standardized memory scale for clinical use. *J. Psychol.*, 19:87-95.

Wernicke, C. (1881). *Lehrbuch der Gehirnkrankheiten für Ärzte und Studierende.* Berlin: Fischer.

Wernicke, C. (1900). *Grundriss der Psychiatrie.* Leipzig: Thieme.

White, T. H. (1952). *The scandalmonger.* New York: Putnam.

Wieck, H. H. (1955). *Zur Psychologie und Psychopathologie der Erinnerungen.* Stuttgart: Thieme.

Wilcoxon, F. (1949). *Some rapid approximate statistical procedures.* New York: Amer. Cyanamid Co.

Williams, H. W., and Rupp, C. (1938). Observations on confabulation. *Amer. J. Psychiat.*, 95:395-405.

Williams, M., and Pennybacker, J. (1954). Memory disturbances in third ventricle tumors. *J. Neurol. Neurosurg. Psychiat.*, 17:115-124.

Williams, M., and Smith, H. V. (1954). Mental disturbances in tuberculous meningitis. *J. Neurol. Neurosurg. Psychiat.* 17: 173-182.

Williams, M., and Zangwill, O. L. (1950). Disorders of temporal judgment associated with amnesic states. *J. ment. Sci.*, 96:484-493.

Woodworth, R. S., and Schlosberg, H. (1954). *Experimental psychology.* New York: Holt.

Wulf, F. (1922). Über der Veränderung der Vorstellungen. *Psychol. Forsch.*, 1:333-389.

Wyke, M., and Warrington, E. (1960). An experimental analysis of confabulation in a case of Korsakoff's syndrome using a tachistoscopic method. *J. Neurol. Neurosurg. Psychiat.*, 23:327-333.

Zangwill, O. L. (1941). On a peculiarity of recognition in three cases of Korsakow's psychosis. *Brit. J. Psychol.*, 31:230-248.

Zangwill, O. L. (1946). Some clinical applications of the Rey-Davis performance test. *J. ment. Sci.*, 92:19-34.

Zangwill, O. L. (1950). Amnesia and the generic image. *Quart. J. Exp. Psychol.*, 2:7-12.

Zangwill, O. L. (1953). Disorientation for age. *J. ment Sci.*, 99:698-701.

Zubin, J. (1948). Memory function in patients treated with electric shock therapy. *J. Pers.*, 17:33-41.

# AUTHOR INDEX

Numbers in italic indicate the page on which complete reference is cited.

# SUBJECT INDEX